DOCTOR WHO
THE FOURTH DOCTOR

VOL 1: GAZE OF THE MEDUSA

"If you're a classic Doctor Who fan, you will love this book!"
KABOOOOOM

"Writers Gordon Rennie and Emma Beeby delivered the goods!"
FANBOY NATION

"I'd recommend this to any fan new or old."
COMIC CRUSADERS

"Nails the Fourth Doctor's voice."
WE THE NERDY

"Writers Gordon Rennie and Emma Beeby deliver another thrilling Classic Doctor Who installment. 8/10"
AMINO APPS

"It gets the Doctor "right," and does it with a smile and a wink."
CHUCKY'S COMIC OF THE DAY

"The Fourth Doctor is bold and invigorating!"
SNAPPOW

"The writing is still amazing and on point and features incredible art."
GEEKY GIRL WORLD

"Titan Comics have truly done the Fourth Doctor justice."
SCI FI PULSE

"Great dialogue and great characterisation propelled this story along, and near perfect pacing makes this a great read from cover to cover."
NERDLY

TITAN COMICS

SENIOR COMICS EDITOR
Andrew James

ASSISTANT EDITORS
Jessica Burton, Amoona Saohin

COLLECTION DESIGNER
Andrew Leung

TITAN COMICS EDITORIAL
Tom Williams

PRODUCTION ASSISTANT
Peter James

PRODUCTION SUPERVISORS
Maria Pearson, Jackie Flook

PRODUCTION MANAGER
Obi Onuora

ART DIRECTOR
Oz Browne

SENIOR SALES MANAGER
Steve Tothill

PRESS OFFICER
Will O'Mullane

COMICS BRAND MANAGER
Lucy Ripper

DIRECT SALES & MARKETING MANAGER Ricky Claydon

COMMERCIAL MANAGER
Michelle Fairlamb

HEAD OF RIGHTS
Jenny Boyce

PUBLISHING MANAGER
Darryl Tothill

PUBLISHING DIRECTOR
Chris Teather

OPERATIONS DIRECTOR
Leigh Baulch

EXECUTIVE DIRECTOR
Vivian Cheung

PUBLISHER
Nick Landau

FOR RIGHTS INFORMATION CONTACT jenny.boyce@titanemail.com

Special thanks to Steven Moffat, Brian Minchin, Mandy Thwaites, Matt Nicholls, James Dudley, Edward Russell, Derek Ritchie, Scott Handcock, Kirsty Mullan, Kate Bush, Julia Nocciolino, and Ed Casey, for their invaluable assistance.

BBC WORLDWIDE

DIRECTOR OF EDITORIAL GOVERNANCE
Nicolas Brett

DIRECTOR OF CONSUMER PRODUCTS AND PUBLISHING
Andrew Moultrie

HEAD OF UK PUBLISHING
Chris Kerwin

PUBLISHER
Mandy Thwaites

PUBLISHING CO-ORDINATOR
Eva Abramik

DOCTOR WHO: THE FOURTH DOCTOR
VOL 1: GAZE OF THE MEDUSA
HB ISBN: 9781782767558 SB ISBN: 9781785852909
Published by Titan Comics, a division of Titan Publishing Group, Ltd.
144 Southwark Street, London, SE1 0UP.

A CIP catalogue record for this title is available from the British Library.
First edition: January 2017.

10 9 8 7 6 5 4 3 2 1

Printed in China.

Titan Comics does not read or accept unsolicited DOCTOR WHO submissions of ideas, stories or artwork.

DOCTOR WHO
THE FOURTH DOCTOR

VOL 1: GAZE OF THE MEDUSA

WRITERS: GORDON RENNIE & EMMA BEEBY

ARTIST: BRIAN WILLIAMSON

COLORIST: HI FI

LETTERS: RICHARD STARKINGS AND COMICRAFT'S JIMMY BETANCOURT

TITAN COMICS   BBC

www.titan-comics.com

BBC

DOCTOR WHO

THE FOURTH DOCTOR

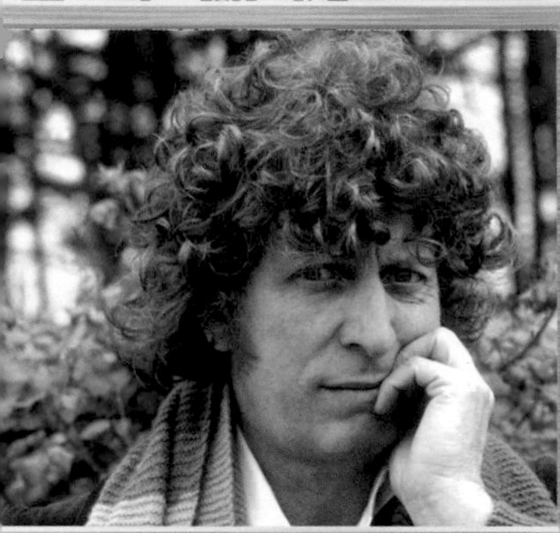

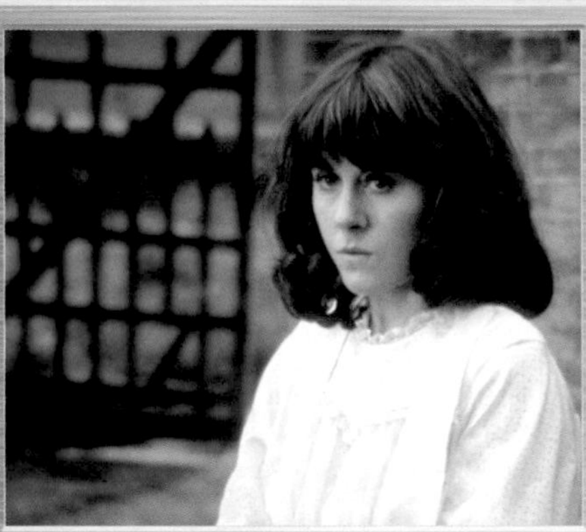

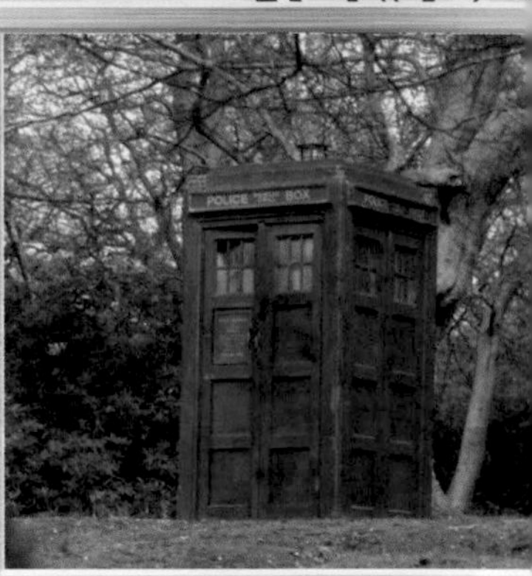

THE DOCTOR

A Time Lord of Gallifrey, the Fourth Doctor is a charming, unpredictable force of insatiable curiosity, let loose upon the cosmos. Filled with a new wanderlust after years exiled to Earth, this manlike mass of teeth and curls baffles friends and flummoxes foes in equal measure!

SARAH JANE SMITH

Bold and brave, Sarah Jane is a journalist and investigator of the highest calibre. Possessed of a keen analytical mind, she never loses touch with her human side – or her fears – and never lets the Doctor forget his greater responsibilities.

THE TARDIS

'Time and Relative Dimension in Space'. Bigger on the inside, this battered blue police box is your ticket to unforgettable adventure! The Doctor likes to think he's in control, but often the TARDIS takes him where and when he needs to be...

PREVIOUSLY...

The Fourth Doctor and Sarah Jane Smith have had many adventures together, roaming across time, space, and the furthest boundaries of the universe! From facing the K1 Experimental Prototype Robot to battling the Wirrn on Space Station Nerva, and defeating the terror of the Sontarans to battling Sutekh and his robot mummies, the Doctor and Sarah have triumphed over many threats.

But now they must face... the Medusa's Gaze!

When you've finished reading the collection, please email your thoughts to doctorwhocomic@titanemail.com

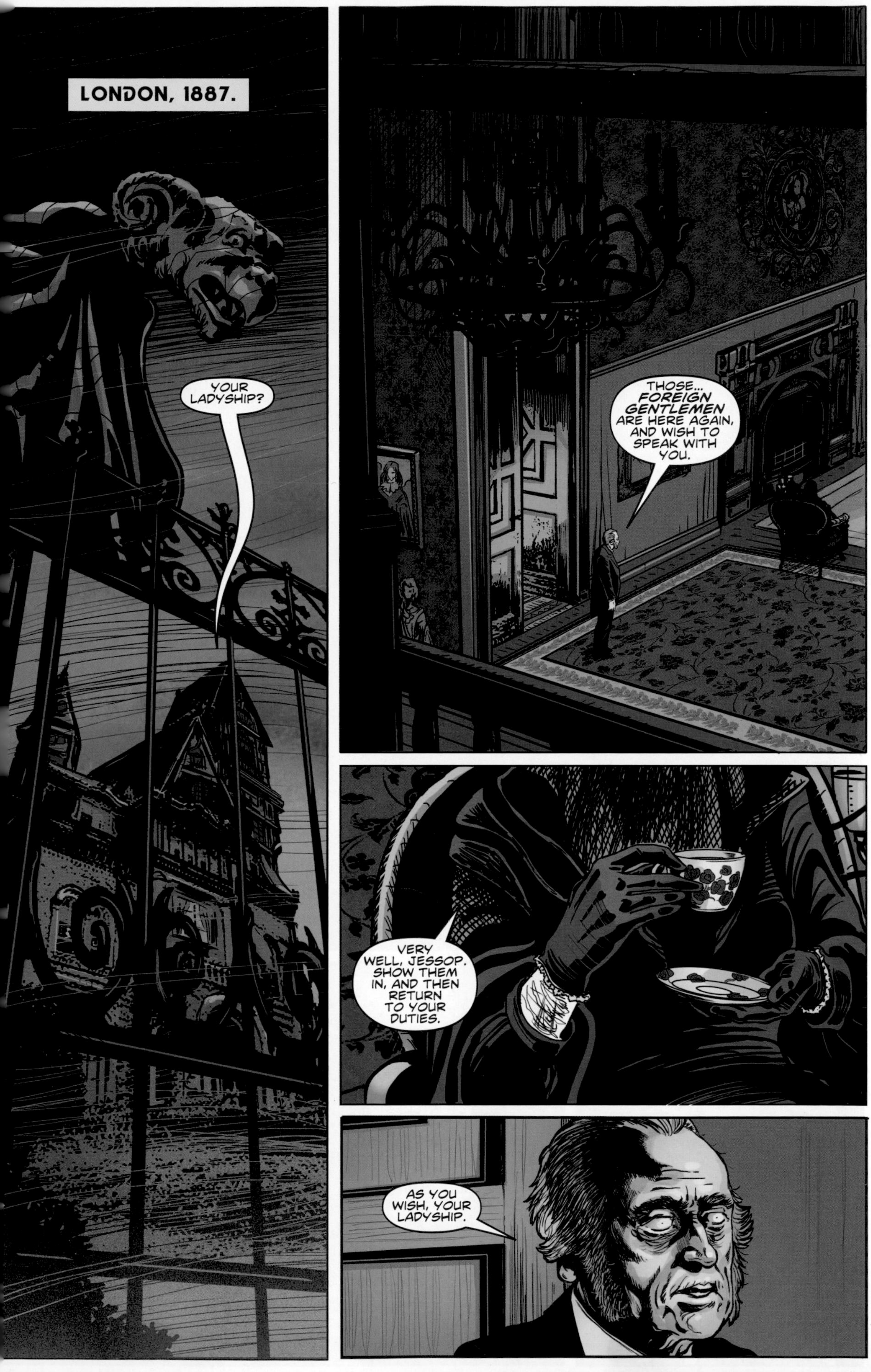
LONDON, 1887.
YOUR LADYSHIP?
THOSE... FOREIGN GENTLEMEN ARE HERE AGAIN, AND WISH TO SPEAK WITH YOU.
VERY WELL, JESSOP. SHOW THEM IN, AND THEN RETURN TO YOUR DUTIES.
AS YOU WISH, YOUR LADYSHIP.

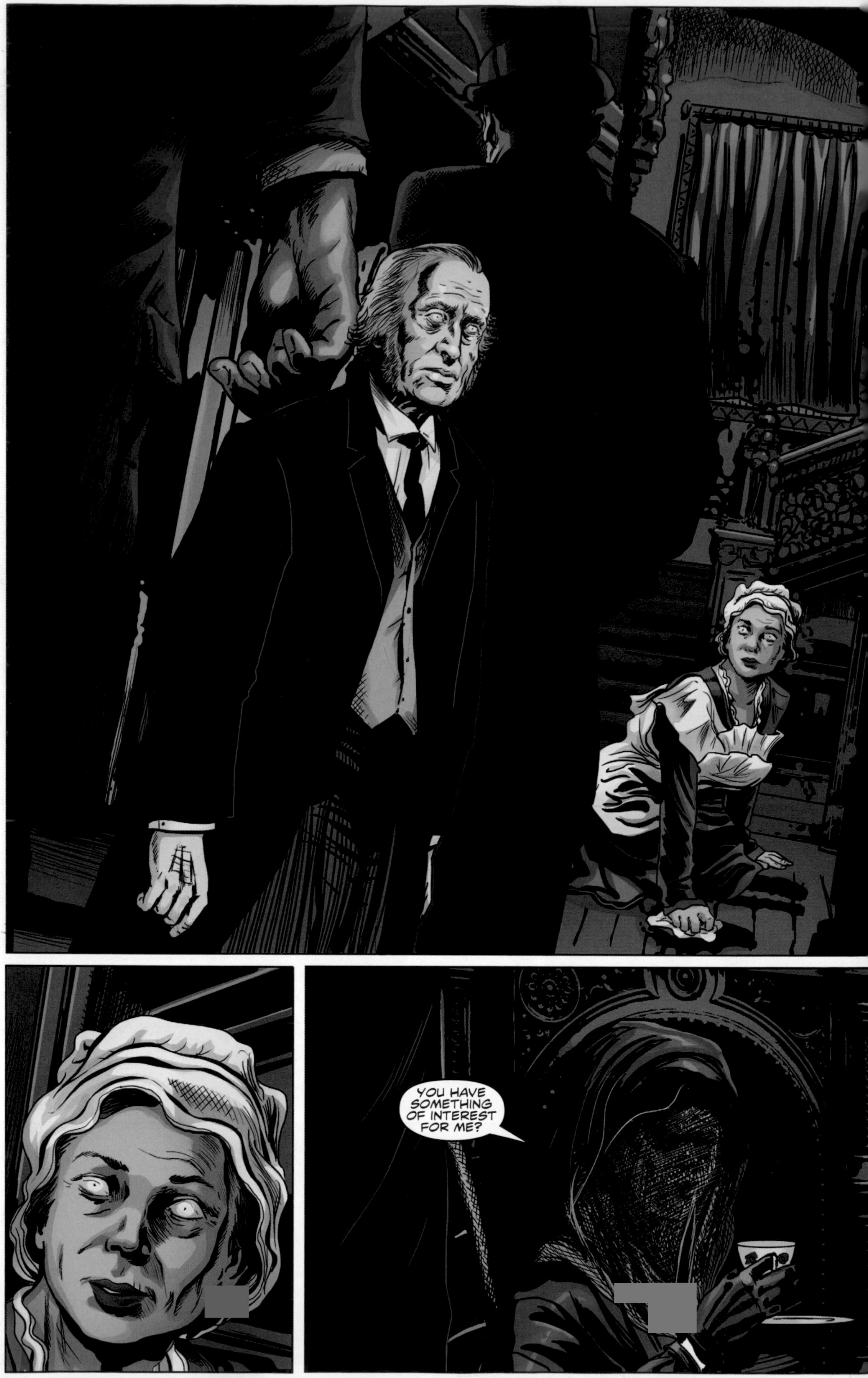
YOU HAVE SOMETHING OF INTEREST FOR ME?

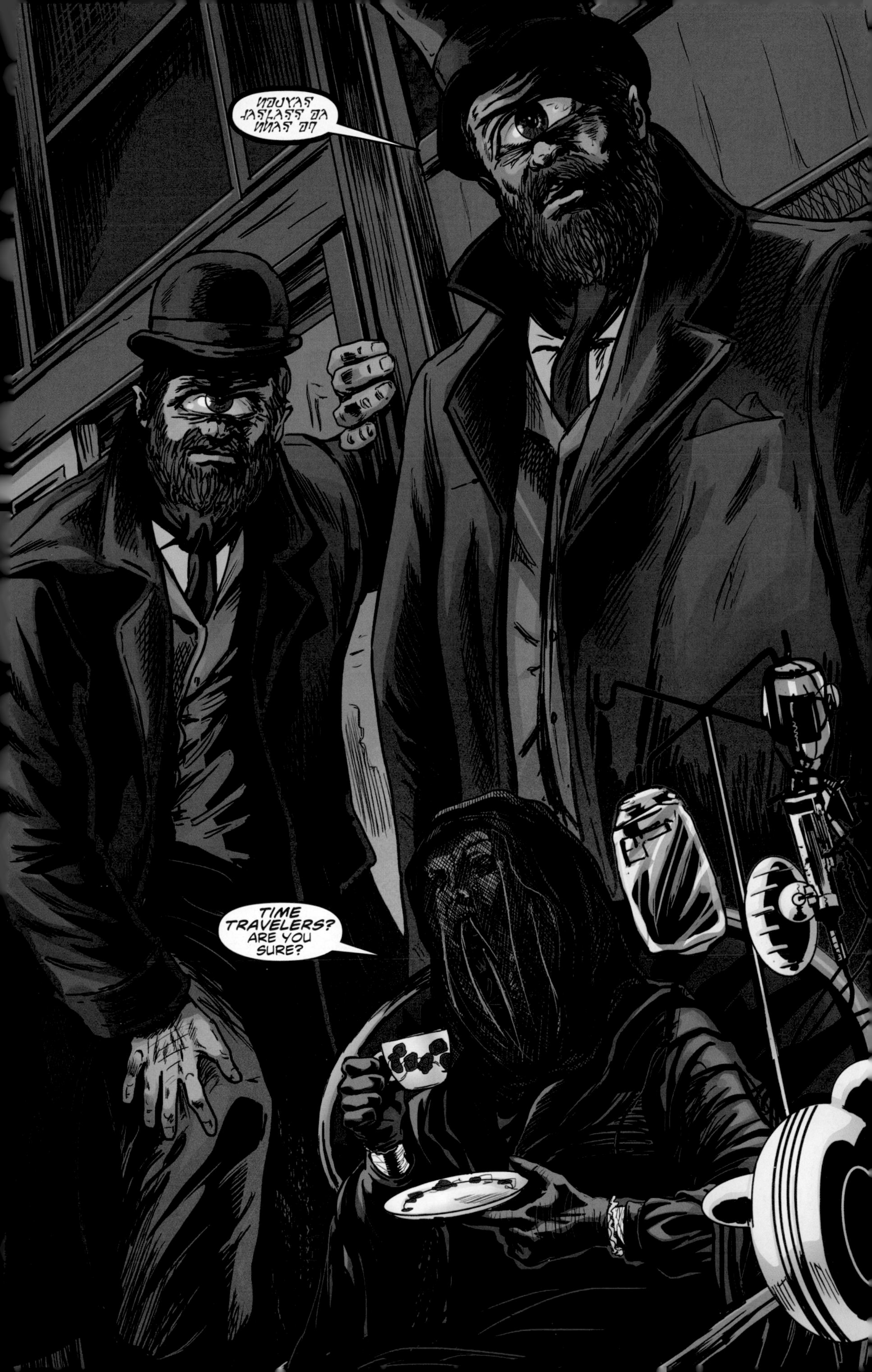
TIME TRAVELERS? ARE YOU SURE?

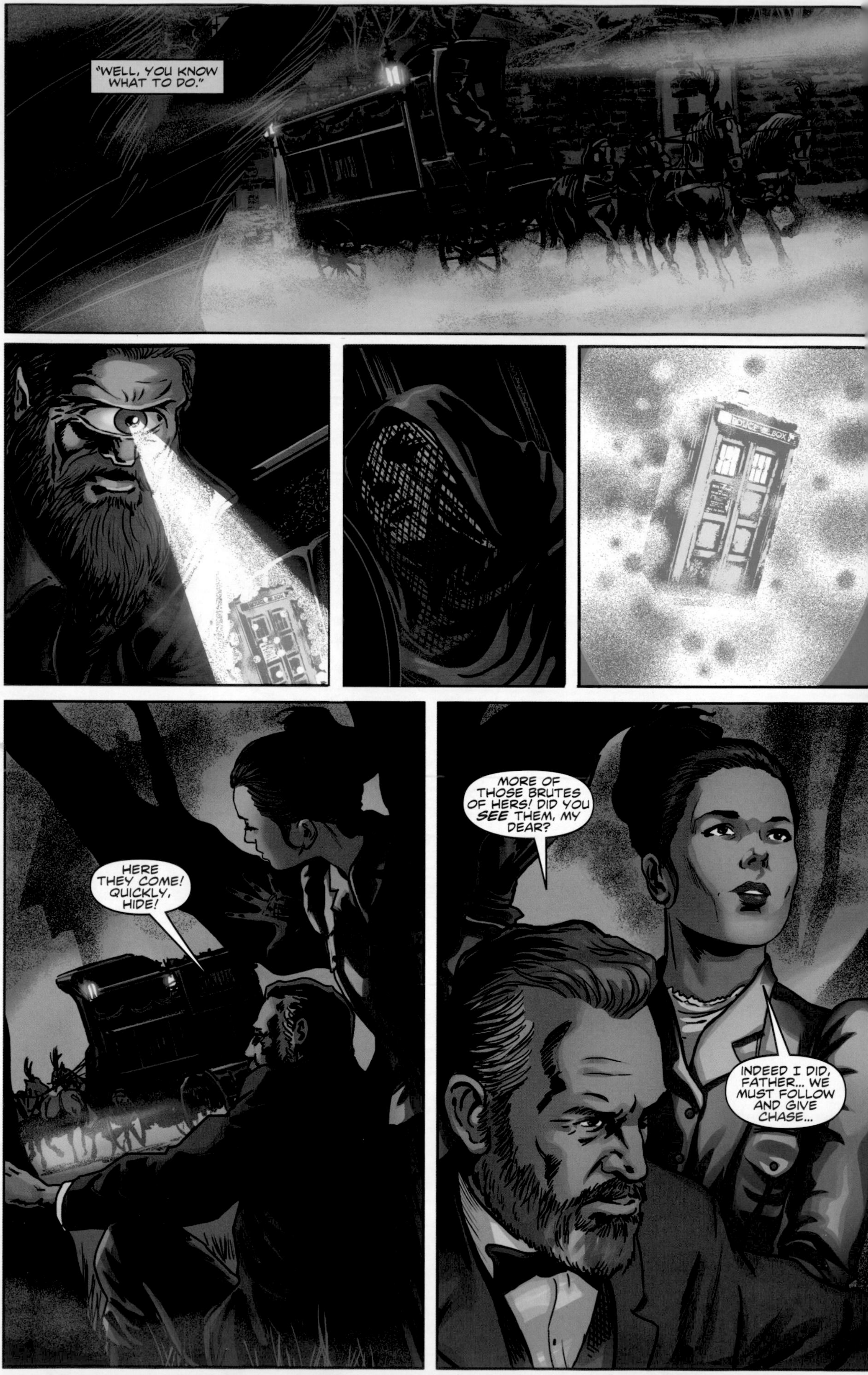
"WELL, YOU KNOW WHAT TO DO."
HERE THEY COME! QUICKLY, HIDE!
MORE OF THOSE BRUTES OF HERS! DID YOU *SEE* THEM, MY DEAR?
INDEED I DID, FATHER... WE MUST FOLLOW AND GIVE CHASE...

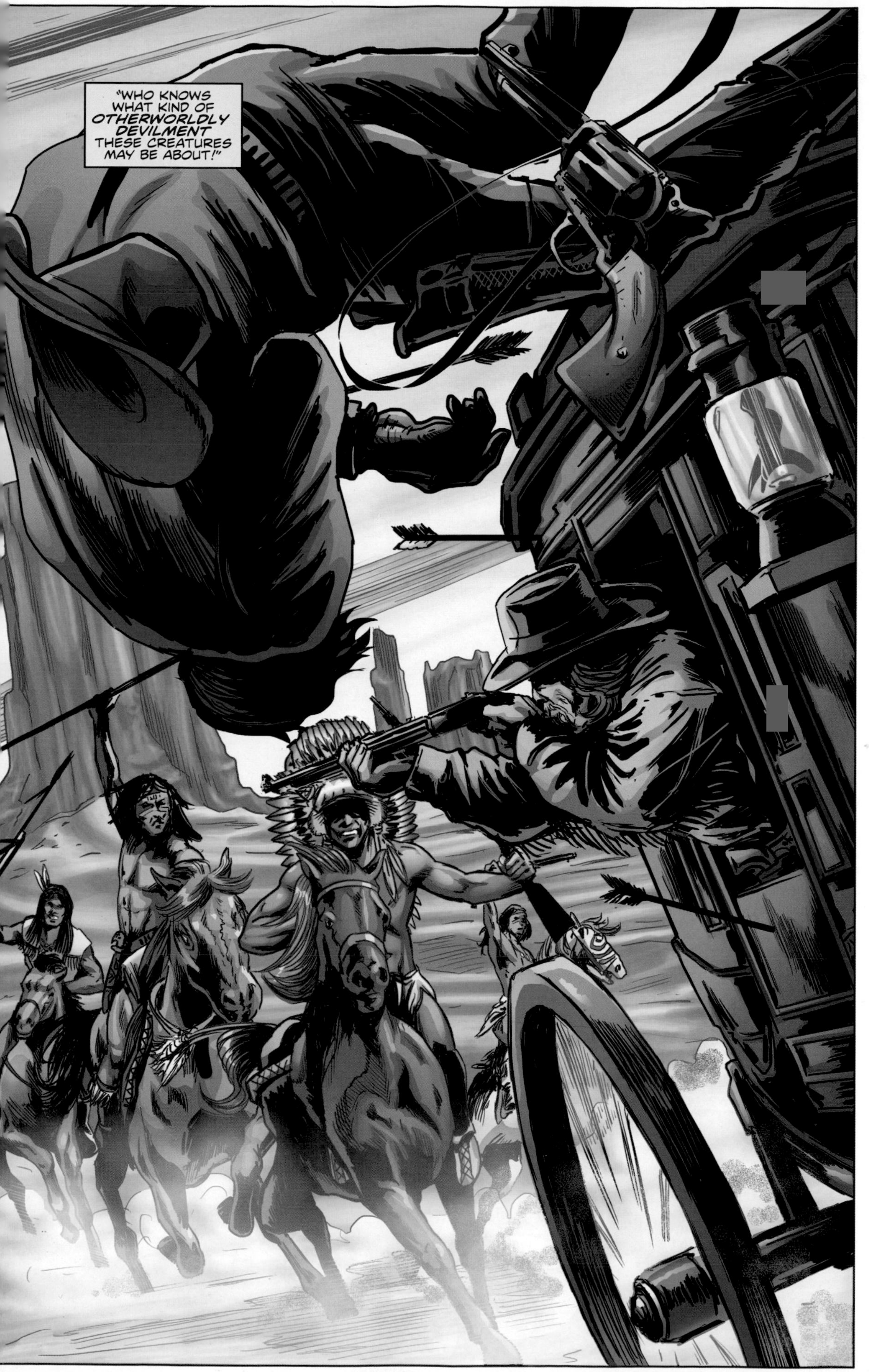
"WHO KNOWS WHAT KIND OF OTHERWORLDLY DEVILMENT THESE CREATURES MAY BE ABOUT!"

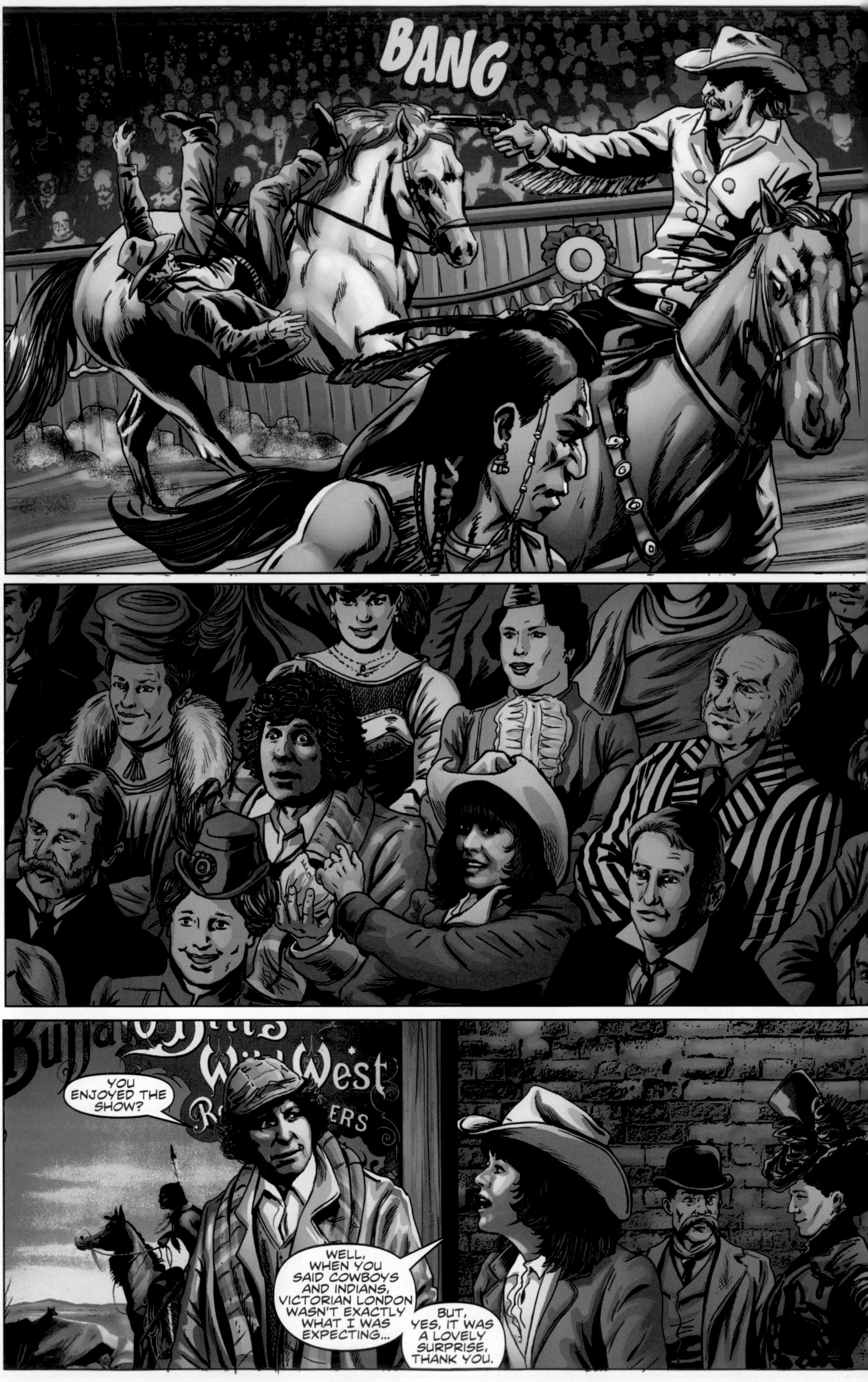
BANG
YOU ENJOYED THE SHOW?
WELL, WHEN YOU SAID COWBOYS AND INDIANS, VICTORIAN LONDON WASN'T EXACTLY WHAT I WAS EXPECTING...
BUT, YES, IT WAS A LOVELY SURPRISE, THANK YOU.

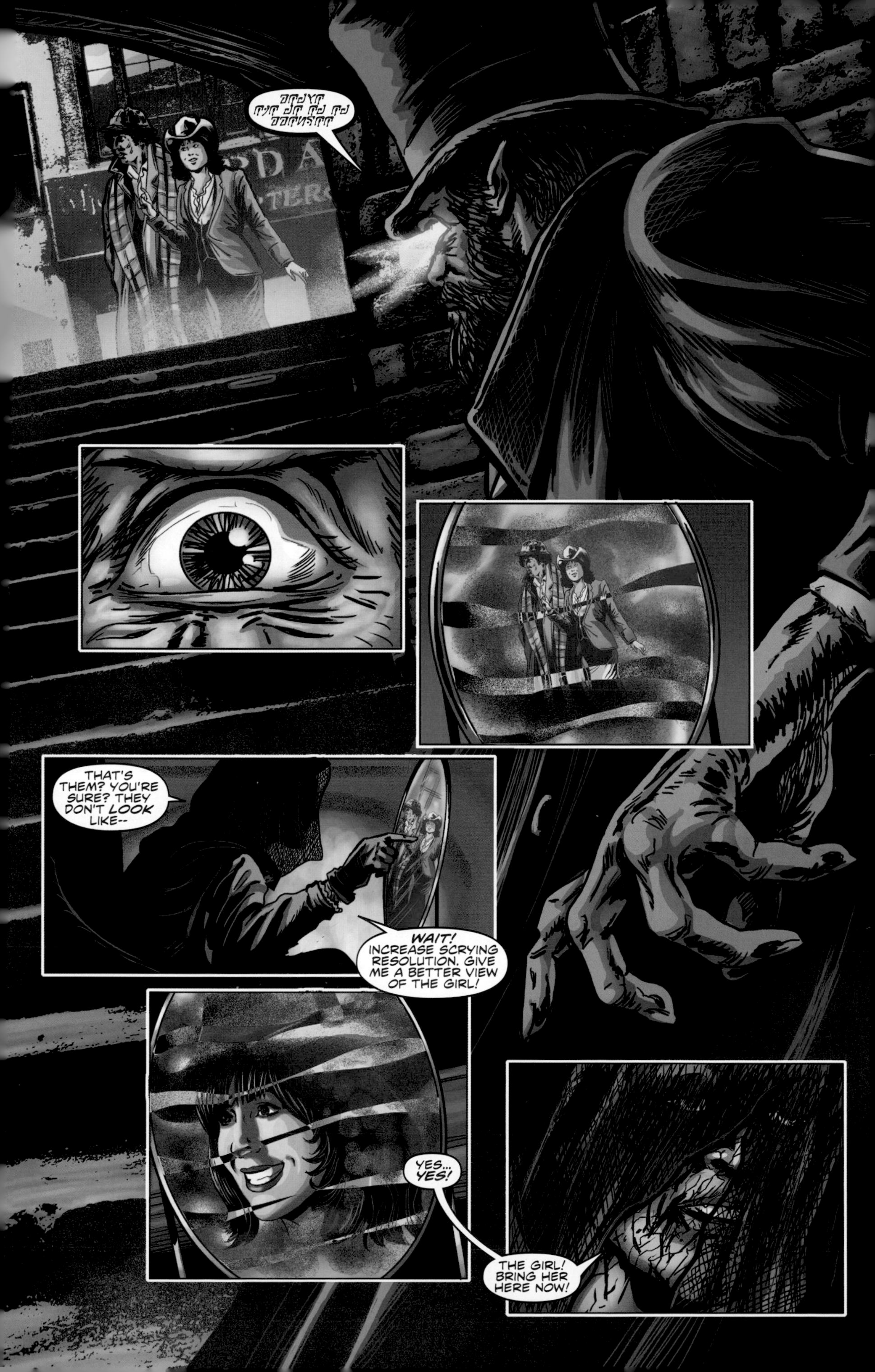
THAT'S THEM? YOU'RE SURE? THEY DON'T LOOK LIKE--
WAIT! INCREASE SCRYING RESOLUTION. GIVE ME A BETTER VIEW OF THE GIRL!
YES... YES!
THE GIRL! BRING HER HERE NOW!

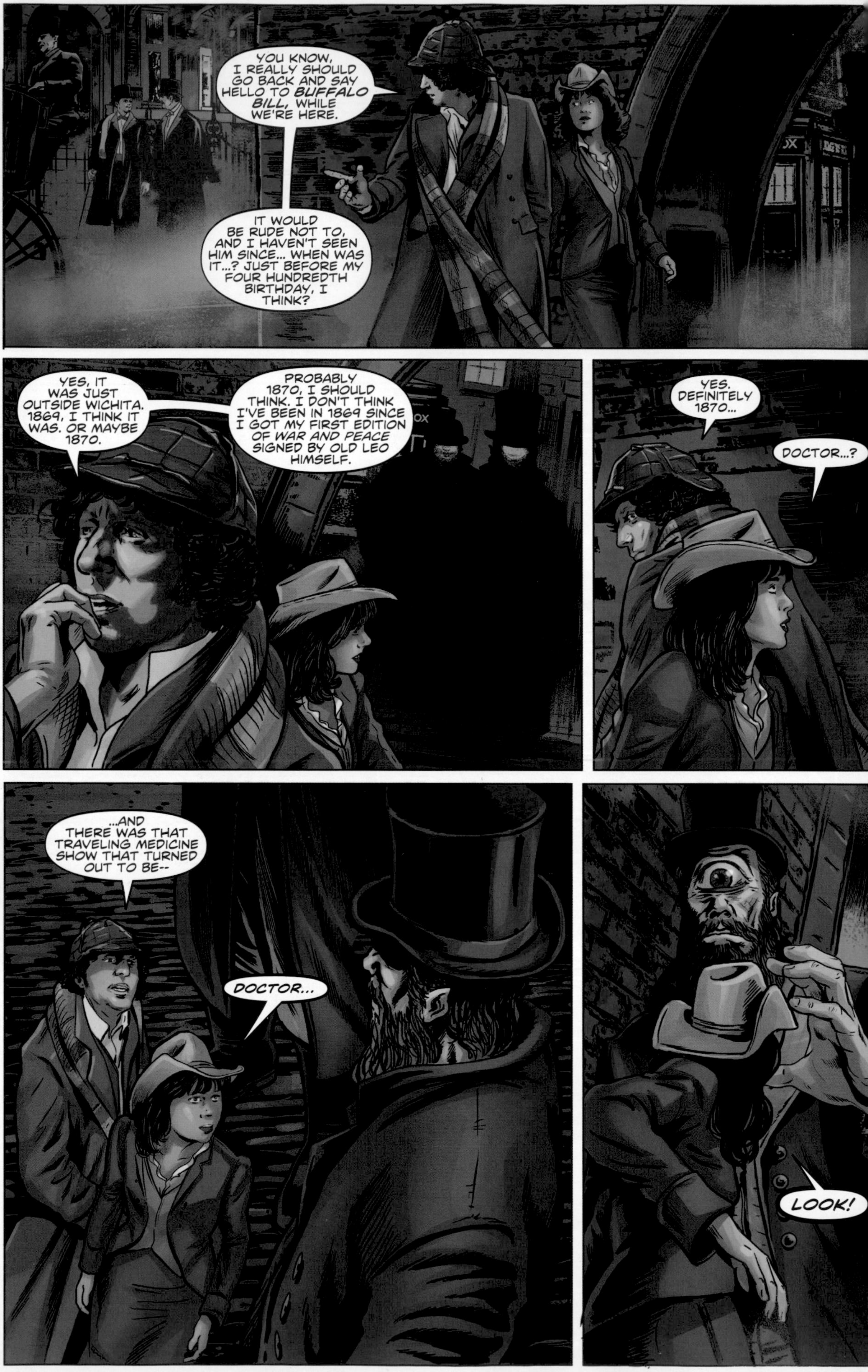
YOU KNOW, I REALLY SHOULD GO BACK AND SAY HELLO TO *BUFFALO BILL*, WHILE WE'RE HERE.
IT WOULD BE RUDE NOT TO, AND I HAVEN'T SEEN HIM SINCE... WHEN WAS IT...? JUST BEFORE MY FOUR HUNDREDTH BIRTHDAY, I THINK?
YES, IT WAS JUST OUTSIDE WICHITA. 1869, I THINK IT WAS. OR MAYBE 1870.
PROBABLY 1870, I SHOULD THINK. I DON'T THINK I'VE BEEN IN 1869 SINCE I GOT MY FIRST EDITION OF *WAR AND PEACE* SIGNED BY OLD LEO HIMSELF.
YES. DEFINITELY 1870...
DOCTOR...?
...AND THERE WAS THAT TRAVELING MEDICINE SHOW THAT TURNED OUT TO BE--
DOCTOR...
LOOK!

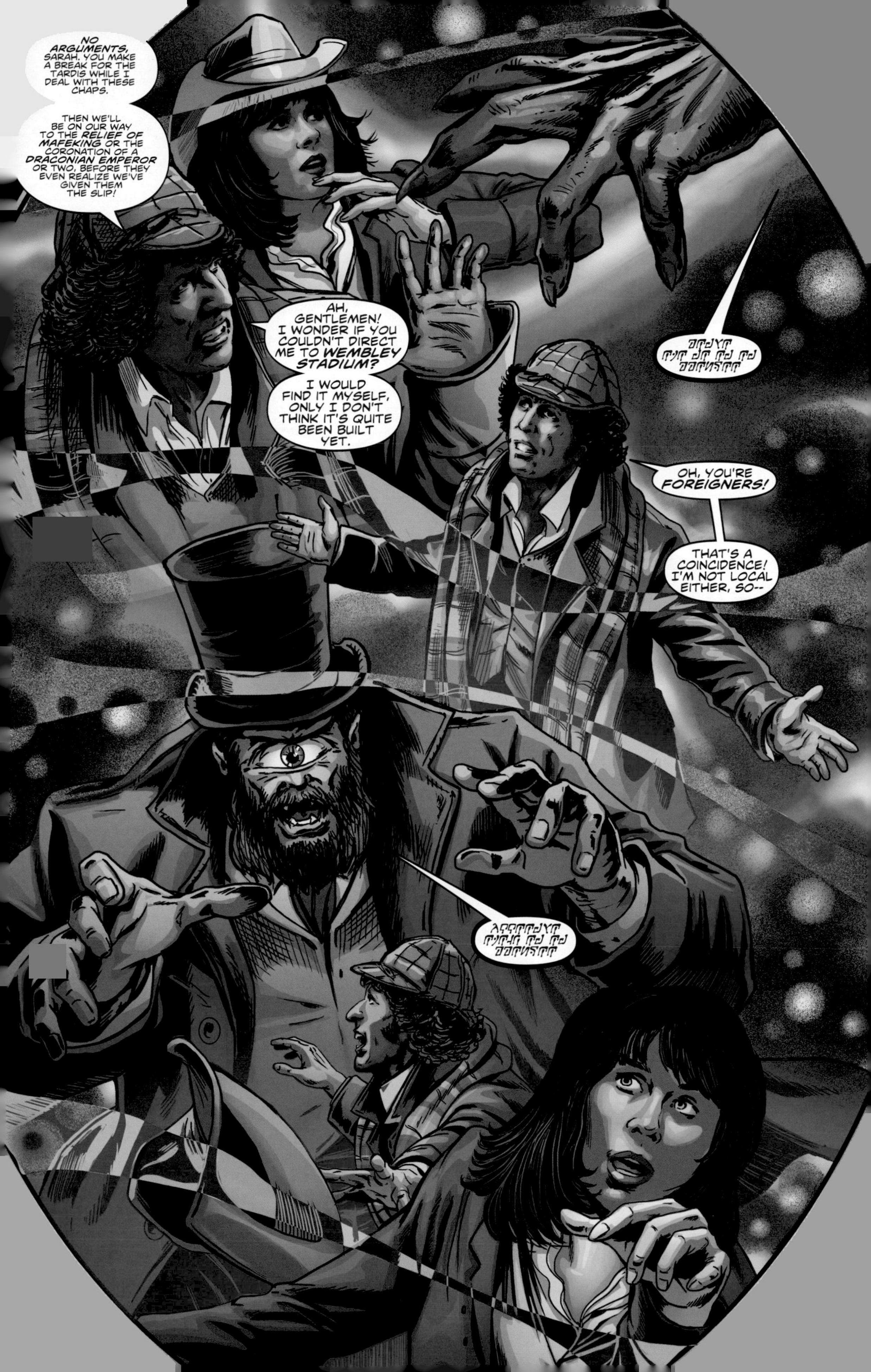
NO ARGUMENTS, SARAH. YOU MAKE A BREAK FOR THE TARDIS WHILE I DEAL WITH THESE CHAPS.
THEN WE'LL BE ON OUR WAY TO THE RELIEF OF MAFEKING OR THE CORONATION OF A DRACONIAN EMPEROR OR TWO, BEFORE THEY EVEN REALIZE WE'VE GIVEN THEM THE SLIP!
AH, GENTLEMEN! I WONDER IF YOU COULDN'T DIRECT ME TO WEMBLEY STADIUM?
I WOULD FIND IT MYSELF, ONLY I DON'T THINK IT'S QUITE BEEN BUILT YET.
OH, YOU'RE FOREIGNERS!
THAT'S A COINCIDENCE! I'M NOT LOCAL EITHER, SO--

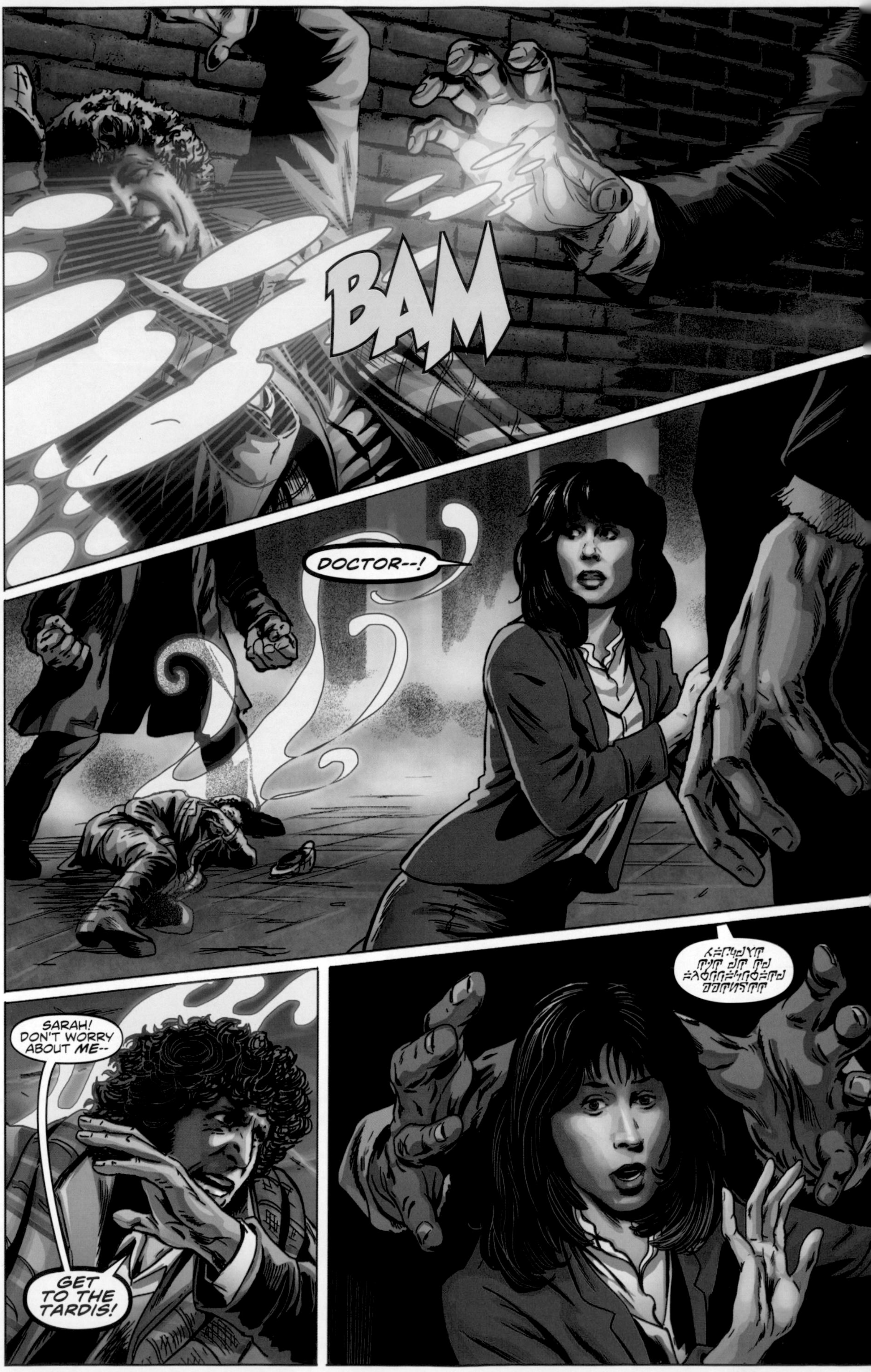
BAM
DOCTOR--!
SARAH! DON'T WORRY ABOUT ME--
GET TO THE TARDIS!

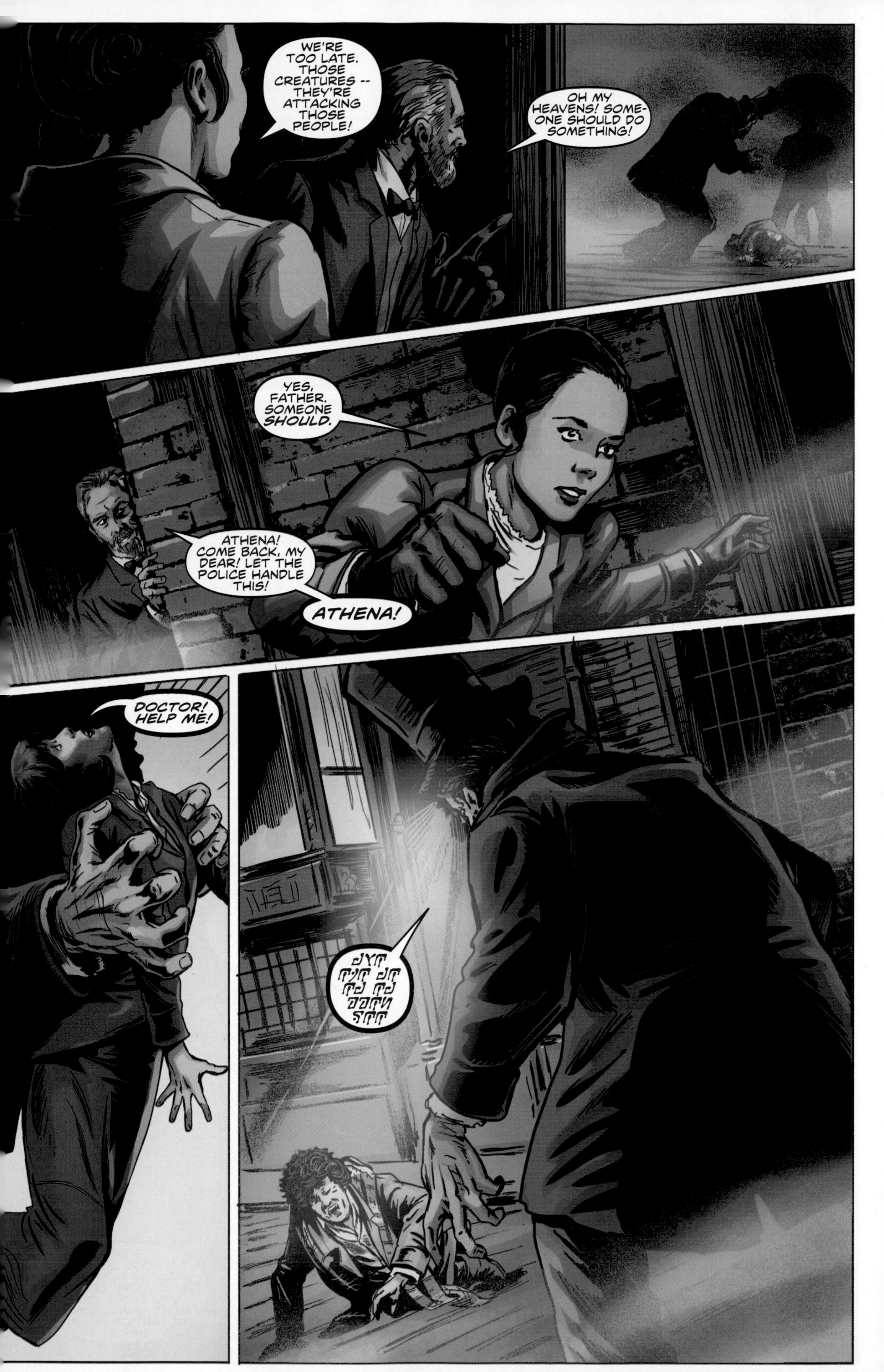
WE'RE TOO LATE. THOSE CREATURES -- THEY'RE ATTACKING THOSE PEOPLE!
OH MY HEAVENS! SOME-ONE SHOULD DO SOMETHING!
YES, FATHER. SOMEONE *SHOULD.*
ATHENA! COME BACK, MY DEAR! LET THE POLICE HANDLE THIS!
ATHENA!
DOCTOR! HELP ME!

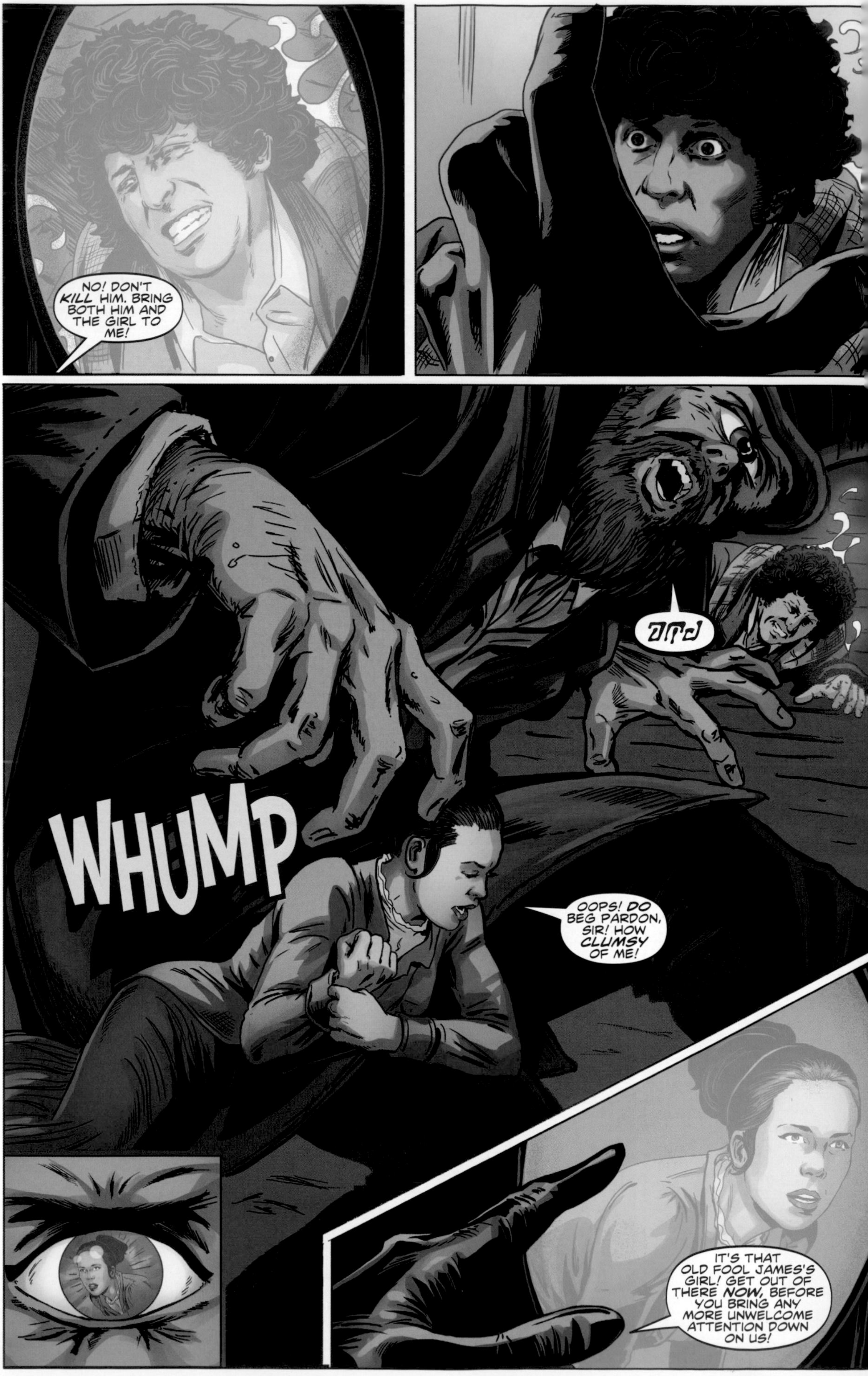
NO! DON'T KILL HIM. BRING BOTH HIM AND THE GIRL TO ME!
WHUMP
OOPS! DO BEG PARDON, SIR! HOW CLUMSY OF ME!
IT'S THAT OLD FOOL JAMES'S GIRL! GET OUT OF THERE NOW, BEFORE YOU BRING ANY MORE UNWELCOME ATTENTION DOWN ON US!

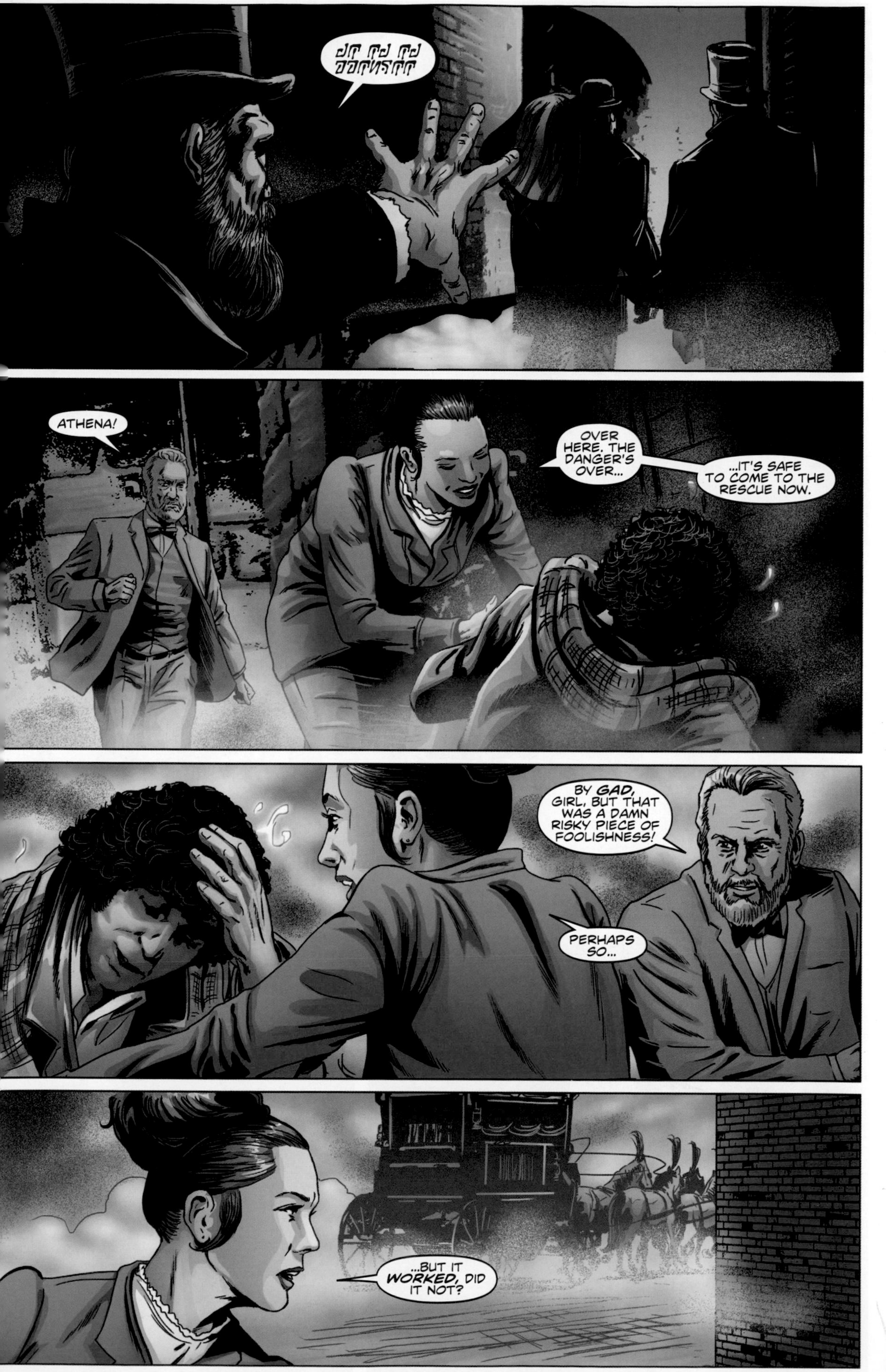
ATHENA!
OVER HERE. THE DANGER'S OVER...
...IT'S SAFE TO COME TO THE RESCUE NOW.
BY GAD, GIRL, BUT THAT WAS A DAMN RISKY PIECE OF FOOLISHNESS!
PERHAPS SO...
...BUT IT WORKED, DID IT NOT?

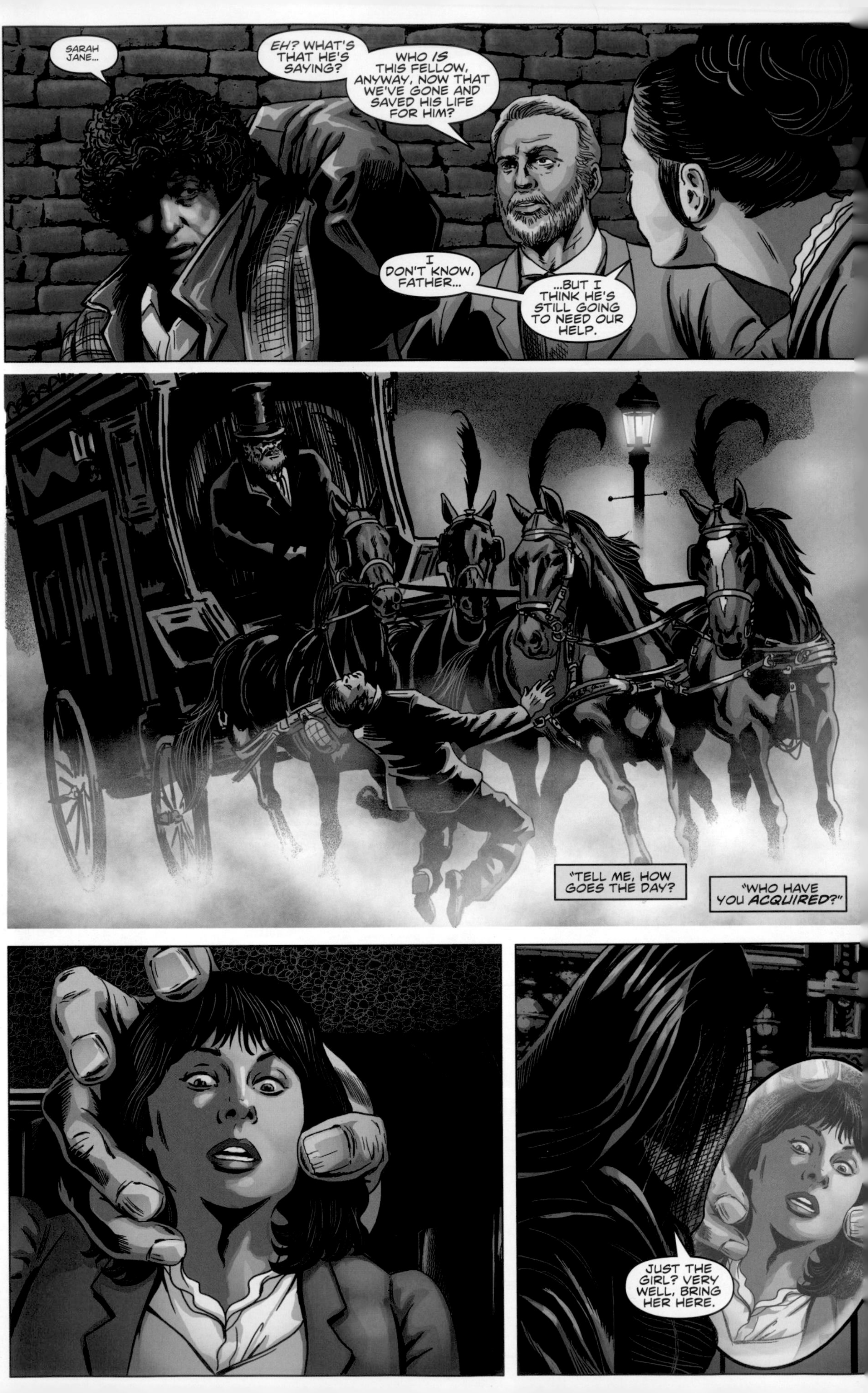
SARAH JANE...
EH? WHAT'S THAT HE'S SAYING?
WHO IS THIS FELLOW, ANYWAY, NOW THAT WE'VE GONE AND SAVED HIS LIFE FOR HIM?
I DON'T KNOW, FATHER...
...BUT I THINK HE'S STILL GOING TO NEED OUR HELP.
"TELL ME, HOW GOES THE DAY?
"WHO HAVE YOU ACQUIRED?"
JUST THE GIRL? VERY WELL, BRING HER HERE.

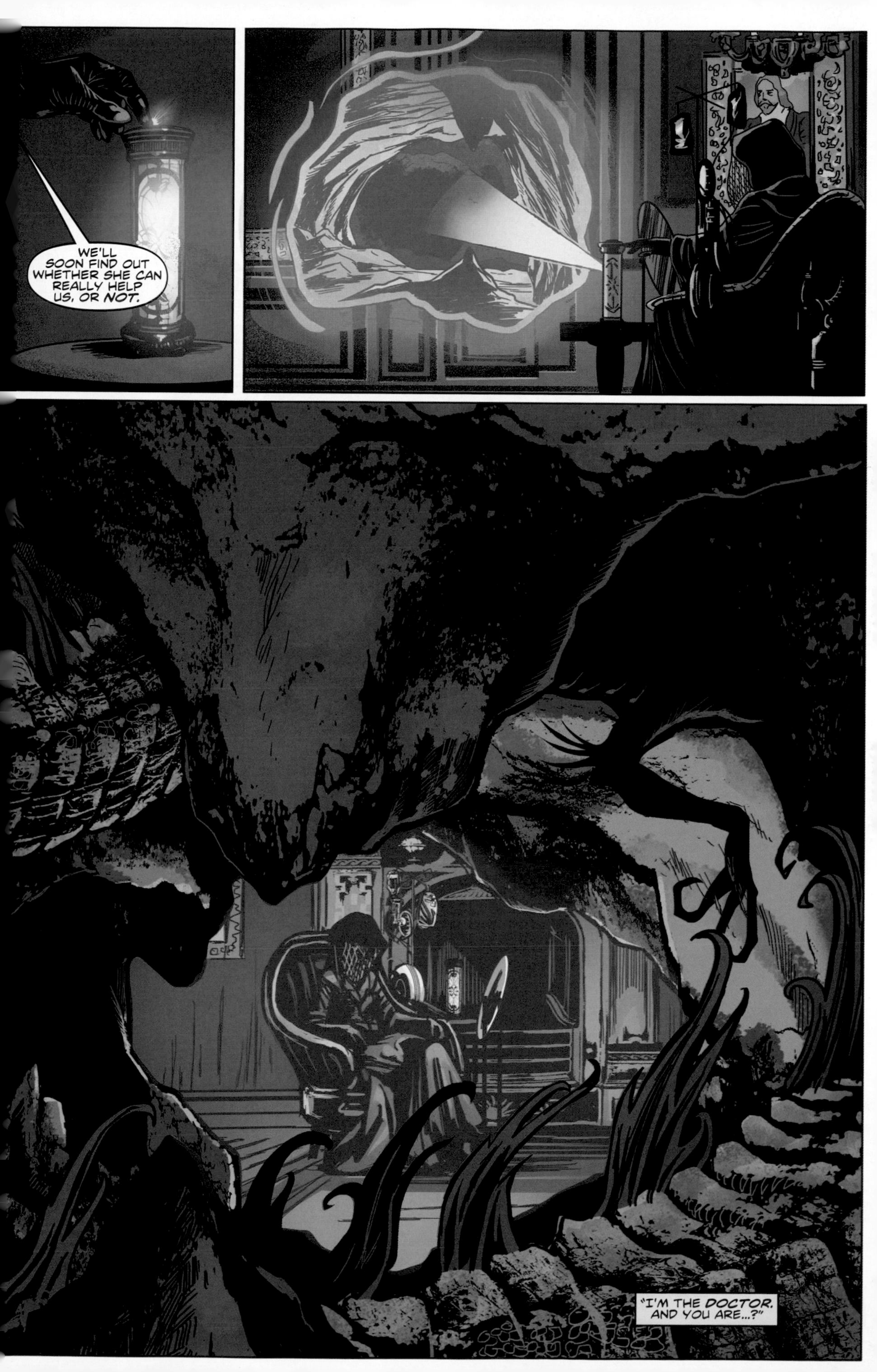
WE'LL SOON FIND OUT WHETHER SHE CAN REALLY HELP US, OR NOT.
"I'M THE DOCTOR. AND YOU ARE...?"

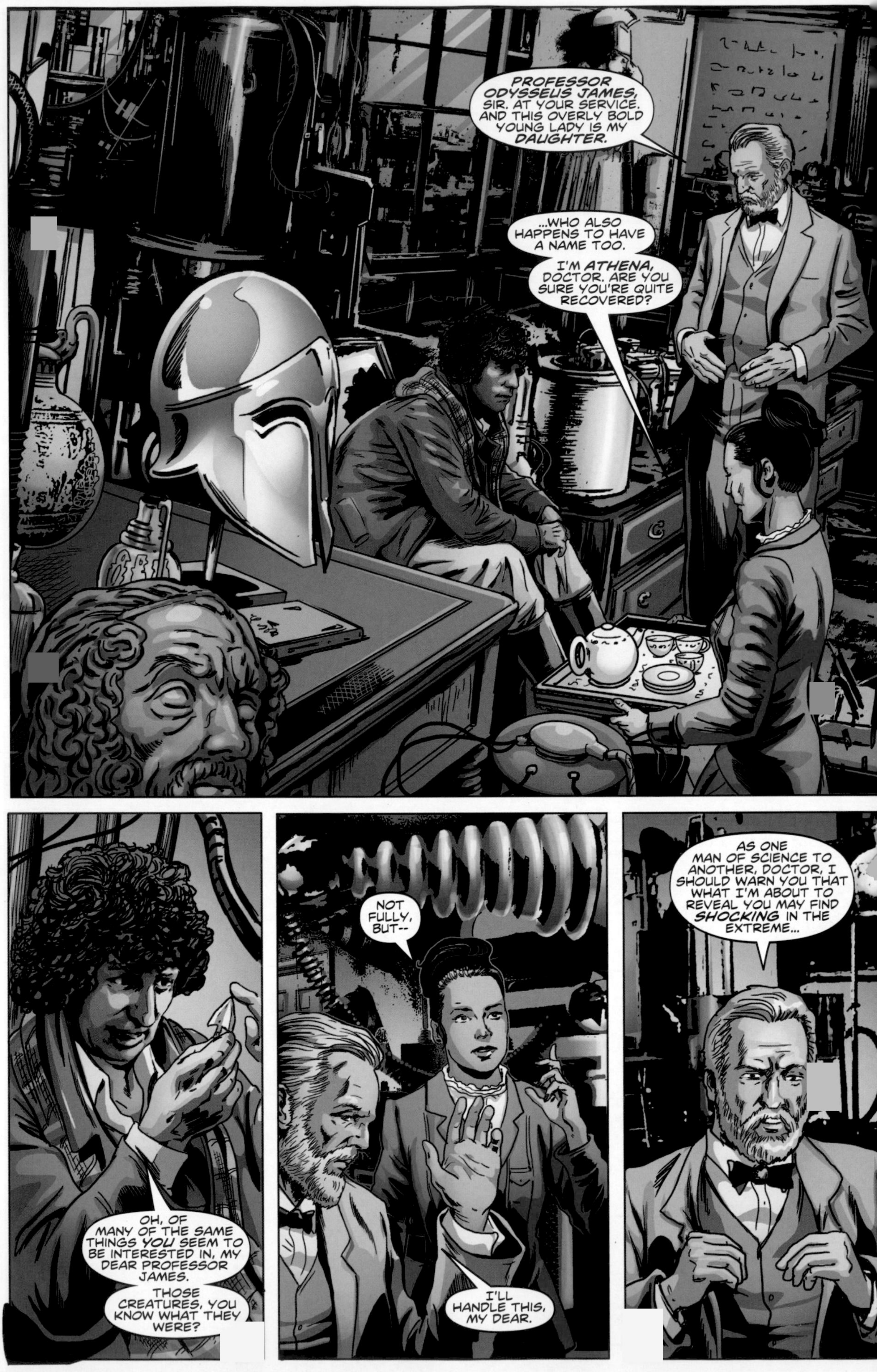
PROFESSOR ODYSSEUS JAMES, SIR. AT YOUR SERVICE. AND THIS OVERLY BOLD YOUNG LADY IS MY DAUGHTER.
...WHO ALSO HAPPENS TO HAVE A NAME TOO.
I'M ATHENA, DOCTOR. ARE YOU SURE YOU'RE QUITE RECOVERED?
OH, OF MANY OF THE SAME THINGS YOU SEEM TO BE INTERESTED IN, MY DEAR PROFESSOR JAMES.
THOSE CREATURES, YOU KNOW WHAT THEY WERE?
NOT FULLY, BUT--
I'LL HANDLE THIS, MY DEAR.
AS ONE MAN OF SCIENCE TO ANOTHER, DOCTOR, I SHOULD WARN YOU THAT WHAT I'M ABOUT TO REVEAL YOU MAY FIND SHOCKING IN THE EXTREME...

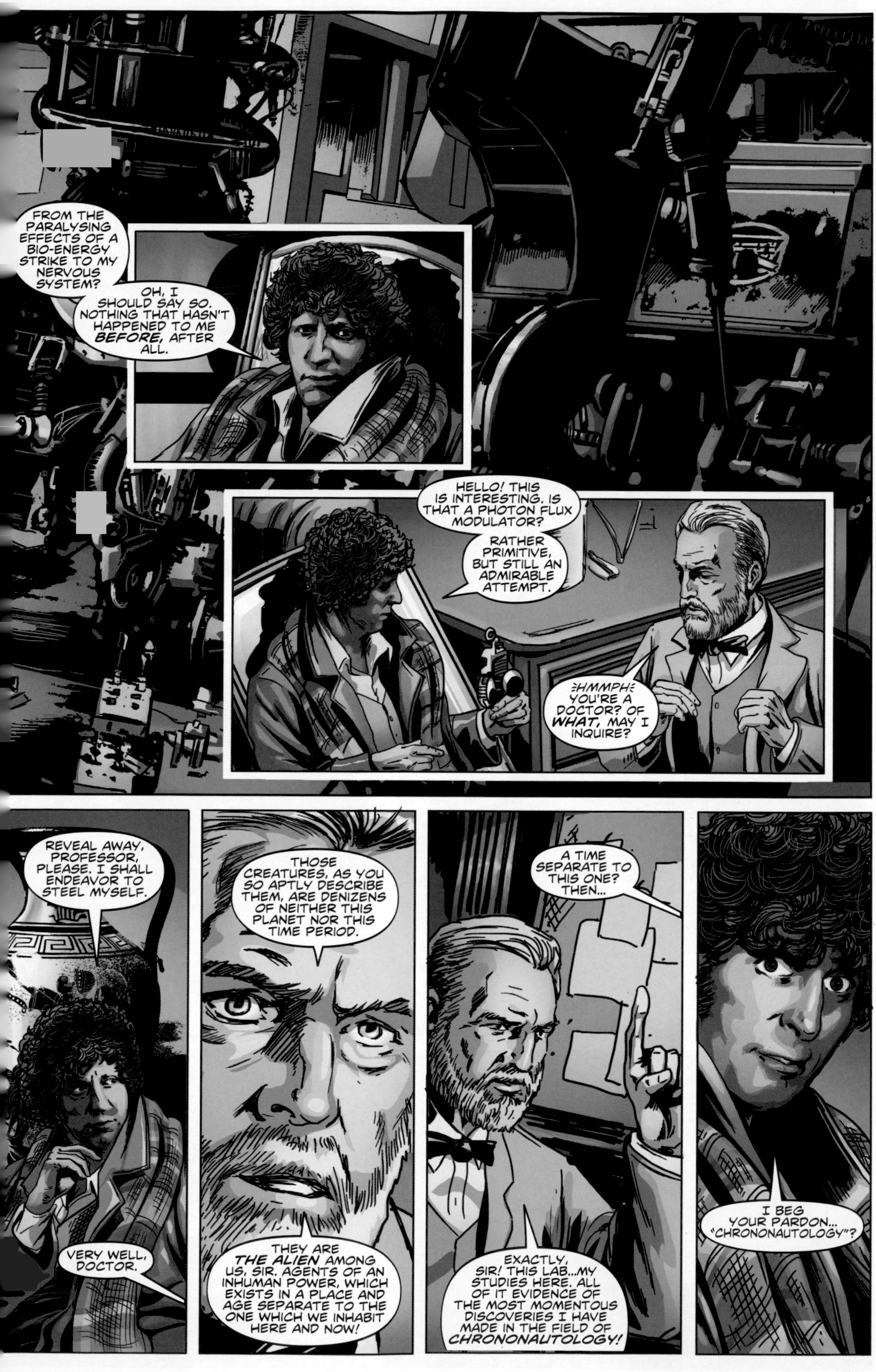
FROM THE PARALYSING EFFECTS OF A BIO-ENERGY STRIKE TO MY NERVOUS SYSTEM?
OH, I SHOULD SAY SO. NOTHING THAT HASN'T HAPPENED TO ME ***BEFORE,*** AFTER ALL.
HELLO! THIS IS INTERESTING. IS THAT A PHOTON FLUX MODULATOR?
RATHER PRIMITIVE, BUT STILL AN ADMIRABLE ATTEMPT.
HMMPH. YOU'RE A DOCTOR? OF ***WHAT,*** MAY I INQUIRE?
REVEAL AWAY, PROFESSOR, PLEASE. I SHALL ENDEAVOR TO STEEL MYSELF.
VERY WELL, DOCTOR.
THOSE CREATURES, AS YOU SO APTLY DESCRIBE THEM, ARE DENIZENS OF NEITHER THIS PLANET NOR THIS TIME PERIOD.
THEY ARE ***THE ALIEN*** AMONG US, SIR. AGENTS OF AN INHUMAN POWER, WHICH EXISTS IN A PLACE AND AGE SEPARATE TO THE ONE WHICH WE INHABIT HERE AND NOW!
A TIME SEPARATE TO THIS ONE? THEN...
EXACTLY, SIR! THIS LAB...MY STUDIES HERE. ALL OF IT EVIDENCE OF THE MOST MOMENTOUS DISCOVERIES I HAVE MADE IN THE FIELD OF ***CHRONONAUTOLOGY!***
I BEG YOUR PARDON... "CHRONONAUTOLOGY"?

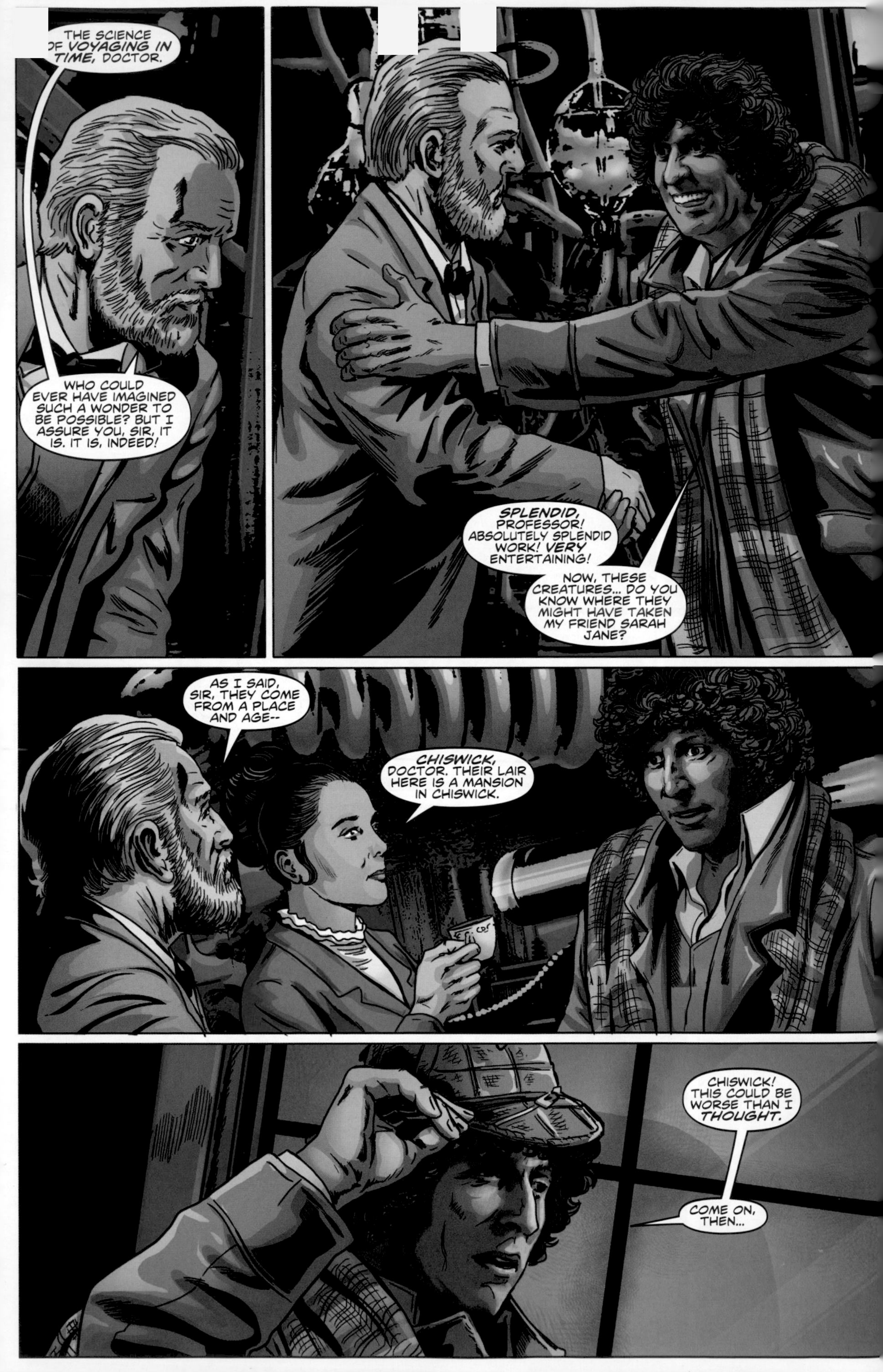
THE SCIENCE OF VOYAGING IN TIME, DOCTOR.
WHO COULD EVER HAVE IMAGINED SUCH A WONDER TO BE POSSIBLE? BUT I ASSURE YOU, SIR, IT IS. IT IS, INDEED!
SPLENDID, PROFESSOR! ABSOLUTELY SPLENDID WORK! VERY ENTERTAINING!
NOW, THESE CREATURES... DO YOU KNOW WHERE THEY MIGHT HAVE TAKEN MY FRIEND SARAH JANE?
AS I SAID, SIR, THEY COME FROM A PLACE AND AGE--
CHISWICK, DOCTOR. THEIR LAIR HERE IS A MANSION IN CHISWICK.
CHISWICK! THIS COULD BE WORSE THAN I THOUGHT.
COME ON, THEN...

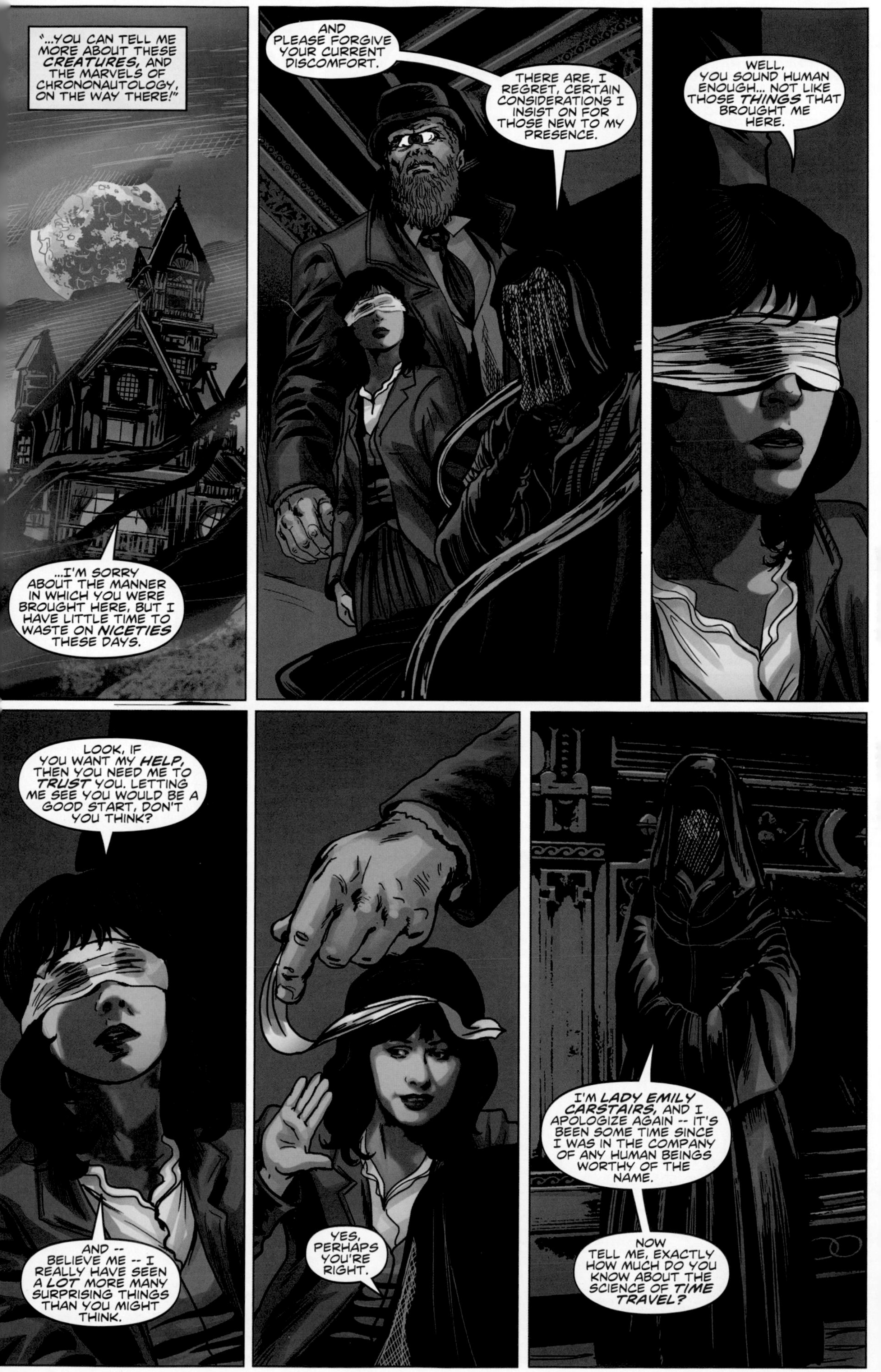
"...YOU CAN TELL ME MORE ABOUT THESE CREATURES, AND THE MARVELS OF CHRONONAUTOLOGY, ON THE WAY THERE!"
...I'M SORRY ABOUT THE MANNER IN WHICH YOU WERE BROUGHT HERE, BUT I HAVE LITTLE TIME TO WASTE ON NICETIES THESE DAYS.
AND PLEASE FORGIVE YOUR CURRENT DISCOMFORT.
THERE ARE, I REGRET, CERTAIN CONSIDERATIONS I INSIST ON FOR THOSE NEW TO MY PRESENCE.
WELL, YOU SOUND HUMAN ENOUGH... NOT LIKE THOSE THINGS THAT BROUGHT ME HERE.
LOOK, IF YOU WANT MY HELP, THEN YOU NEED ME TO TRUST YOU. LETTING ME SEE YOU WOULD BE A GOOD START, DON'T YOU THINK?
AND -- BELIEVE ME -- I REALLY HAVE SEEN A LOT MORE MANY SURPRISING THINGS THAN YOU MIGHT THINK.
YES, PERHAPS YOU'RE RIGHT.
I'M LADY EMILY CARSTAIRS, AND I APOLOGIZE AGAIN -- IT'S BEEN SOME TIME SINCE I WAS IN THE COMPANY OF ANY HUMAN BEINGS WORTHY OF THE NAME.
NOW TELL ME, EXACTLY HOW MUCH DO YOU KNOW ABOUT THE SCIENCE OF TIME TRAVEL?

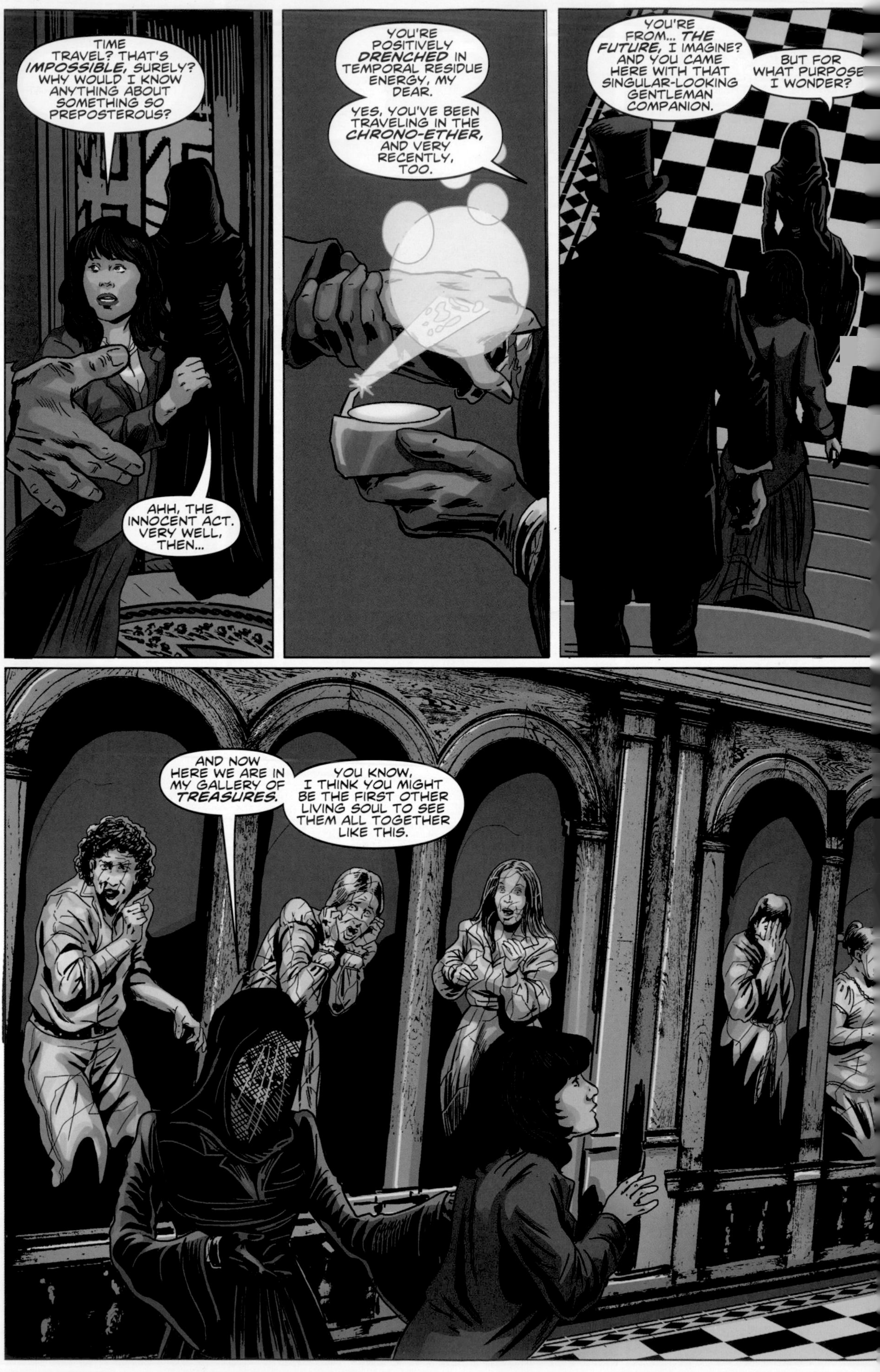
TIME TRAVEL? THAT'S IMPOSSIBLE, SURELY? WHY WOULD I KNOW ANYTHING ABOUT SOMETHING SO PREPOSTEROUS?
AHH, THE INNOCENT ACT. VERY WELL, THEN...
YOU'RE POSITIVELY DRENCHED IN TEMPORAL RESIDUE ENERGY, MY DEAR.
YES, YOU'VE BEEN TRAVELING IN THE CHRONO-ETHER, AND VERY RECENTLY, TOO.
YOU'RE FROM... THE FUTURE, I IMAGINE? AND YOU CAME HERE WITH THAT SINGULAR-LOOKING GENTLEMAN COMPANION.
BUT FOR WHAT PURPOSE I WONDER?
AND NOW HERE WE ARE IN MY GALLERY OF TREASURES.
YOU KNOW, I THINK YOU MIGHT BE THE FIRST OTHER LIVING SOUL TO SEE THEM ALL TOGETHER LIKE THIS.

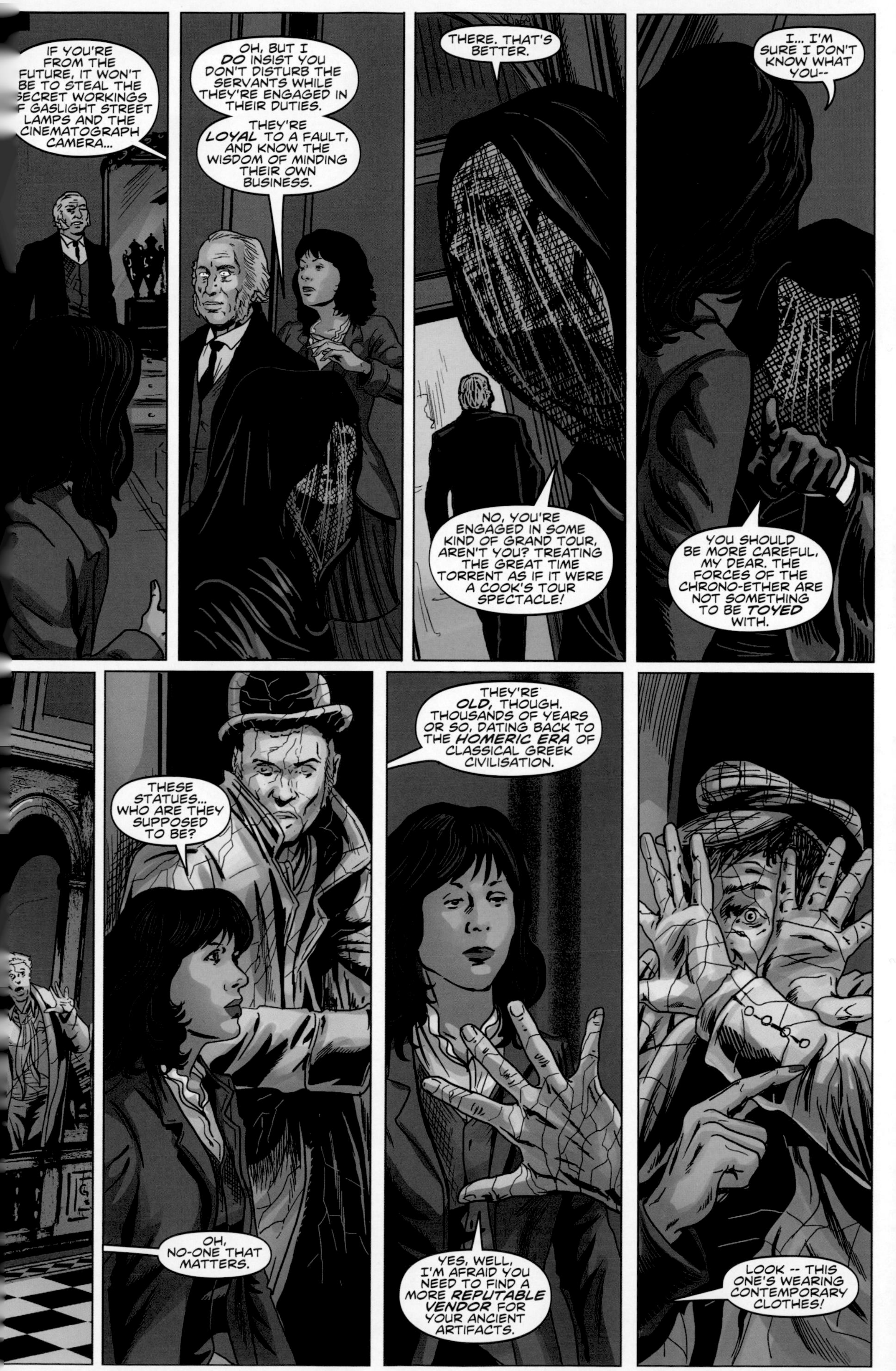

IF YOU'RE FROM THE FUTURE, IT WON'T BE TO STEAL THE SECRET WORKINGS OF GASLIGHT STREET LAMPS AND THE CINEMATOGRAPH CAMERA...
OH, BUT I DO INSIST YOU DON'T DISTURB THE SERVANTS WHILE THEY'RE ENGAGED IN THEIR DUTIES.
THEY'RE LOYAL TO A FAULT, AND KNOW THE WISDOM OF MINDING THEIR OWN BUSINESS.
THERE. THAT'S BETTER.
NO, YOU'RE ENGAGED IN SOME KIND OF GRAND TOUR, AREN'T YOU? TREATING THE GREAT TIME TORRENT AS IF IT WERE A COOK'S TOUR SPECTACLE!
I... I'M SURE I DON'T KNOW WHAT YOU--
YOU SHOULD BE MORE CAREFUL, MY DEAR. THE FORCES OF THE CHRONO-ETHER ARE NOT SOMETHING TO BE TOYED WITH.
THESE STATUES... WHO ARE THEY SUPPOSED TO BE?
OH, NO-ONE THAT MATTERS.
THEY'RE OLD, THOUGH. THOUSANDS OF YEARS OR SO, DATING BACK TO THE HOMERIC ERA OF CLASSICAL GREEK CIVILISATION.
YES, WELL, I'M AFRAID YOU NEED TO FIND A MORE REPUTABLE VENDOR FOR YOUR ANCIENT ARTIFACTS.
LOOK -- THIS ONE'S WEARING CONTEMPORARY CLOTHES!

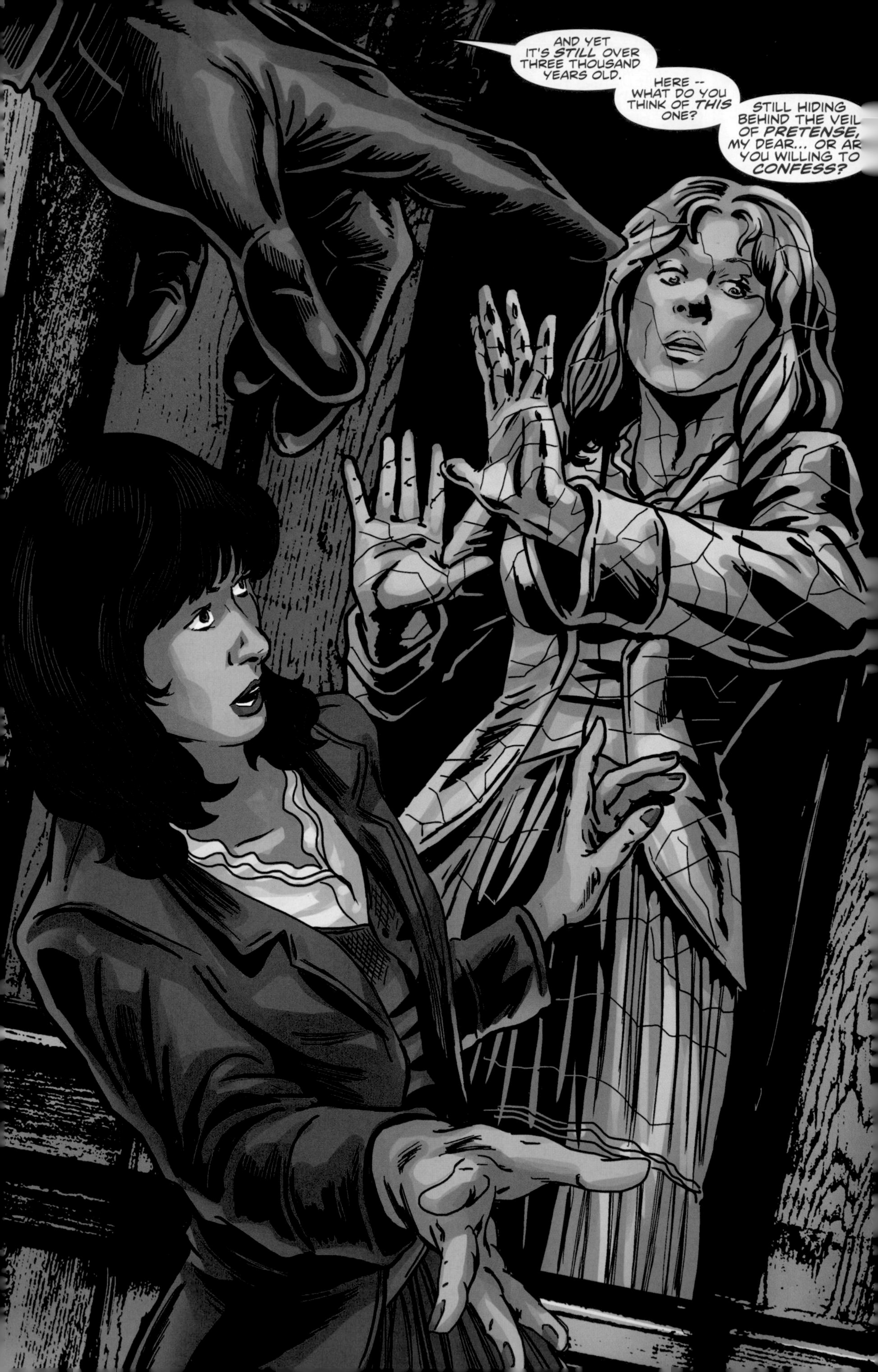
AND YET IT'S *STILL* OVER THREE THOUSAND YEARS OLD.
HERE -- WHAT DO YOU THINK OF *THIS* ONE?
STILL HIDING BEHIND THE VEIL OF *PRETENSE,* MY DEAR... OR AR YOU WILLING TO *CONFESS?*

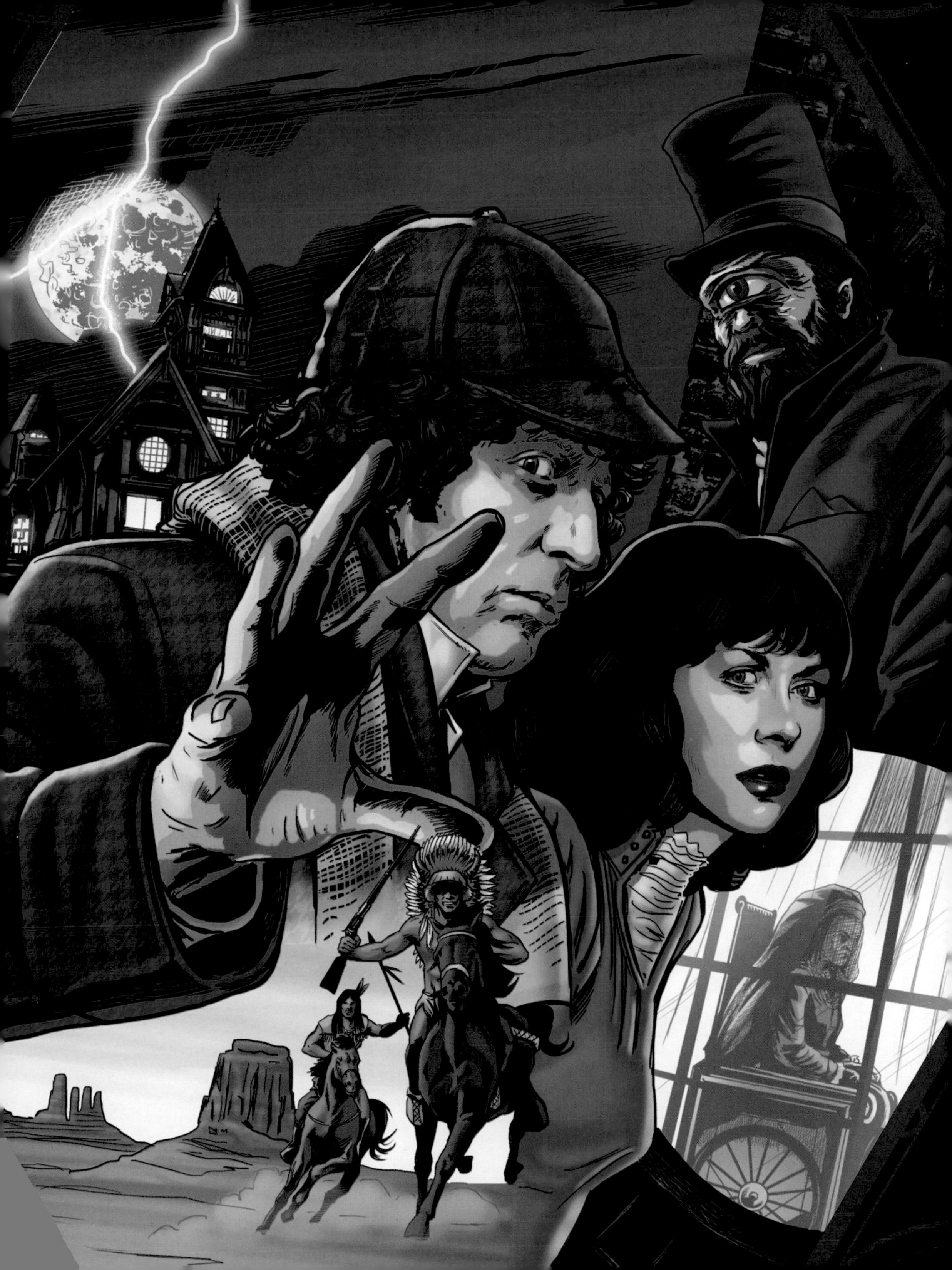

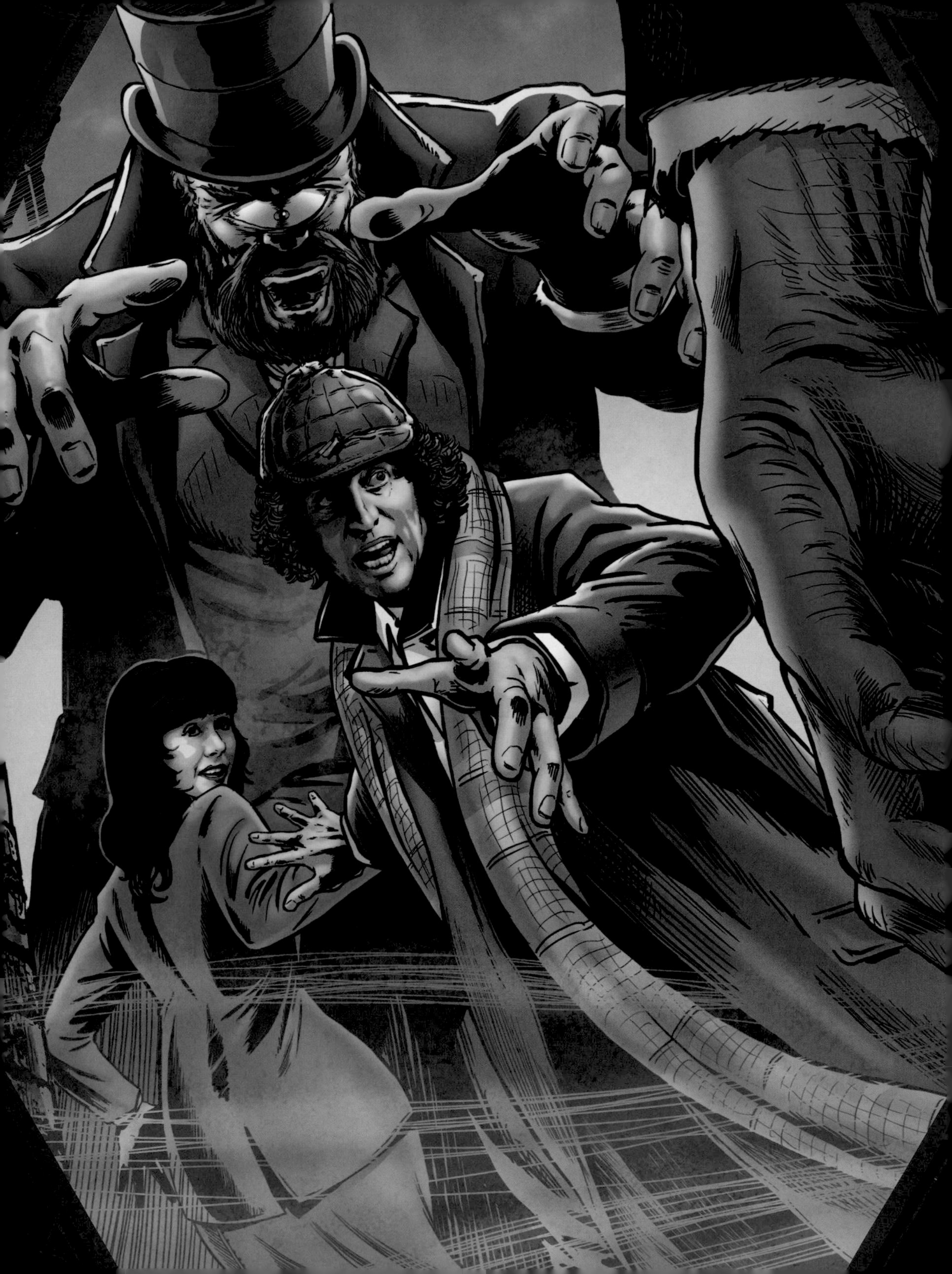

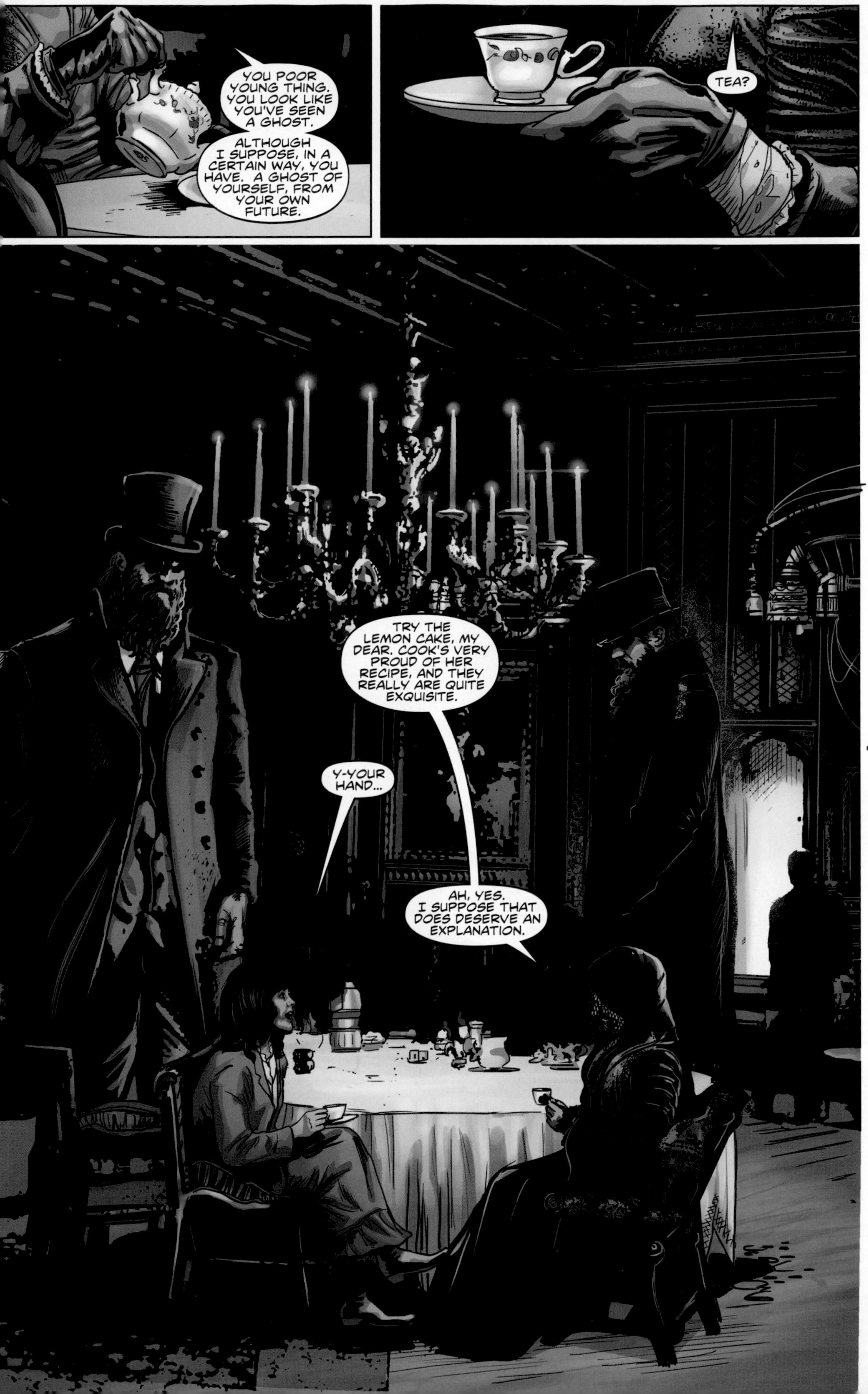
YOU POOR YOUNG THING. YOU LOOK LIKE YOU'VE SEEN A GHOST.
ALTHOUGH I SUPPOSE, IN A CERTAIN WAY, YOU HAVE. A GHOST OF YOURSELF, FROM YOUR OWN FUTURE.
TEA?
TRY THE LEMON CAKE, MY DEAR. COOK'S VERY PROUD OF HER RECIPE, AND THEY REALLY ARE QUITE EXQUISITE.
Y-YOUR HAND...
AH, YES. I SUPPOSE THAT DOES DESERVE AN EXPLANATION.

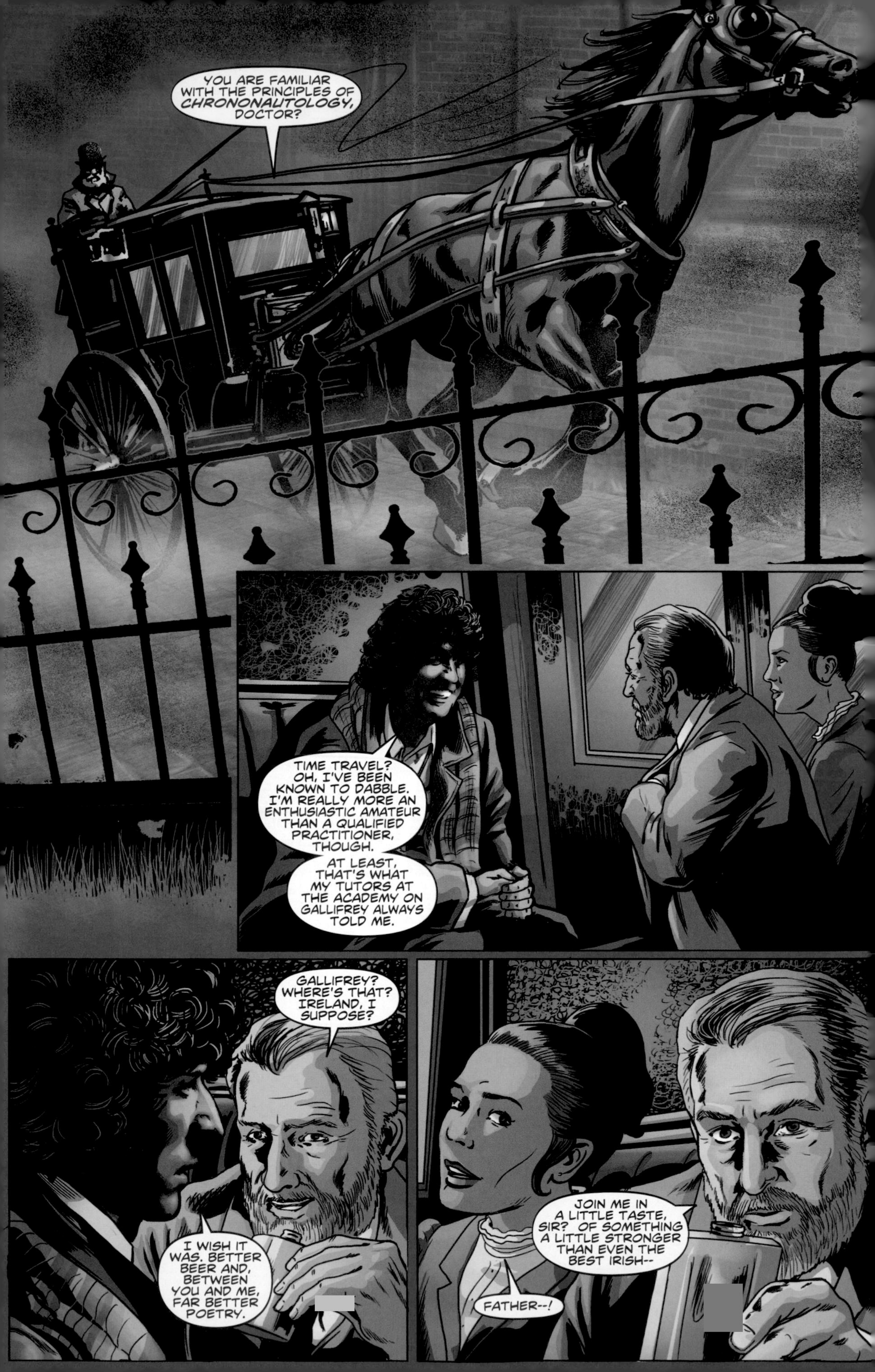
YOU ARE FAMILIAR WITH THE PRINCIPLES OF CHRONONAUTOLOGY, DOCTOR?
TIME TRAVEL? OH, I'VE BEEN KNOWN TO DABBLE. I'M REALLY MORE AN ENTHUSIASTIC AMATEUR THAN A QUALIFIED PRACTITIONER, THOUGH.
AT LEAST, THAT'S WHAT MY TUTORS AT THE ACADEMY ON GALLIFREY ALWAYS TOLD ME.
GALLIFREY? WHERE'S THAT? IRELAND, I SUPPOSE?
I WISH IT WAS. BETTER BEER AND, BETWEEN YOU AND ME, FAR BETTER POETRY.
JOIN ME IN A LITTLE TASTE, SIR? OF SOMETHING A LITTLE STRONGER THAN EVEN THE BEST IRISH--
FATHER--!

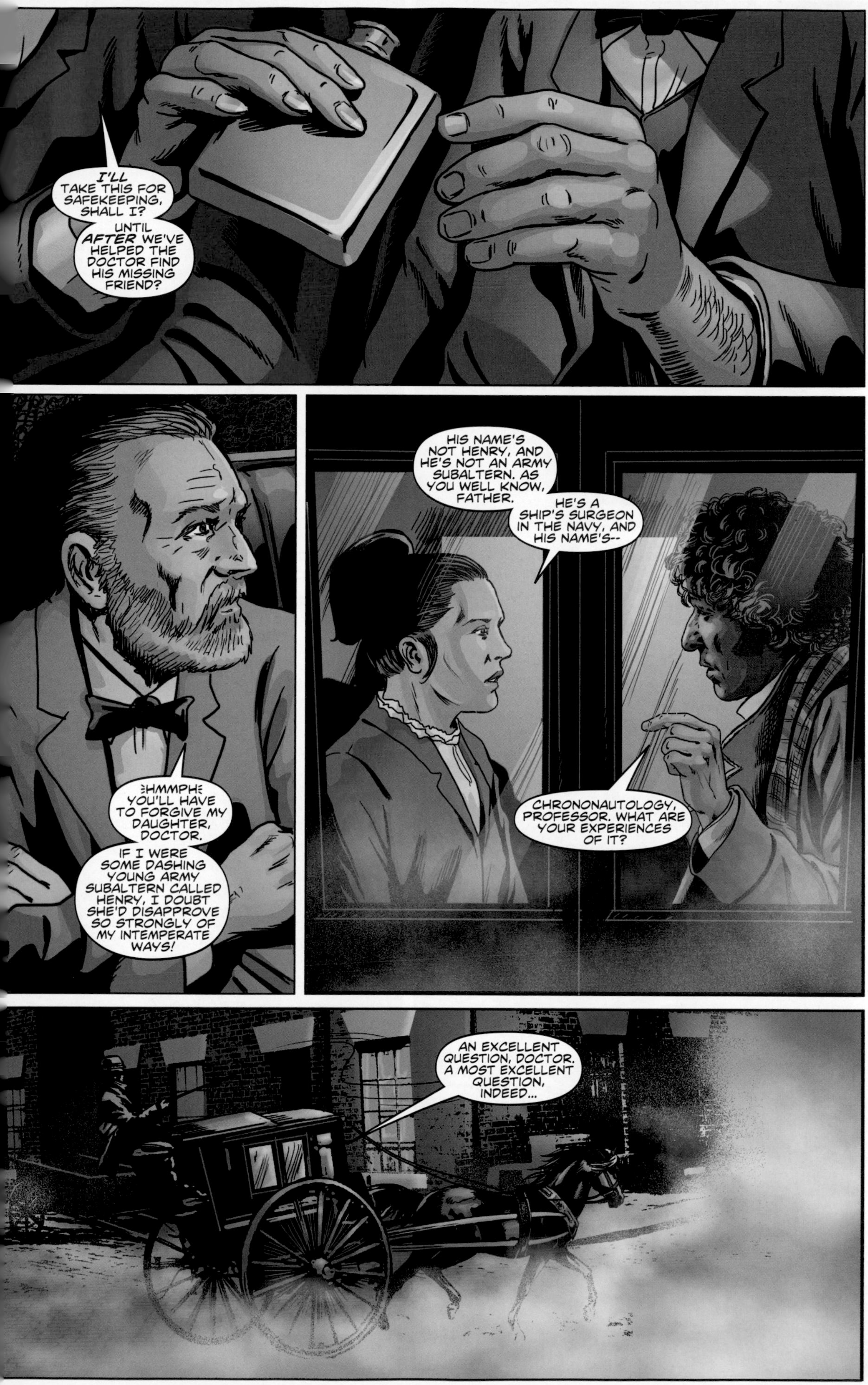

I'LL TAKE THIS FOR SAFEKEEPING, SHALL I?
UNTIL AFTER WE'VE HELPED THE DOCTOR FIND HIS MISSING FRIEND?
HMMPH! YOU'LL HAVE TO FORGIVE MY DAUGHTER, DOCTOR.
IF I WERE SOME DASHING YOUNG ARMY SUBALTERN CALLED HENRY, I DOUBT SHE'D DISAPPROVE SO STRONGLY OF MY INTEMPERATE WAYS!
HIS NAME'S NOT HENRY, AND HE'S NOT AN ARMY SUBALTERN. AS YOU WELL KNOW, FATHER.
HE'S A SHIP'S SURGEON IN THE NAVY, AND HIS NAME'S--
CHRONONAUTOLOGY, PROFESSOR. WHAT ARE YOUR EXPERIENCES OF IT?
AN EXCELLENT QUESTION, DOCTOR. A MOST EXCELLENT QUESTION, INDEED...

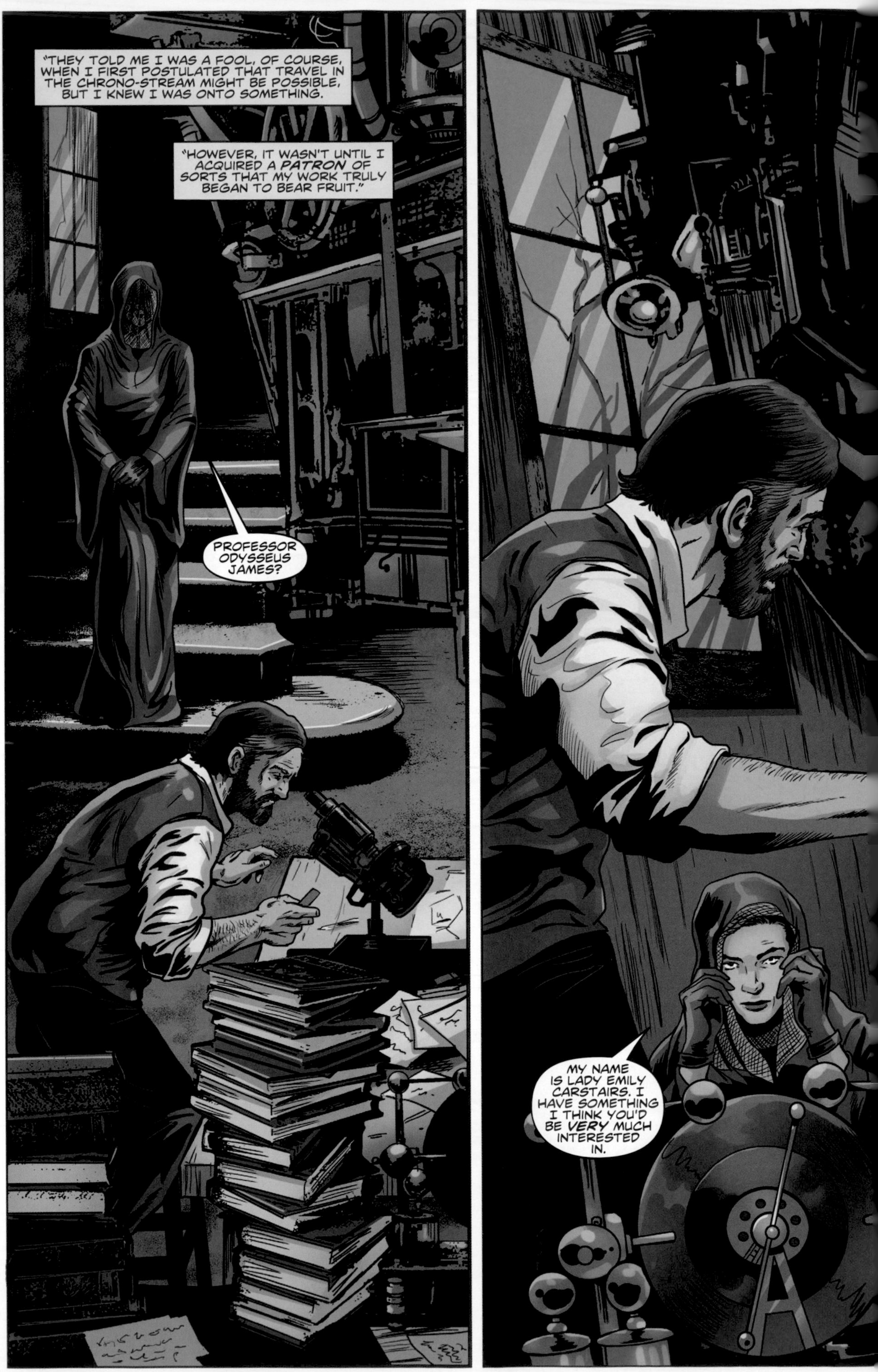
"THEY TOLD ME I WAS A FOOL, OF COURSE, WHEN I FIRST POSTULATED THAT TRAVEL IN THE CHRONO-STREAM MIGHT BE POSSIBLE, BUT I KNEW I WAS ONTO SOMETHING.
"HOWEVER, IT WASN'T UNTIL I ACQUIRED A PATRON OF SORTS THAT MY WORK TRULY BEGAN TO BEAR FRUIT."
PROFESSOR ODYSSEUS JAMES?
MY NAME IS LADY EMILY CARSTAIRS. I HAVE SOMETHING I THINK YOU'D BE VERY MUCH INTERESTED IN.

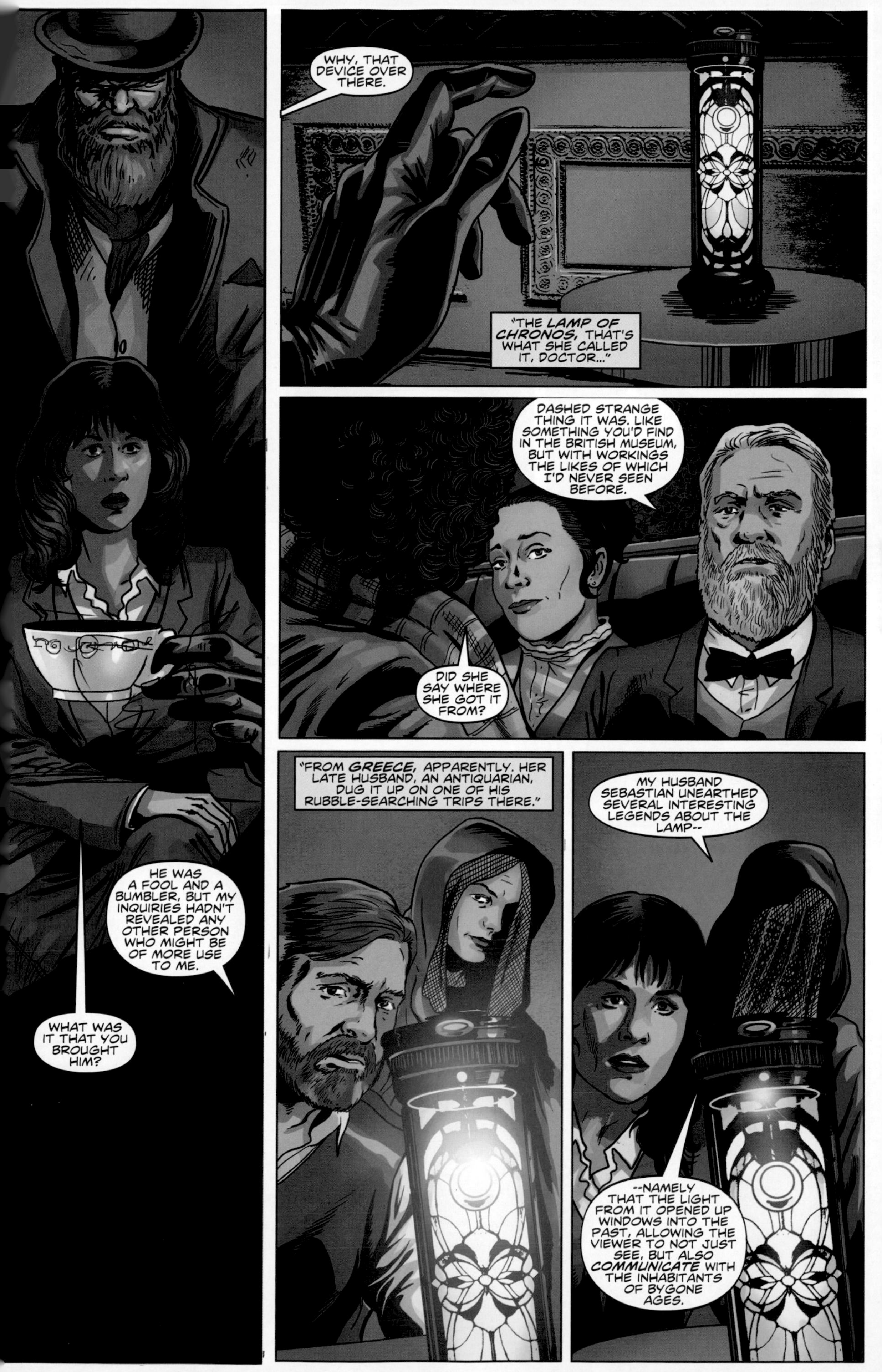
WHY, THAT DEVICE OVER THERE.
"THE LAMP OF CHRONOS, THAT'S WHAT SHE CALLED IT, DOCTOR..."
DASHED STRANGE THING IT WAS. LIKE SOMETHING YOU'D FIND IN THE BRITISH MUSEUM, BUT WITH WORKINGS THE LIKES OF WHICH I'D NEVER SEEN BEFORE.
DID SHE SAY WHERE SHE GOT IT FROM?
"FROM GREECE, APPARENTLY. HER LATE HUSBAND, AN ANTIQUARIAN, DUG IT UP ON ONE OF HIS RUBBLE-SEARCHING TRIPS THERE."
MY HUSBAND SEBASTIAN UNEARTHED SEVERAL INTERESTING LEGENDS ABOUT THE LAMP--
--NAMELY THAT THE LIGHT FROM IT OPENED UP WINDOWS INTO THE PAST, ALLOWING THE VIEWER TO NOT JUST SEE, BUT ALSO COMMUNICATE WITH THE INHABITANTS OF BYGONE AGES.
HE WAS A FOOL AND A BUMBLER, BUT MY INQUIRIES HADN'T REVEALED ANY OTHER PERSON WHO MIGHT BE OF MORE USE TO ME.
WHAT WAS IT THAT YOU BROUGHT HIM?

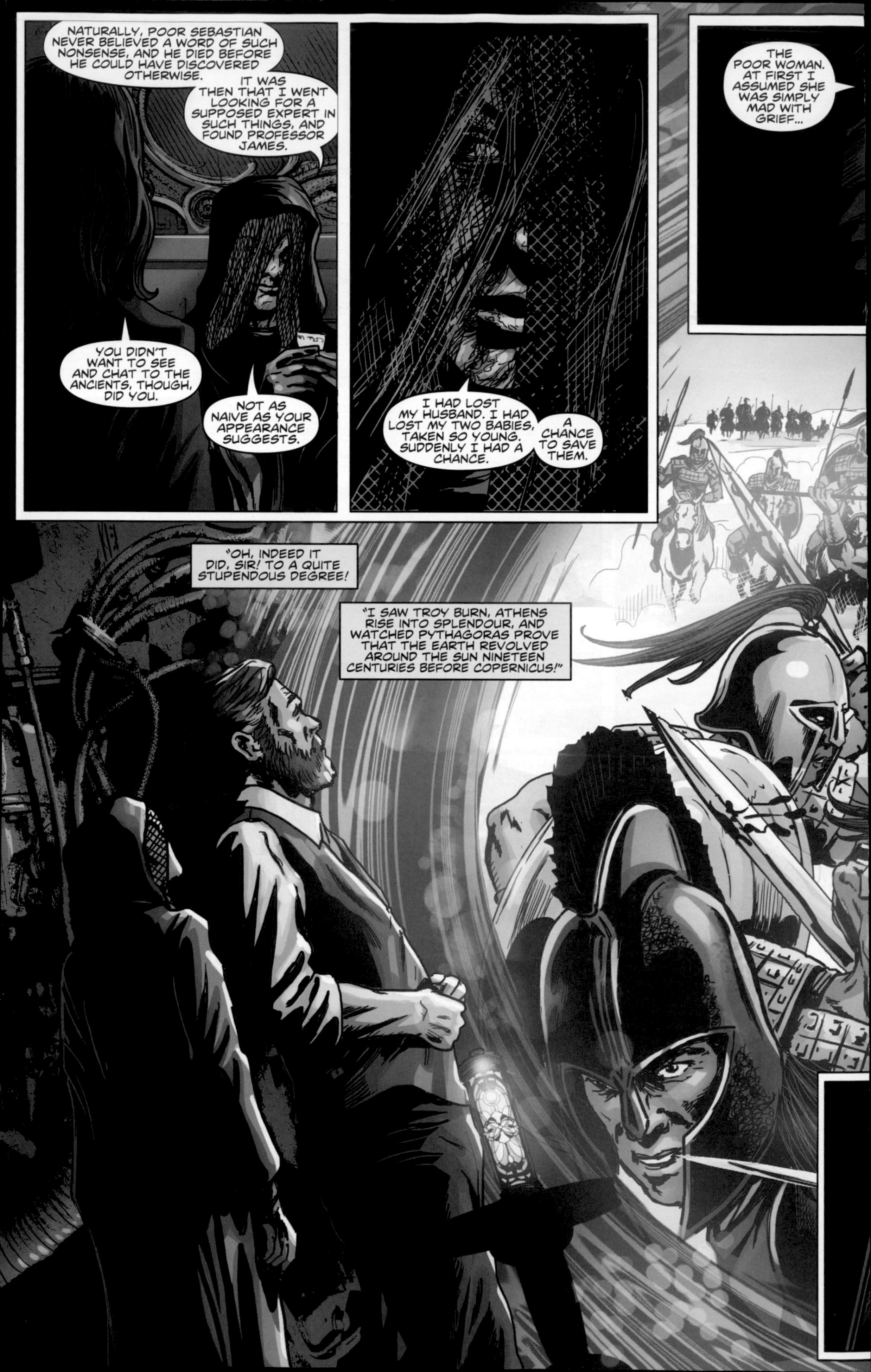
NATURALLY, POOR SEBASTIAN NEVER BELIEVED A WORD OF SUCH NONSENSE, AND HE DIED BEFORE HE COULD HAVE DISCOVERED OTHERWISE.
IT WAS THEN THAT I WENT LOOKING FOR A SUPPOSED EXPERT IN SUCH THINGS, AND FOUND PROFESSOR JAMES.
YOU DIDN'T WANT TO SEE AND CHAT TO THE ANCIENTS, THOUGH, DID YOU.
NOT AS NAIVE AS YOUR APPEARANCE SUGGESTS.
I HAD LOST MY HUSBAND. I HAD LOST MY TWO BABIES, TAKEN SO YOUNG. SUDDENLY I HAD A CHANCE.
A CHANCE TO SAVE THEM.
THE POOR WOMAN. AT FIRST I ASSUMED SHE WAS SIMPLY MAD WITH GRIEF...
"OH, INDEED IT DID, SIR! TO A QUITE STUPENDOUS DEGREE!
"I SAW TROY BURN, ATHENS RISE INTO SPLENDOUR, AND WATCHED PYTHAGORAS PROVE THAT THE EARTH REVOLVED AROUND THE SUN NINETEEN CENTURIES BEFORE COPERNICUS!"

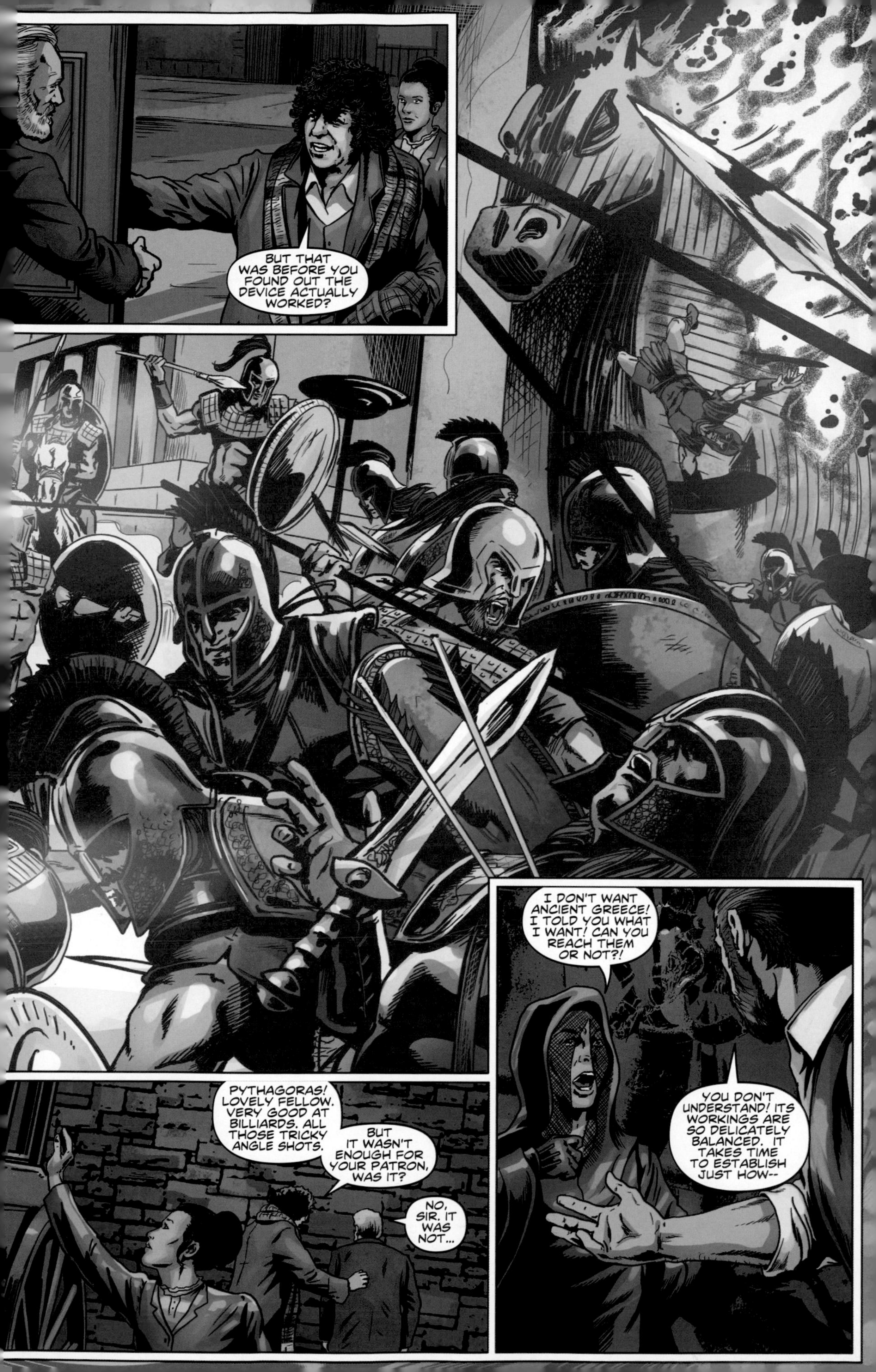
BUT THAT WAS BEFORE YOU FOUND OUT THE DEVICE ACTUALLY WORKED?
I DON'T WANT ANCIENT GREECE! I TOLD YOU WHAT I WANT! CAN YOU REACH THEM OR NOT?!
YOU DON'T UNDERSTAND! ITS WORKINGS ARE SO DELICATELY BALANCED. IT TAKES TIME TO ESTABLISH JUST HOW--
PYTHAGORAS! LOVELY FELLOW. VERY GOOD AT BILLIARDS. ALL THOSE TRICKY ANGLE SHOTS.
BUT IT WASN'T ENOUGH FOR YOUR PATRON, WAS IT?
NO, SIR. IT WAS NOT...

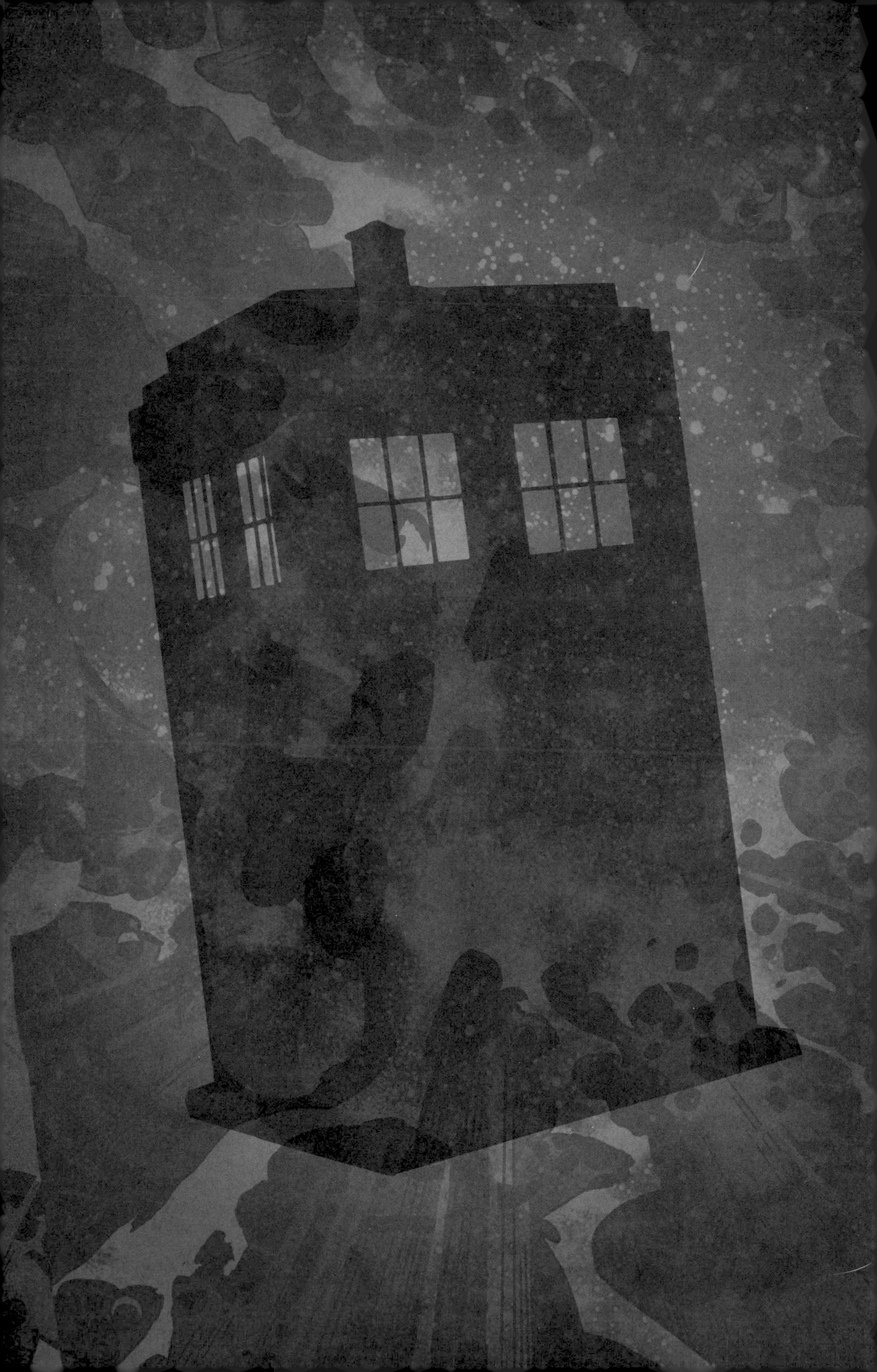

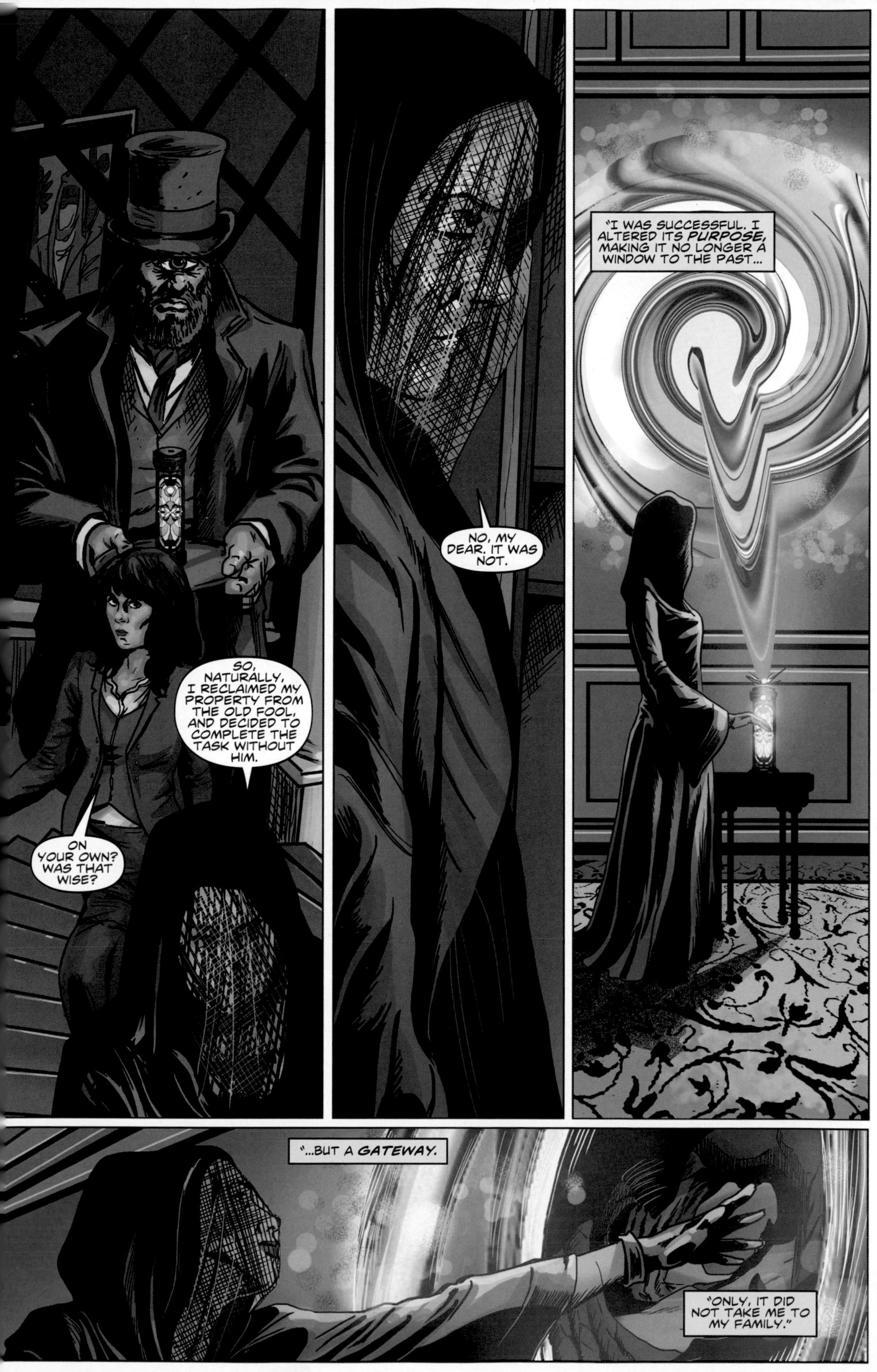
SO, NATURALLY, I RECLAIMED MY PROPERTY FROM THE OLD FOOL, AND DECIDED TO COMPLETE THE TASK WITHOUT HIM.
ON YOUR OWN? WAS THAT WISE?
NO, MY DEAR. IT WAS NOT.
"I WAS SUCCESSFUL. I ALTERED ITS PURPOSE, MAKING IT NO LONGER A WINDOW TO THE PAST...
"...BUT A GATEWAY.
"ONLY, IT DID NOT TAKE ME TO MY FAMILY."

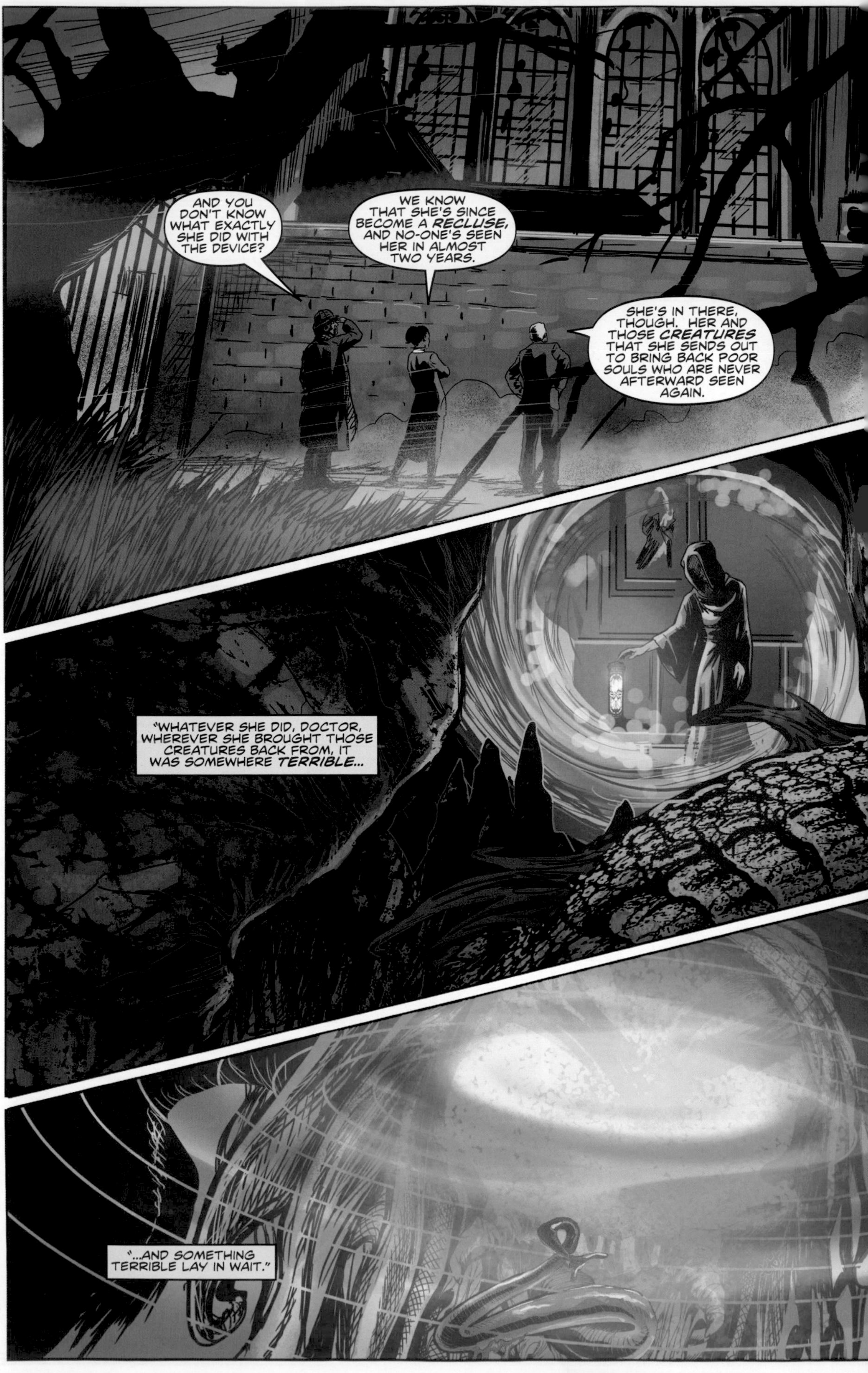
AND YOU DON'T KNOW WHAT EXACTLY SHE DID WITH THE DEVICE?
WE KNOW THAT SHE'S SINCE BECOME A RECLUSE, AND NO-ONE'S SEEN HER IN ALMOST TWO YEARS.
SHE'S IN THERE, THOUGH. HER AND THOSE CREATURES THAT SHE SENDS OUT TO BRING BACK POOR SOULS WHO ARE NEVER AFTERWARD SEEN AGAIN.
"WHATEVER SHE DID, DOCTOR, WHEREVER SHE BROUGHT THOSE CREATURES BACK FROM, IT WAS SOMEWHERE TERRIBLE...
"...AND SOMETHING TERRIBLE LAY IN WAIT."

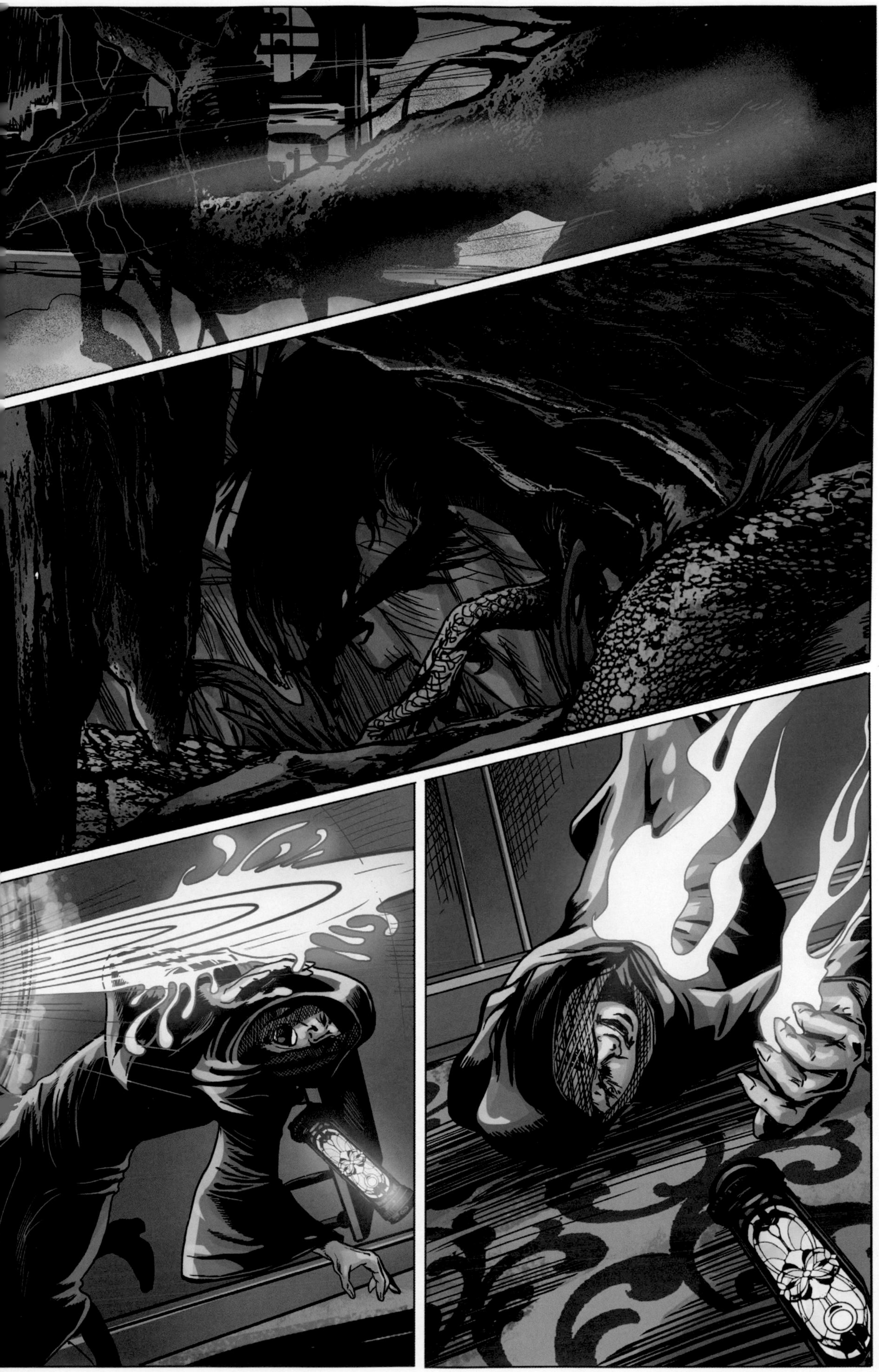

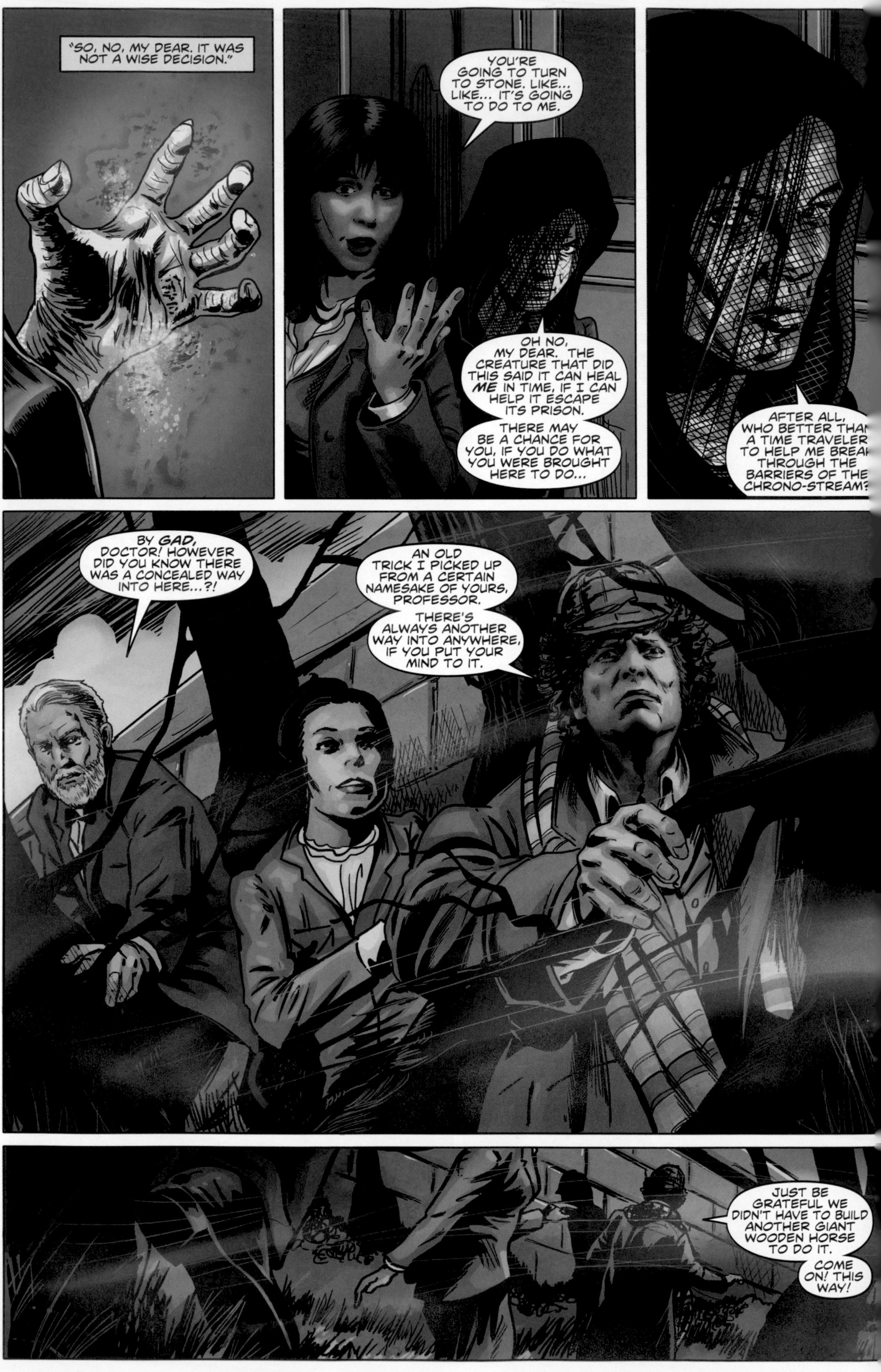
"SO, NO, MY DEAR. IT WAS NOT A WISE DECISION."
YOU'RE GOING TO TURN TO STONE. LIKE... LIKE... IT'S GOING TO DO TO ME.
OH NO, MY DEAR. THE CREATURE THAT DID THIS SAID IT CAN HEAL *ME* IN TIME, IF I CAN HELP IT ESCAPE ITS PRISON.
THERE MAY BE A CHANCE FOR YOU, IF YOU DO WHAT YOU WERE BROUGHT HERE TO DO...
AFTER ALL, WHO BETTER THAN A TIME TRAVELER TO HELP ME BREAK THROUGH THE BARRIERS OF THE CHRONO-STREAM?
BY *GAD*, DOCTOR! HOWEVER DID YOU KNOW THERE WAS A CONCEALED WAY INTO HERE...?!
AN OLD TRICK I PICKED UP FROM A CERTAIN NAMESAKE OF YOURS, PROFESSOR.
THERE'S ALWAYS ANOTHER WAY INTO ANYWHERE, IF YOU PUT YOUR MIND TO IT.
JUST BE GRATEFUL WE DIDN'T HAVE TO BUILD ANOTHER GIANT WOODEN HORSE TO DO IT.
COME ON! THIS WAY!

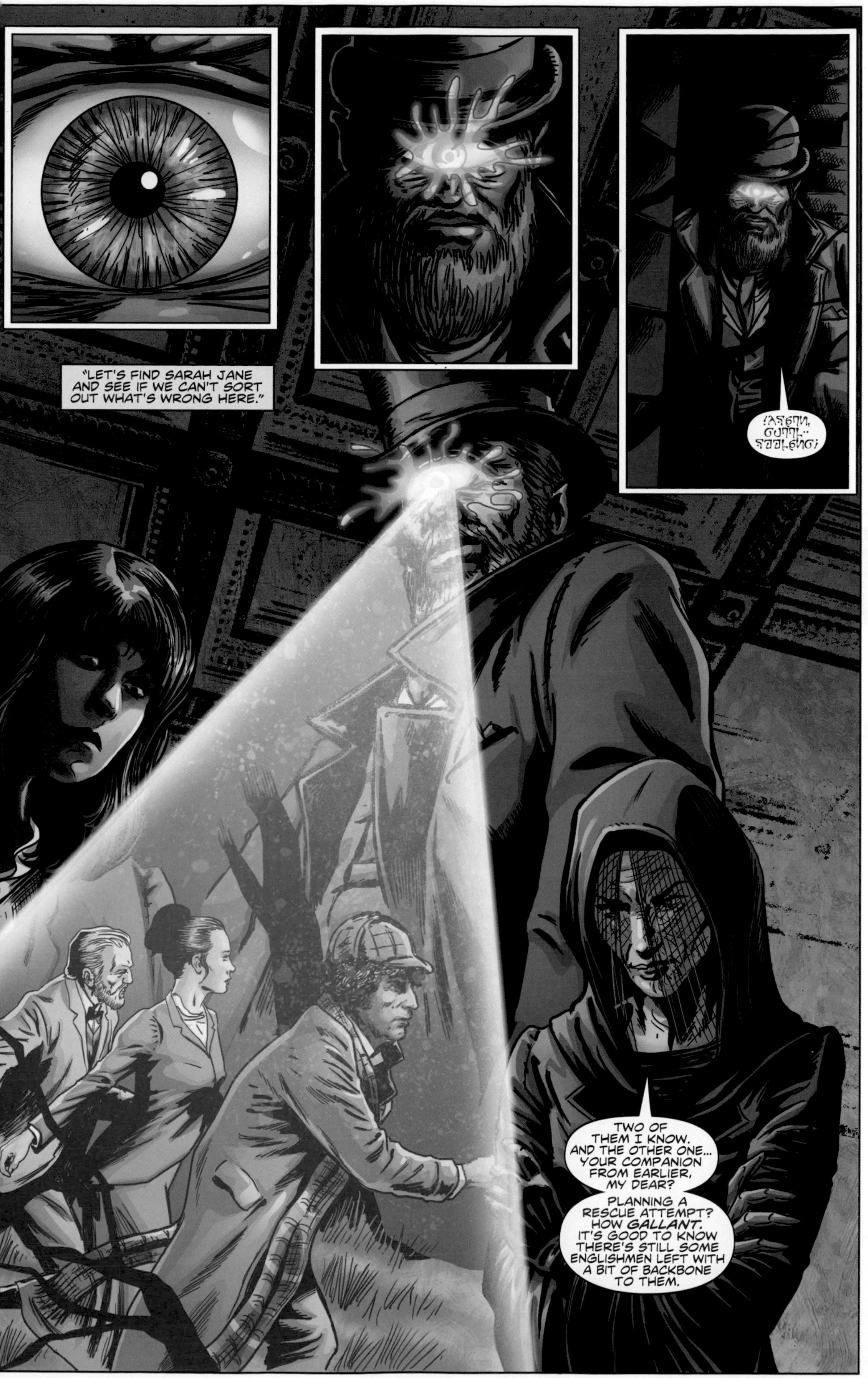
"LET'S FIND SARAH JANE AND SEE IF WE CAN'T SORT OUT WHAT'S WRONG HERE."
TWO OF THEM I KNOW. AND THE OTHER ONE... YOUR COMPANION FROM EARLIER, MY DEAR?
PLANNING A RESCUE ATTEMPT? HOW *GALLANT*. IT'S GOOD TO KNOW THERE'S STILL SOME ENGLISHMEN LEFT WITH A BIT OF BACKBONE TO THEM.

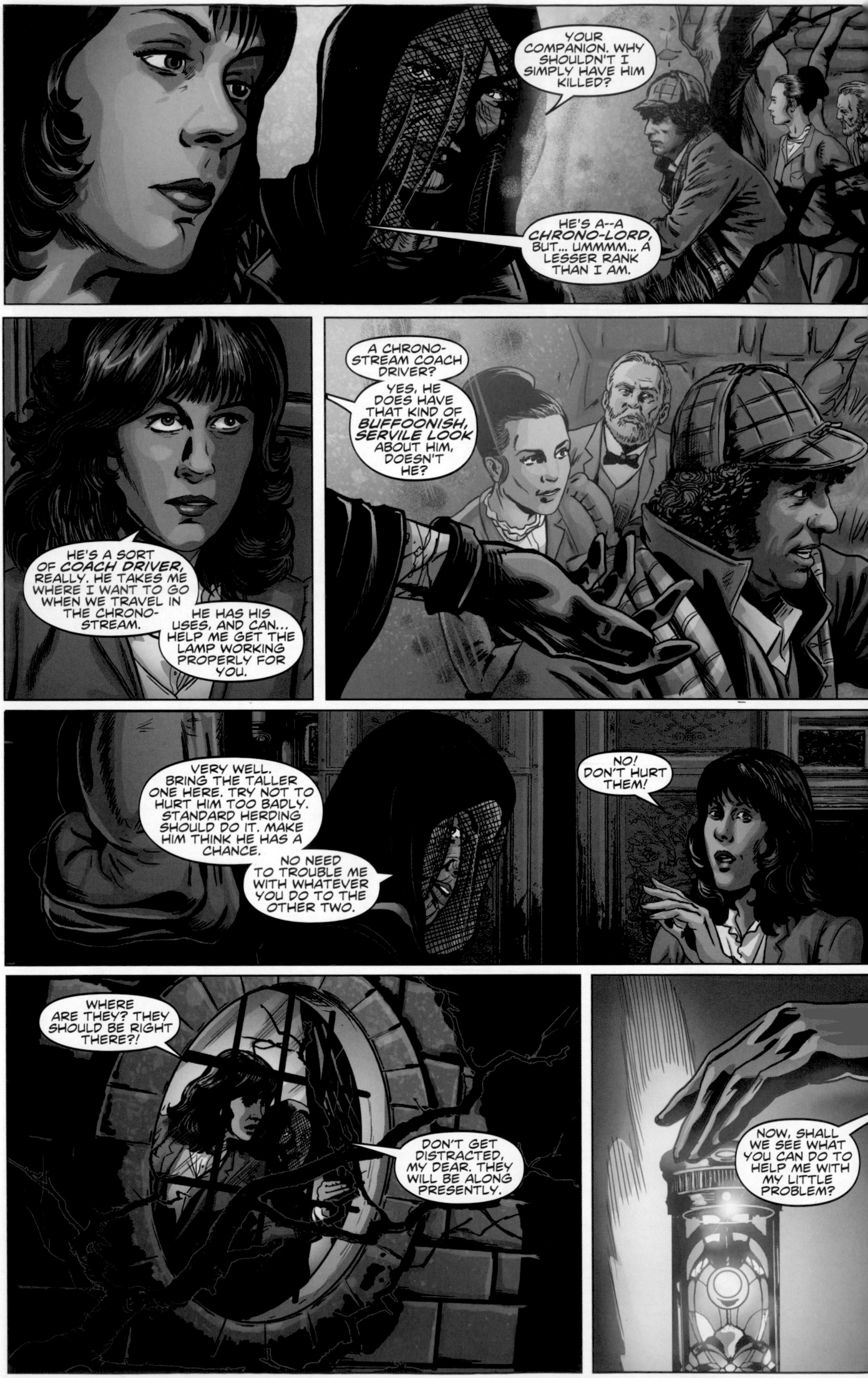
YOUR COMPANION. WHY SHOULDN'T I SIMPLY HAVE HIM KILLED?
HE'S A--A *CHRONO-LORD,* BUT... UMMMM... A LESSER RANK THAN I AM.
HE'S A SORT OF *COACH DRIVER,* REALLY. HE TAKES ME WHERE I WANT TO GO WHEN WE TRAVEL IN THE CHRONO-STREAM.
HE HAS HIS USES, AND CAN... HELP ME GET THE LAMP WORKING PROPERLY FOR YOU.
A CHRONO-STREAM COACH DRIVER?
YES, HE DOES HAVE THAT KIND OF *BUFFOONISH, SERVILE LOOK* ABOUT HIM, DOESN'T HE?
VERY WELL. BRING THE TALLER ONE HERE. TRY NOT TO HURT HIM TOO BADLY. STANDARD HERDING SHOULD DO IT. MAKE HIM THINK HE HAS A CHANCE.
NO NEED TO TROUBLE ME WITH WHATEVER YOU DO TO THE OTHER TWO.
NO! DON'T HURT THEM!
WHERE ARE THEY? THEY SHOULD BE RIGHT THERE?!
DON'T GET DISTRACTED, MY DEAR. THEY WILL BE ALONG PRESENTLY.
NOW, SHALL WE SEE WHAT YOU CAN DO TO HELP ME WITH MY LITTLE PROBLEM?

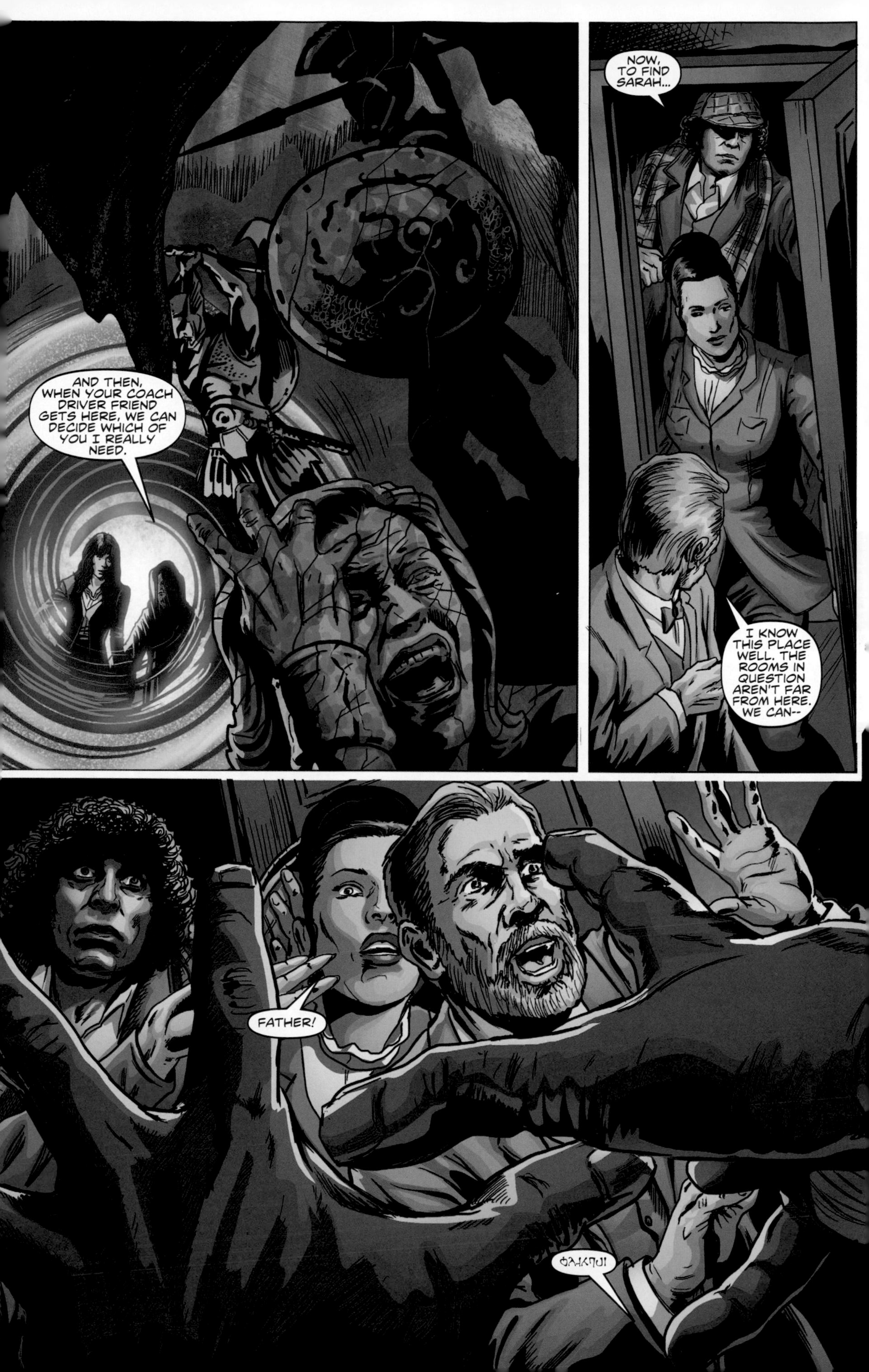
AND THEN, WHEN YOUR COACH DRIVER FRIEND GETS HERE, WE CAN DECIDE WHICH OF YOU I REALLY NEED.
NOW, TO FIND SARAH...
I KNOW THIS PLACE WELL. THE ROOMS IN QUESTION AREN'T FAR FROM HERE. WE CAN--
FATHER!

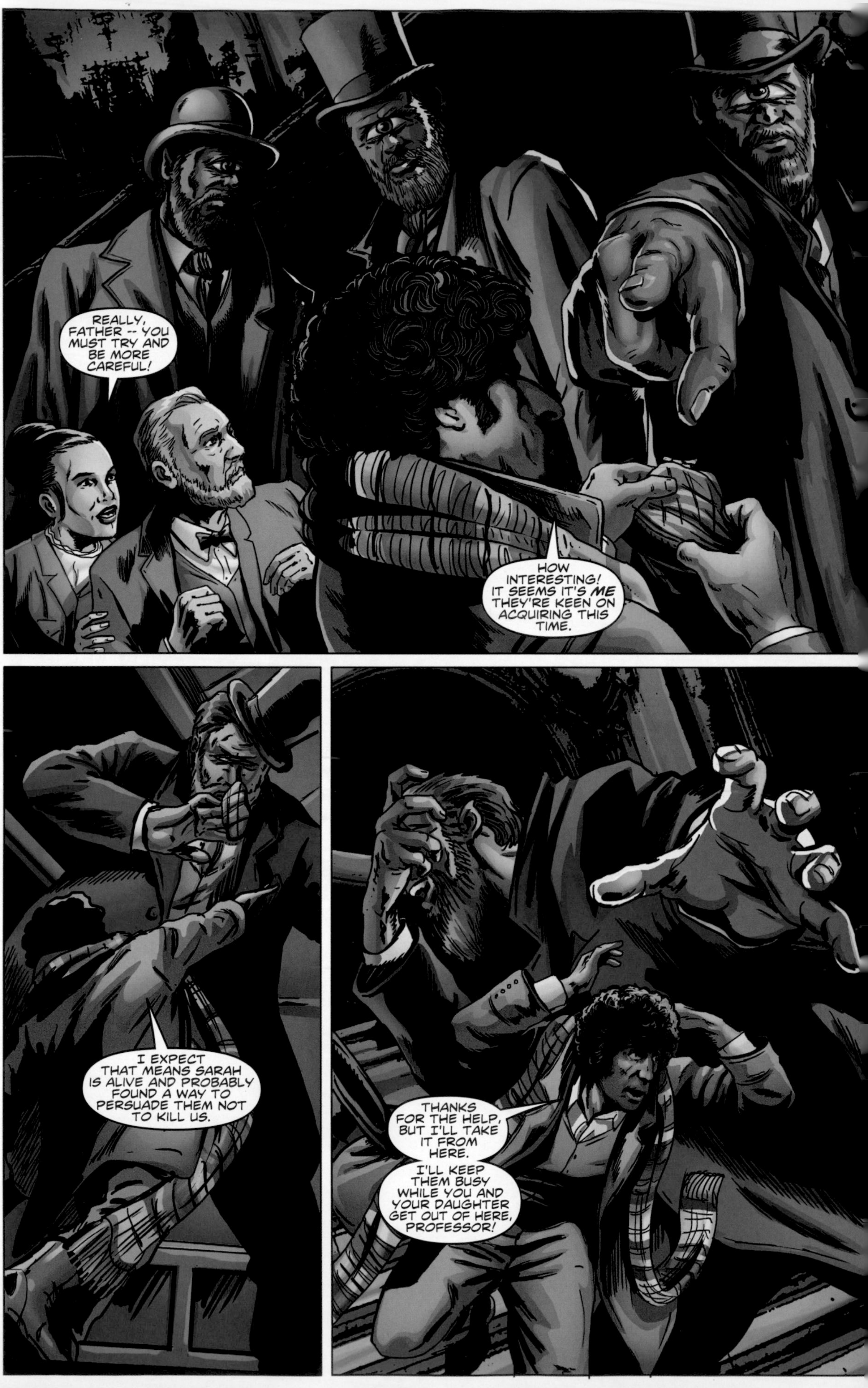
REALLY, FATHER -- YOU MUST TRY AND BE MORE CAREFUL!
HOW INTERESTING! IT SEEMS IT'S *ME* THEY'RE KEEN ON ACQUIRING THIS TIME.
I EXPECT THAT MEANS SARAH IS ALIVE AND PROBABLY FOUND A WAY TO PERSUADE THEM NOT TO KILL US.
THANKS FOR THE HELP, BUT I'LL TAKE IT FROM HERE.
I'LL KEEP THEM BUSY WHILE YOU AND YOUR DAUGHTER GET OUT OF HERE, PROFESSOR!

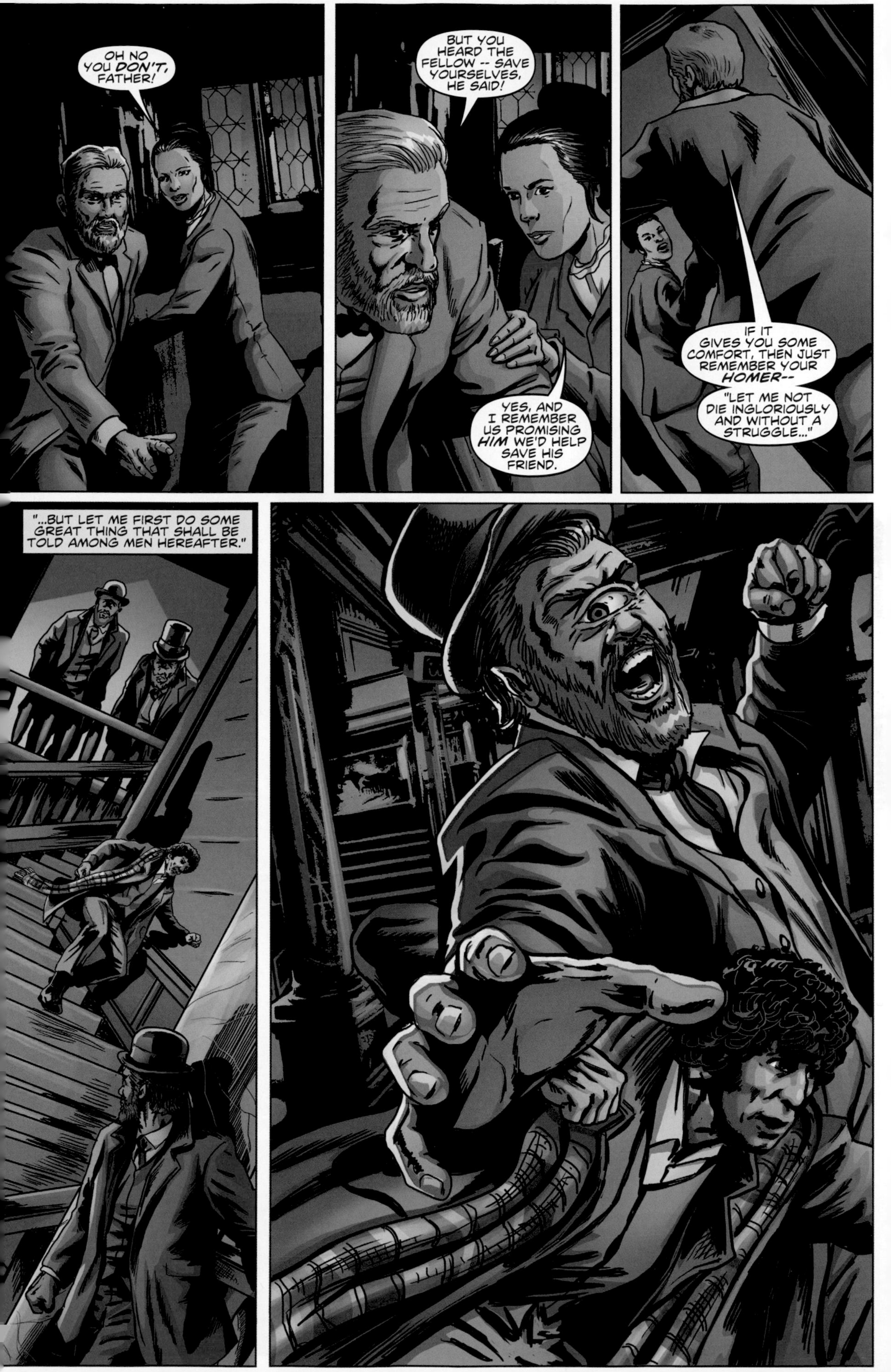
OH NO YOU *DON'T*, FATHER!
BUT YOU HEARD THE FELLOW -- SAVE YOURSELVES, HE SAID!
YES, AND I REMEMBER US PROMISING *HIM* WE'D HELP SAVE HIS FRIEND.
IF IT GIVES YOU SOME COMFORT, THEN JUST REMEMBER YOUR *HOMER*--
"LET ME NOT DIE INGLORIOUSLY AND WITHOUT A STRUGGLE..."
"...BUT LET ME FIRST DO SOME GREAT THING THAT SHALL BE TOLD AMONG MEN HEREAFTER."

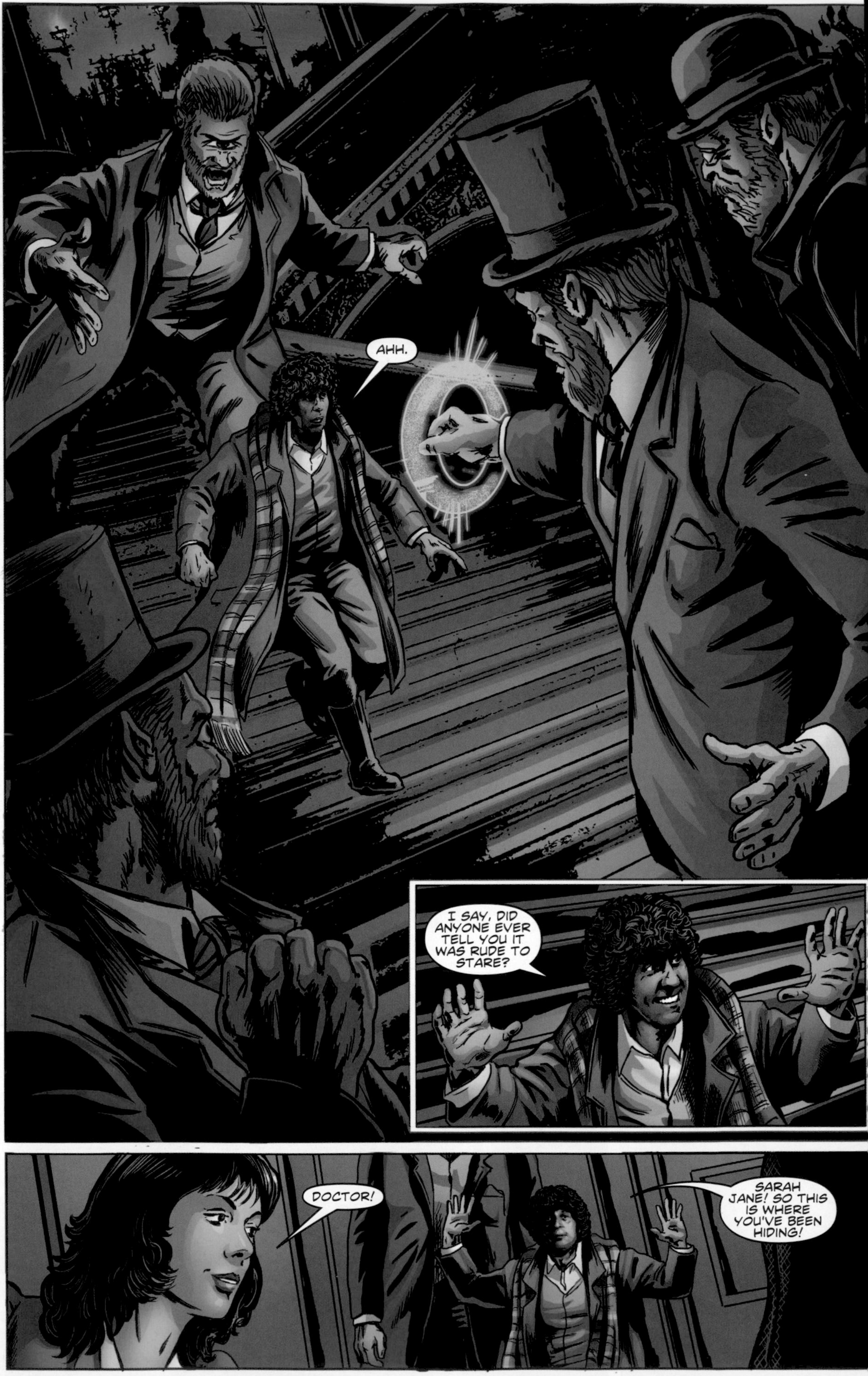
AHH.
I SAY, DID ANYONE EVER TELL YOU IT WAS RUDE TO STARE?
DOCTOR!
SARAH JANE! SO THIS IS WHERE YOU'VE BEEN HIDING!

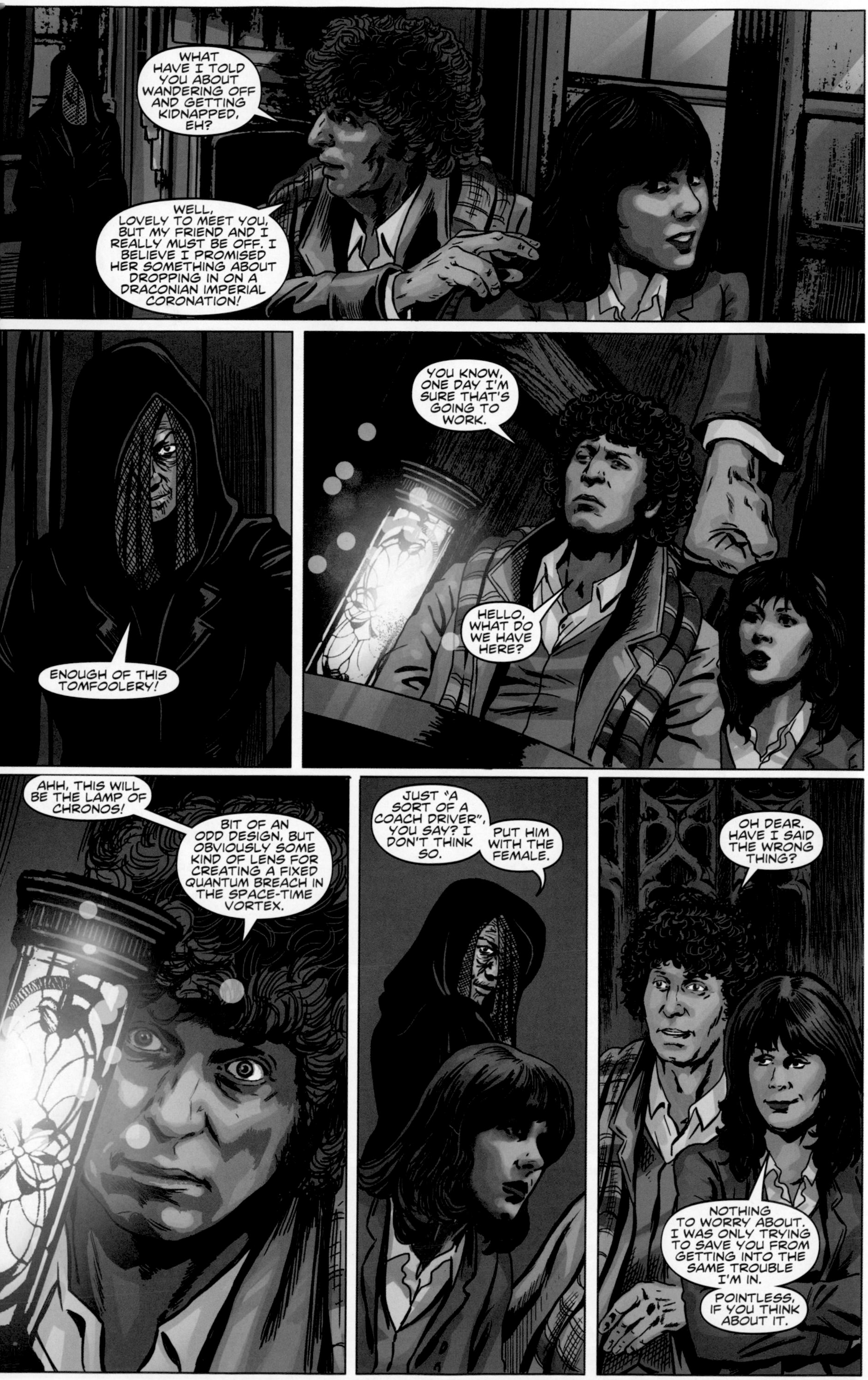
WHAT HAVE I TOLD YOU ABOUT WANDERING OFF AND GETTING KIDNAPPED, EH?
WELL, LOVELY TO MEET YOU, BUT MY FRIEND AND I REALLY MUST BE OFF. I BELIEVE I PROMISED HER SOMETHING ABOUT DROPPING IN ON A DRACONIAN IMPERIAL CORONATION!
ENOUGH OF THIS TOMFOOLERY!
YOU KNOW, ONE DAY I'M SURE THAT'S GOING TO WORK.
HELLO, WHAT DO WE HAVE HERE?
AHH, THIS WILL BE THE LAMP OF CHRONOS!
BIT OF AN ODD DESIGN, BUT OBVIOUSLY SOME KIND OF LENS FOR CREATING A FIXED QUANTUM BREACH IN THE SPACE-TIME VORTEX.
JUST "A SORT OF A COACH DRIVER", YOU SAY? I DON'T THINK SO.
PUT HIM WITH THE FEMALE.
OH DEAR. HAVE I SAID THE WRONG THING?
NOTHING TO WORRY ABOUT. I WAS ONLY TRYING TO SAVE YOU FROM GETTING INTO THE SAME TROUBLE I'M IN.
POINTLESS, IF YOU THINK ABOUT IT.

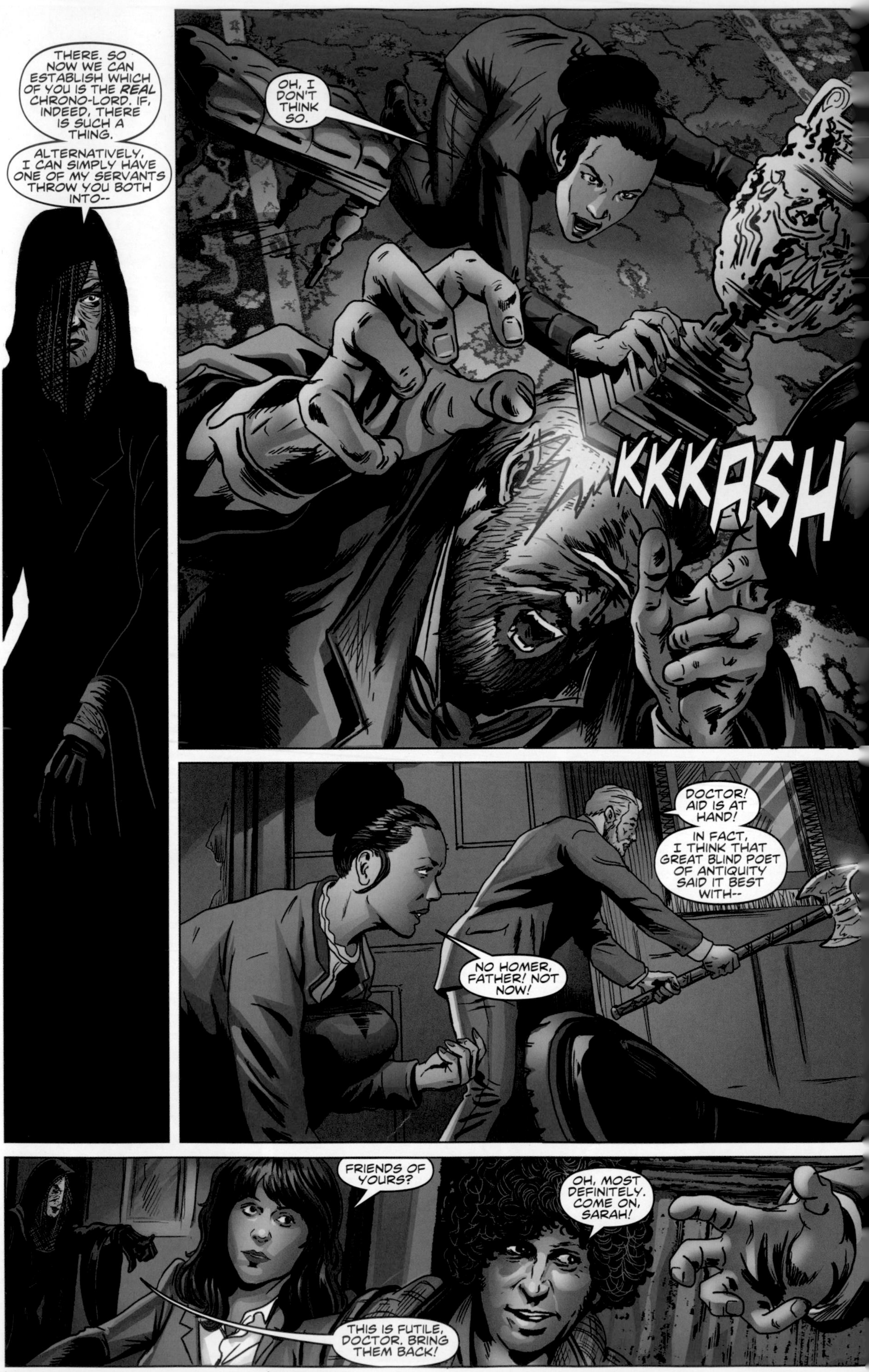

THERE. SO NOW WE CAN ESTABLISH WHICH OF YOU IS THE *REAL* CHRONO-LORD. IF, INDEED, THERE IS SUCH A THING.
ALTERNATIVELY, I CAN SIMPLY HAVE ONE OF MY SERVANTS THROW YOU BOTH INTO--
OH, I DON'T THINK SO.
KKKASH
DOCTOR! AID IS AT HAND!
IN FACT, I THINK THAT GREAT BLIND POET OF ANTIQUITY SAID IT BEST WITH--
NO HOMER, FATHER! NOT NOW!
FRIENDS OF YOURS?
OH, MOST DEFINITELY. COME ON, SARAH!
THIS IS FUTILE, DOCTOR. BRING THEM BACK!

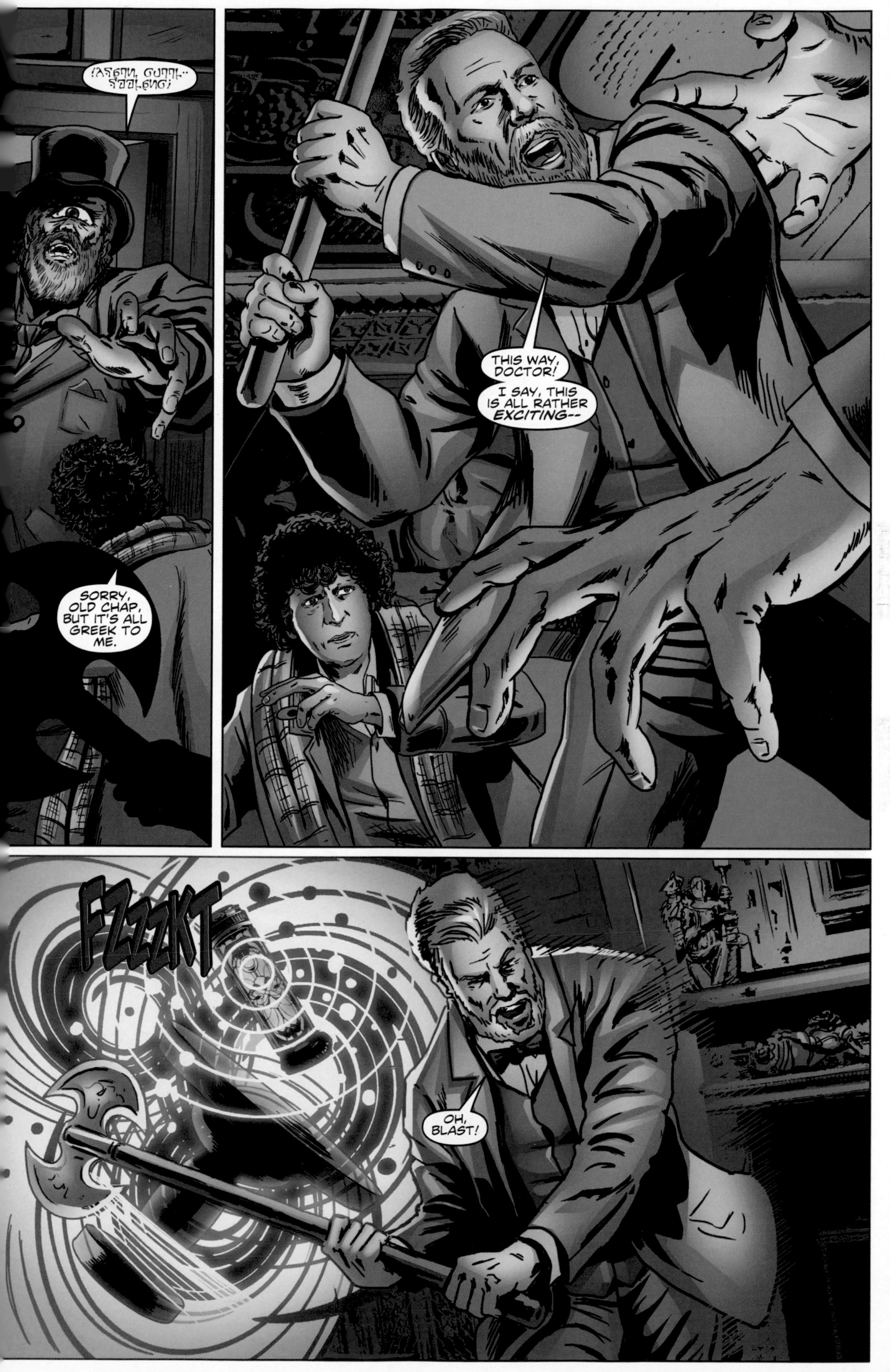
SORRY, OLD CHAP, BUT IT'S ALL GREEK TO ME.
THIS WAY, DOCTOR!
I SAY, THIS IS ALL RATHER *EXCITING*--
FZZZKT
OH, BLAST!

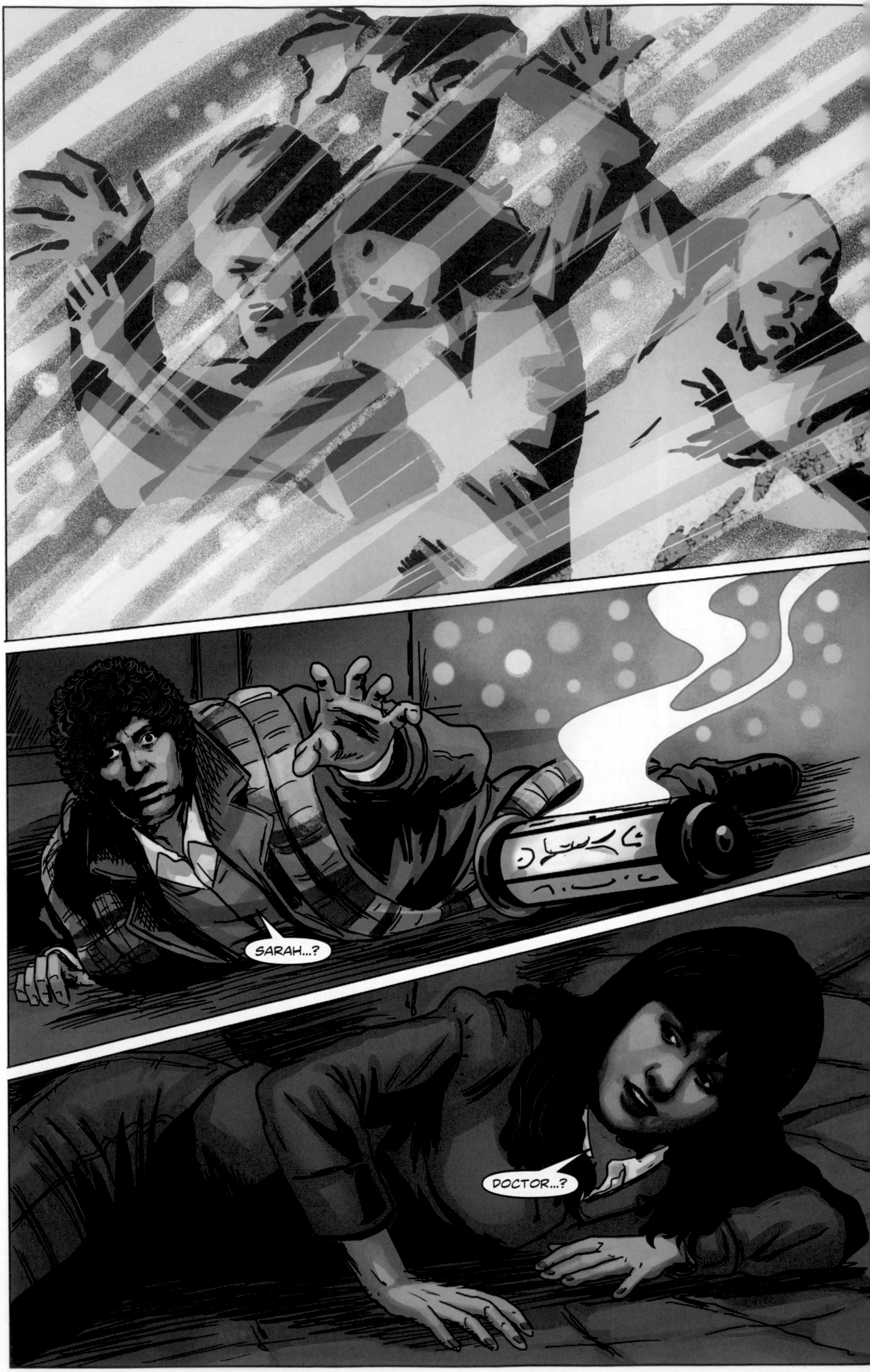
SARAH...?
DOCTOR...?

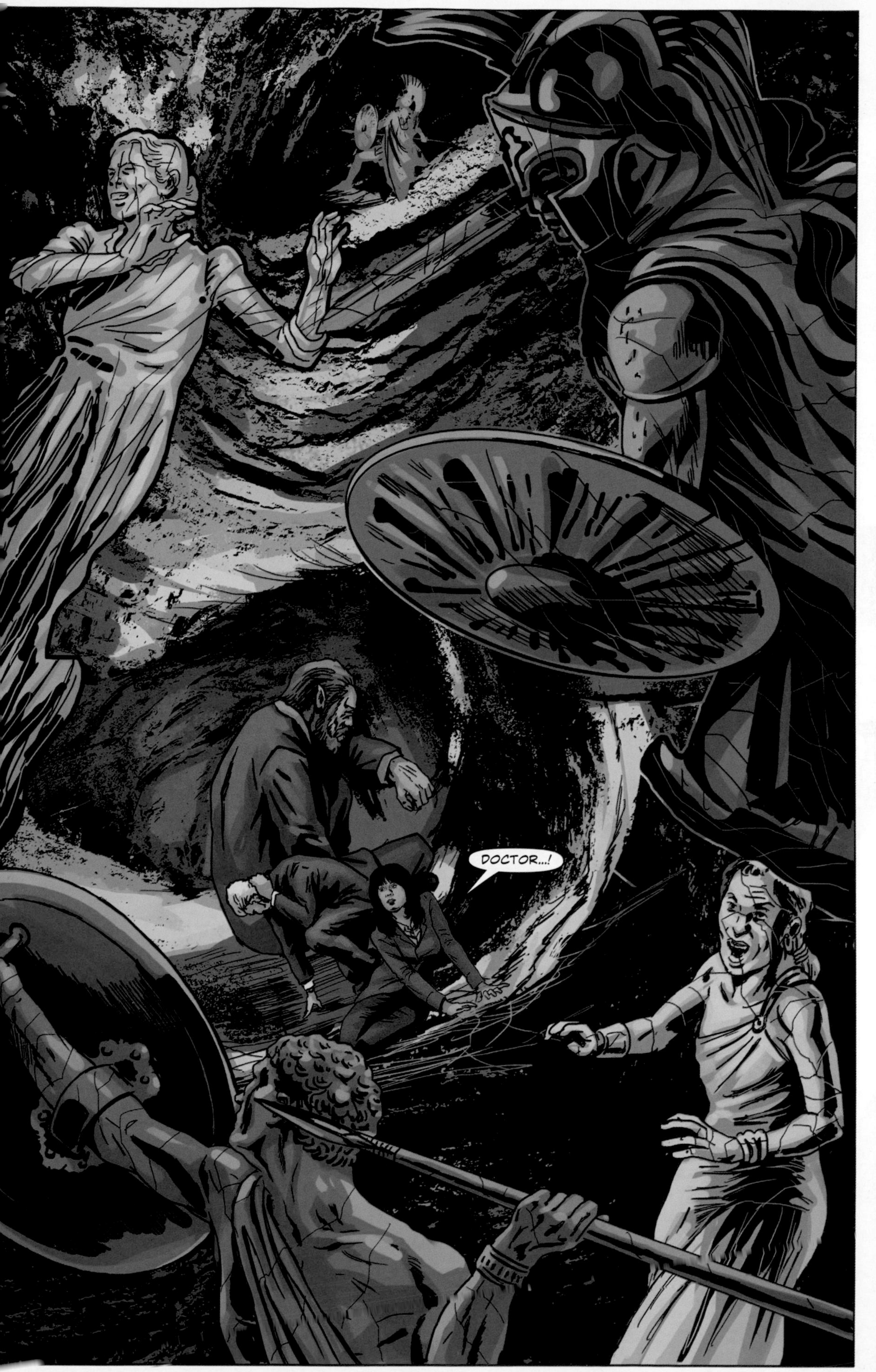
DOCTOR...!

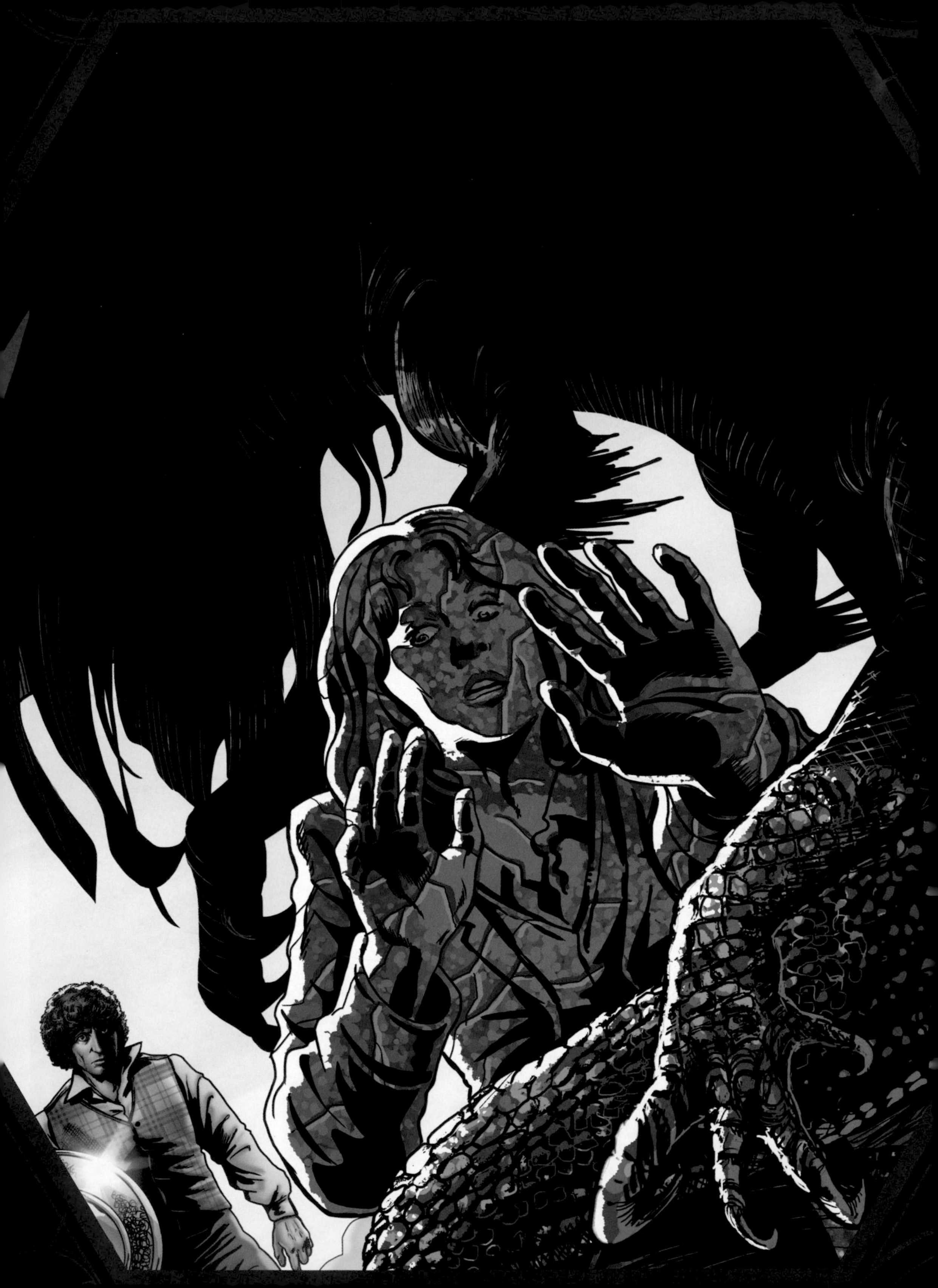

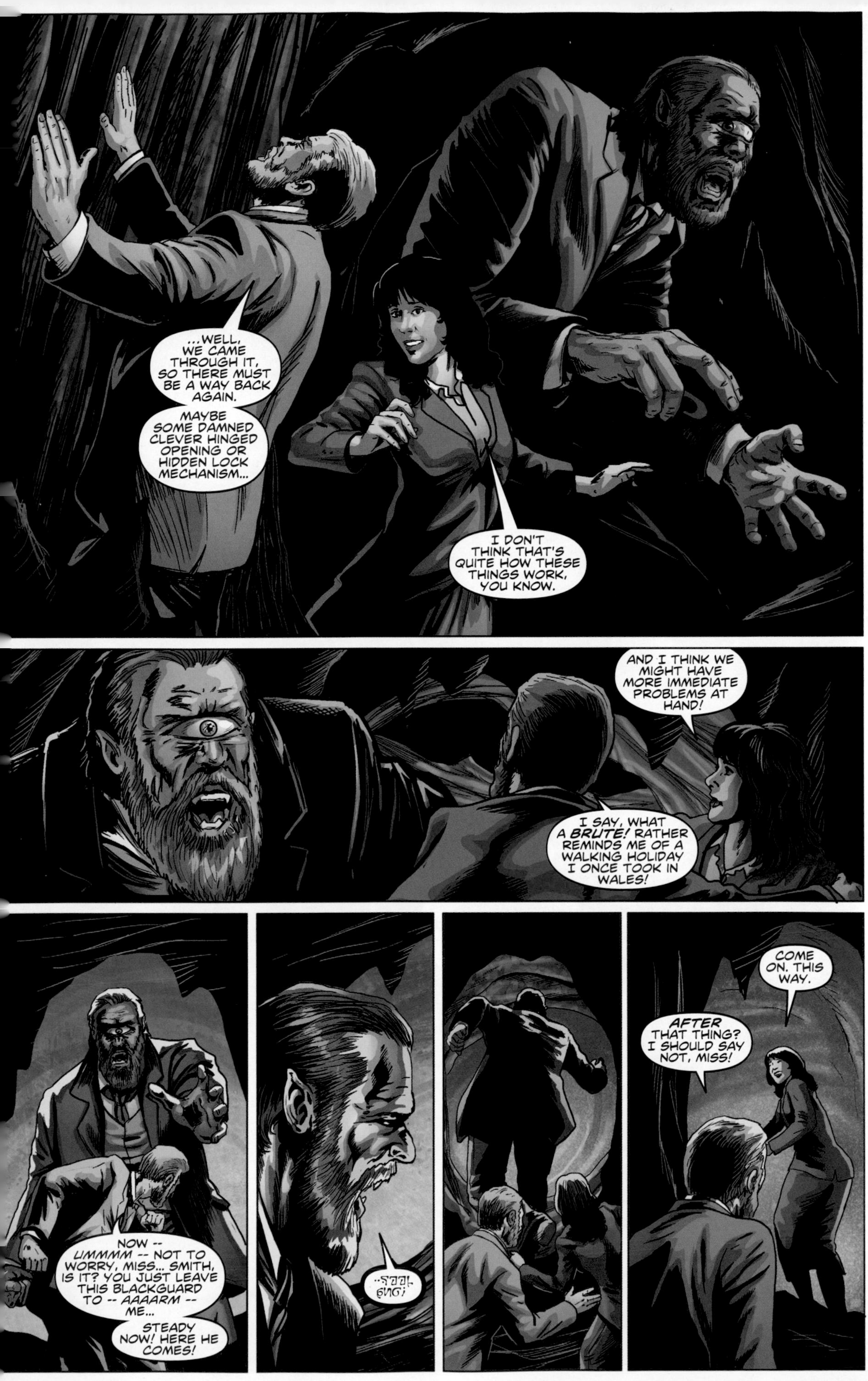
...WELL, WE CAME THROUGH IT, SO THERE MUST BE A WAY BACK AGAIN.
MAYBE SOME DAMNED CLEVER HINGED OPENING OR HIDDEN LOCK MECHANISM...
I DON'T THINK THAT'S QUITE HOW THESE THINGS WORK, YOU KNOW.
AND I THINK WE MIGHT HAVE MORE IMMEDIATE PROBLEMS AT HAND!
I SAY, WHAT A *BRUTE!* RATHER REMINDS ME OF A WALKING HOLIDAY I ONCE TOOK IN WALES!
NOW -- *UMMMM* -- NOT TO WORRY, MISS... SMITH, IS IT? YOU JUST LEAVE THIS BLACKGUARD TO -- *AAAARM* -- ME...
STEADY NOW! HERE HE COMES!
COME ON. THIS WAY.
AFTER THAT THING? I SHOULD SAY NOT, MISS!

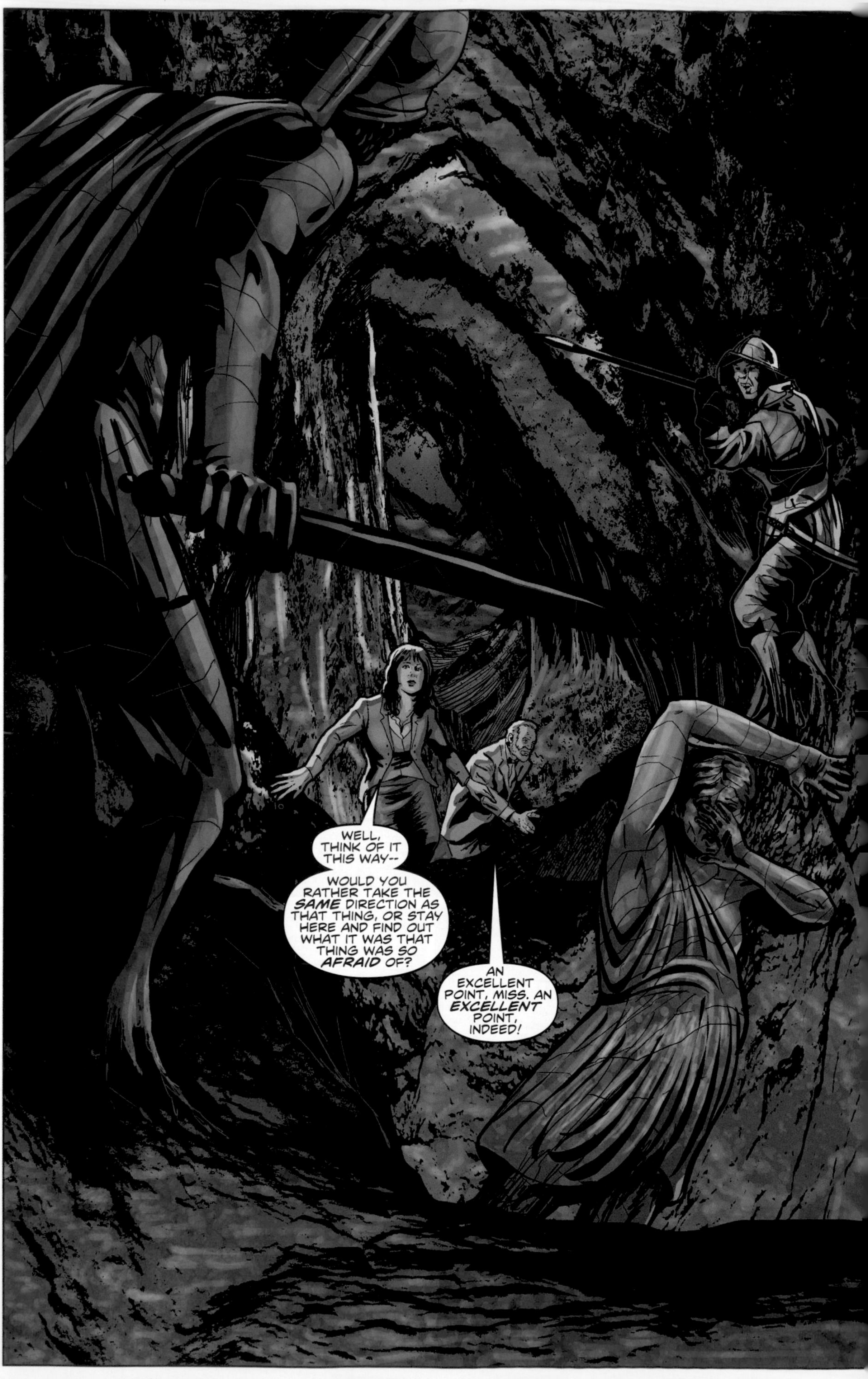
WELL, THINK OF IT THIS WAY--
WOULD YOU RATHER TAKE THE SAME DIRECTION AS THAT THING, OR STAY HERE AND FIND OUT WHAT IT WAS THAT THING WAS SO AFRAID OF?
AN EXCELLENT POINT, MISS. AN EXCELLENT POINT, INDEED!

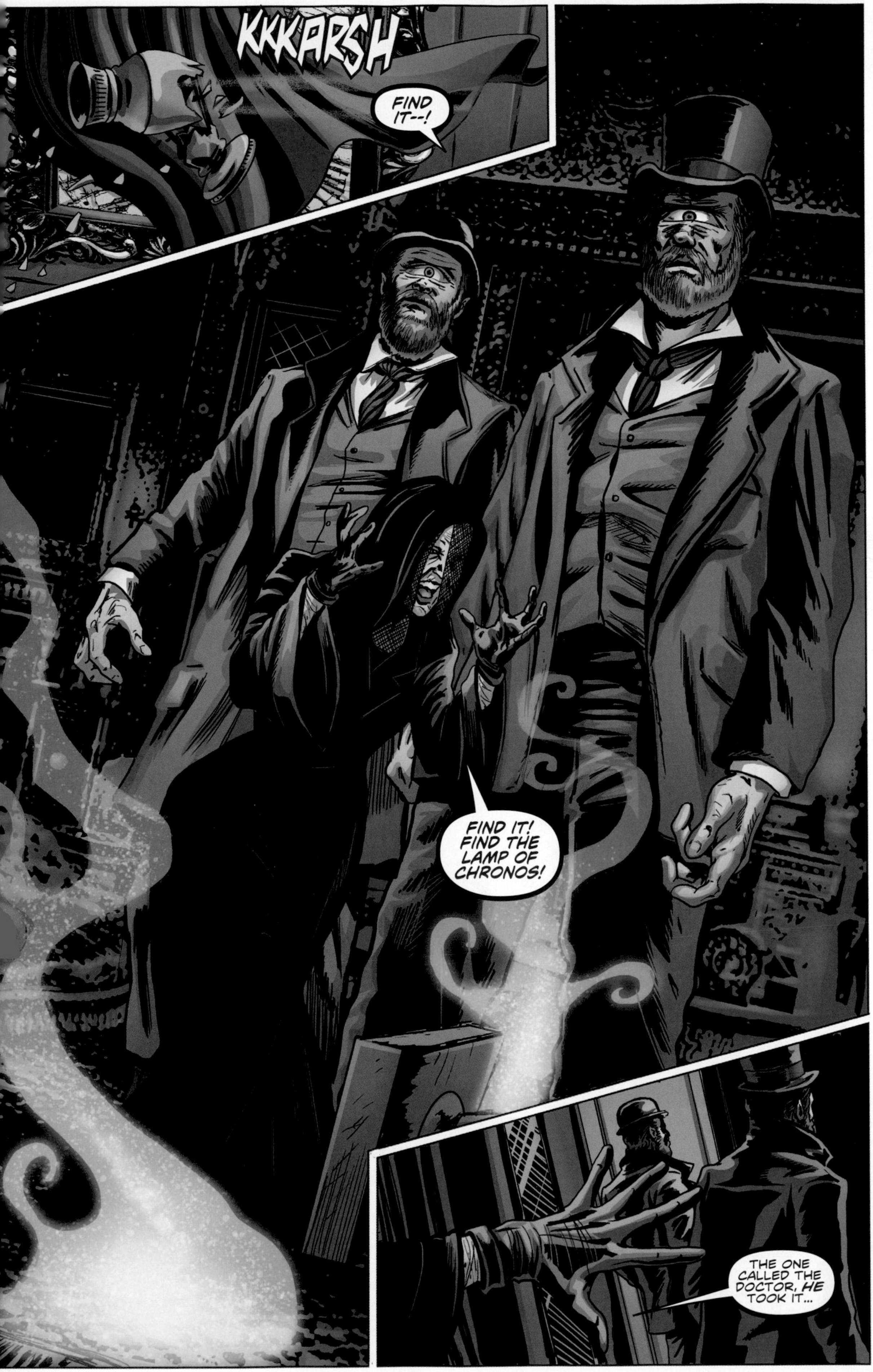
KKKARSH
FIND IT--!
FIND IT! FIND THE LAMP OF CHRONOS!
THE ONE CALLED THE DOCTOR, *HE* TOOK IT...

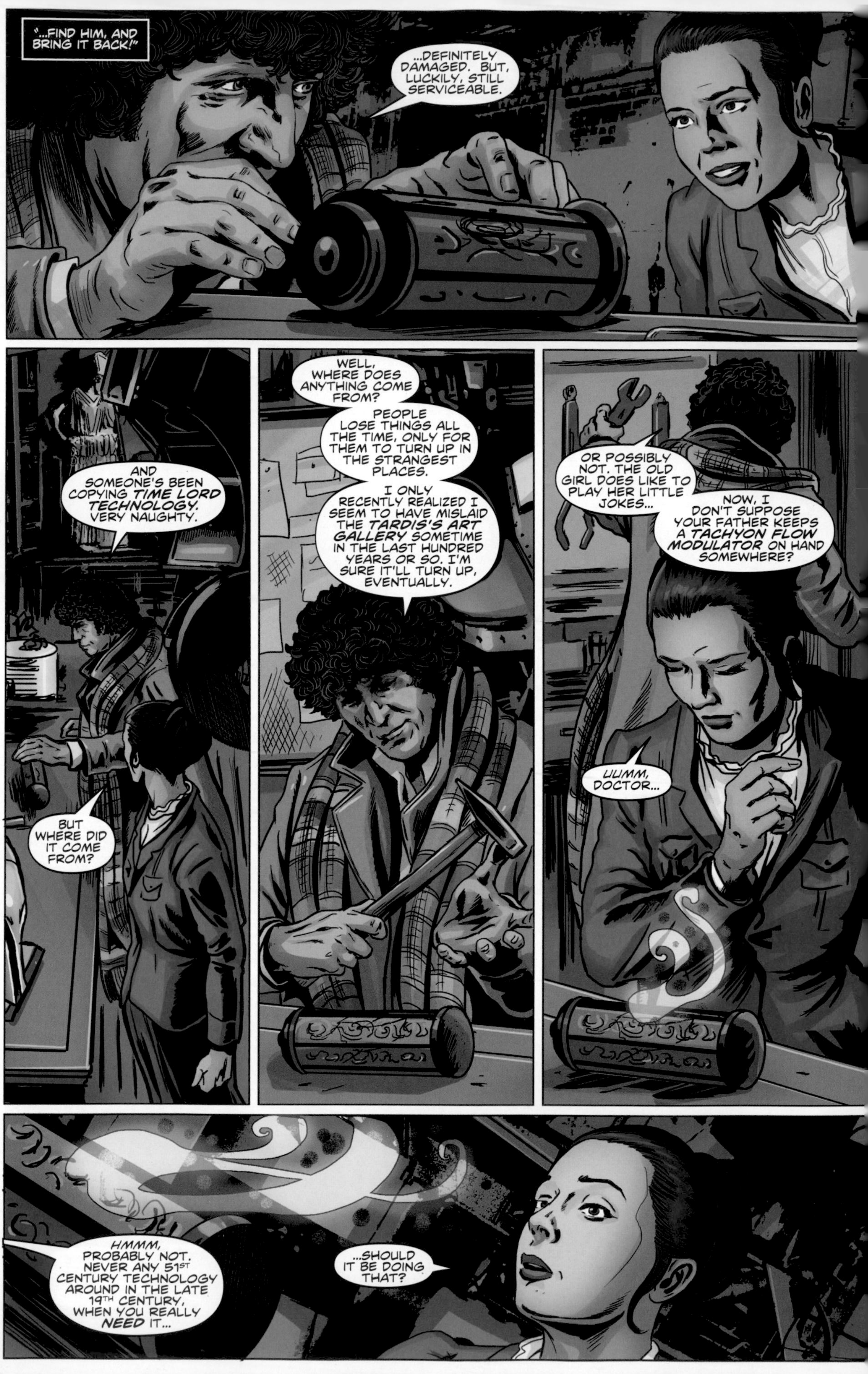
"...FIND HIM, AND BRING IT BACK!"
...DEFINITELY DAMAGED. BUT, LUCKILY, STILL SERVICEABLE.
AND SOMEONE'S BEEN COPYING *TIME LORD TECHNOLOGY*. VERY NAUGHTY.
BUT WHERE DID IT COME FROM?
WELL, WHERE DOES ANYTHING COME FROM?
PEOPLE LOSE THINGS ALL THE TIME, ONLY FOR THEM TO TURN UP IN THE STRANGEST PLACES.
I ONLY RECENTLY REALIZED I SEEM TO HAVE MISLAID THE *TARDIS'S ART GALLERY* SOMETIME IN THE LAST HUNDRED YEARS OR SO. I'M SURE IT'LL TURN UP, EVENTUALLY.
OR POSSIBLY NOT. THE OLD GIRL DOES LIKE TO PLAY HER LITTLE JOKES...
NOW, I DON'T SUPPOSE YOUR FATHER KEEPS A *TACHYON FLOW MODULATOR* ON HAND SOMEWHERE?
UUMM, DOCTOR...
HMMM, PROBABLY NOT. NEVER ANY 51ST CENTURY TECHNOLOGY AROUND IN THE LATE 19TH CENTURY, WHEN YOU REALLY *NEED* IT...
...SHOULD IT BE DOING THAT?

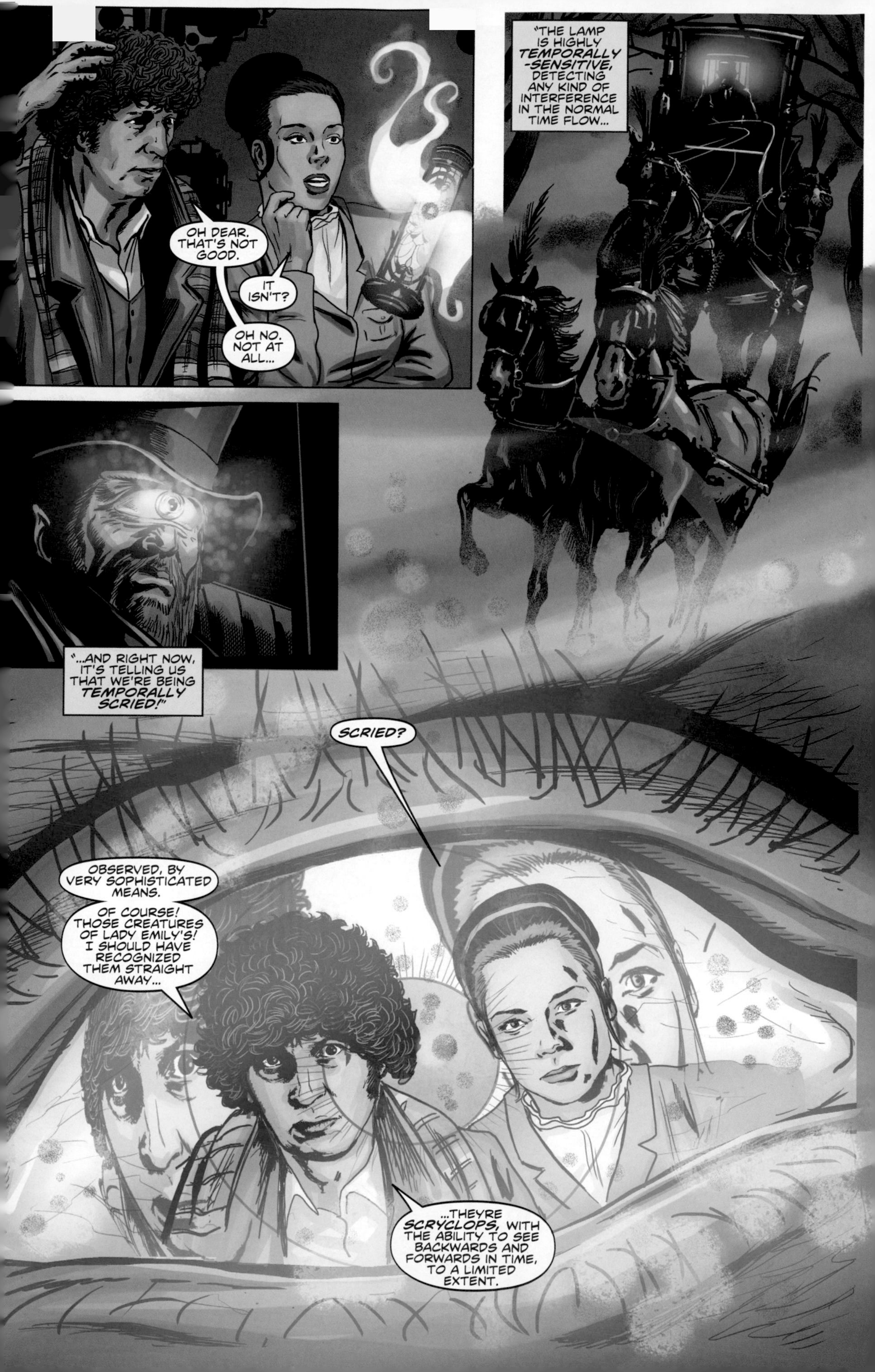
OH DEAR. THAT'S NOT GOOD.
IT ISN'T?
OH NO. NOT AT ALL...
"THE LAMP IS HIGHLY TEMPORALLY -SENSITIVE, DETECTING ANY KIND OF INTERFERENCE IN THE NORMAL TIME FLOW...
"...AND RIGHT NOW, IT'S TELLING US THAT WE'RE BEING TEMPORALLY SCRIED!"
SCRIED?
OBSERVED, BY VERY SOPHISTICATED MEANS.
OF COURSE! THOSE CREATURES OF LADY EMILY'S! I SHOULD HAVE RECOGNIZED THEM STRAIGHT AWAY...
...THEYRE SCRYCLOPS, WITH THE ABILITY TO SEE BACKWARDS AND FORWARDS IN TIME, TO A LIMITED EXTENT.

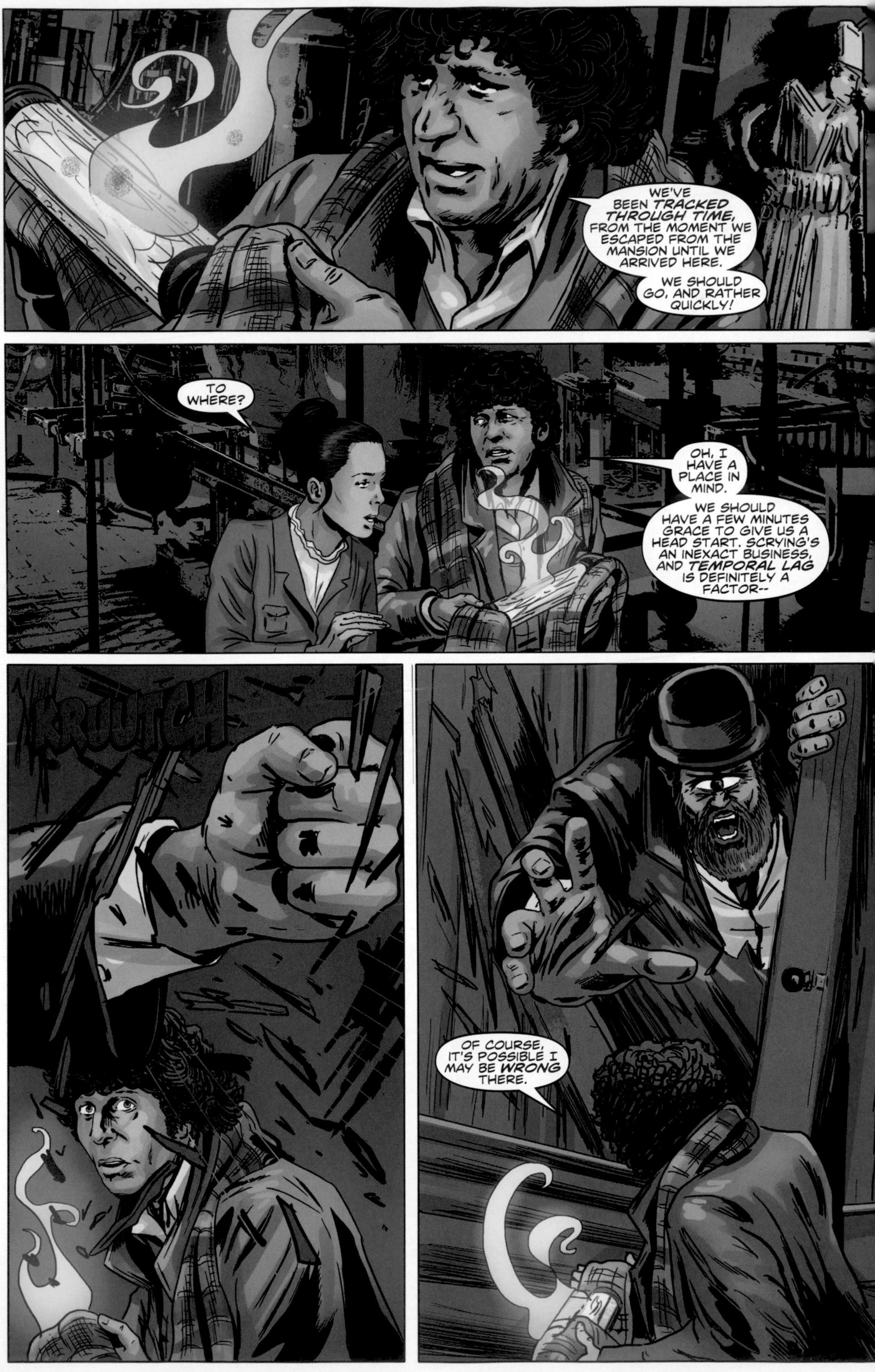
WE'VE BEEN TRACKED THROUGH TIME, FROM THE MOMENT WE ESCAPED FROM THE MANSION UNTIL WE ARRIVED HERE.
WE SHOULD GO, AND RATHER QUICKLY!
TO WHERE?
OH, I HAVE A PLACE IN MIND.
WE SHOULD HAVE A FEW MINUTES GRACE TO GIVE US A HEAD START. SCRYING'S AN INEXACT BUSINESS, AND TEMPORAL LAG IS DEFINITELY A FACTOR--
KRUUTCH
OF COURSE, IT'S POSSIBLE I MAY BE WRONG THERE.

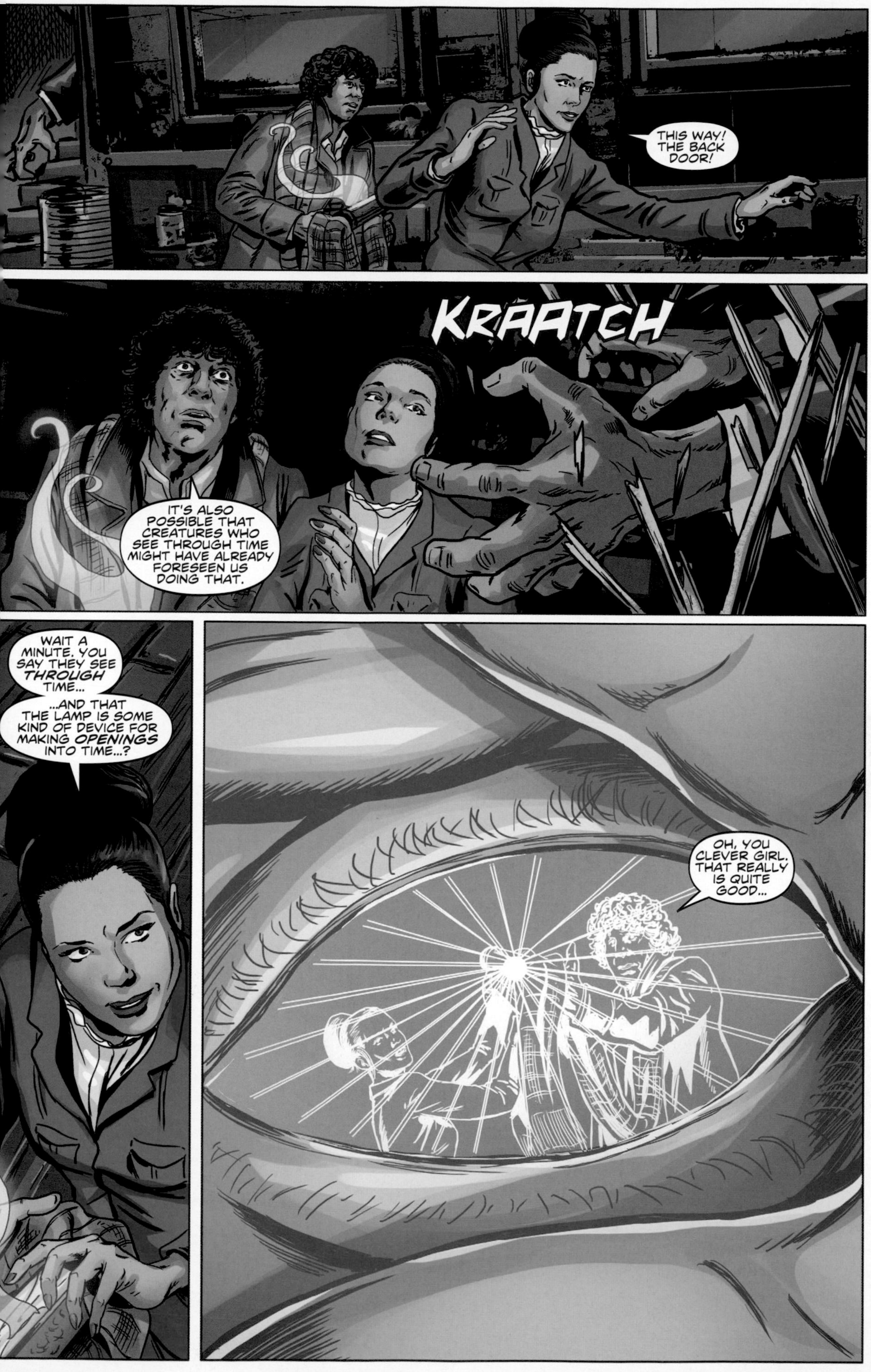
THIS WAY! THE BACK DOOR!
KRAATCH
IT'S ALSO POSSIBLE THAT CREATURES WHO SEE THROUGH TIME MIGHT HAVE ALREADY FORESEEN US DOING THAT.
WAIT A MINUTE. YOU SAY THEY SEE *THROUGH* TIME...
...AND THAT THE LAMP IS SOME KIND OF DEVICE FOR MAKING *OPENINGS* INTO TIME...?
OH, YOU CLEVER GIRL. THAT REALLY IS QUITE GOOD...

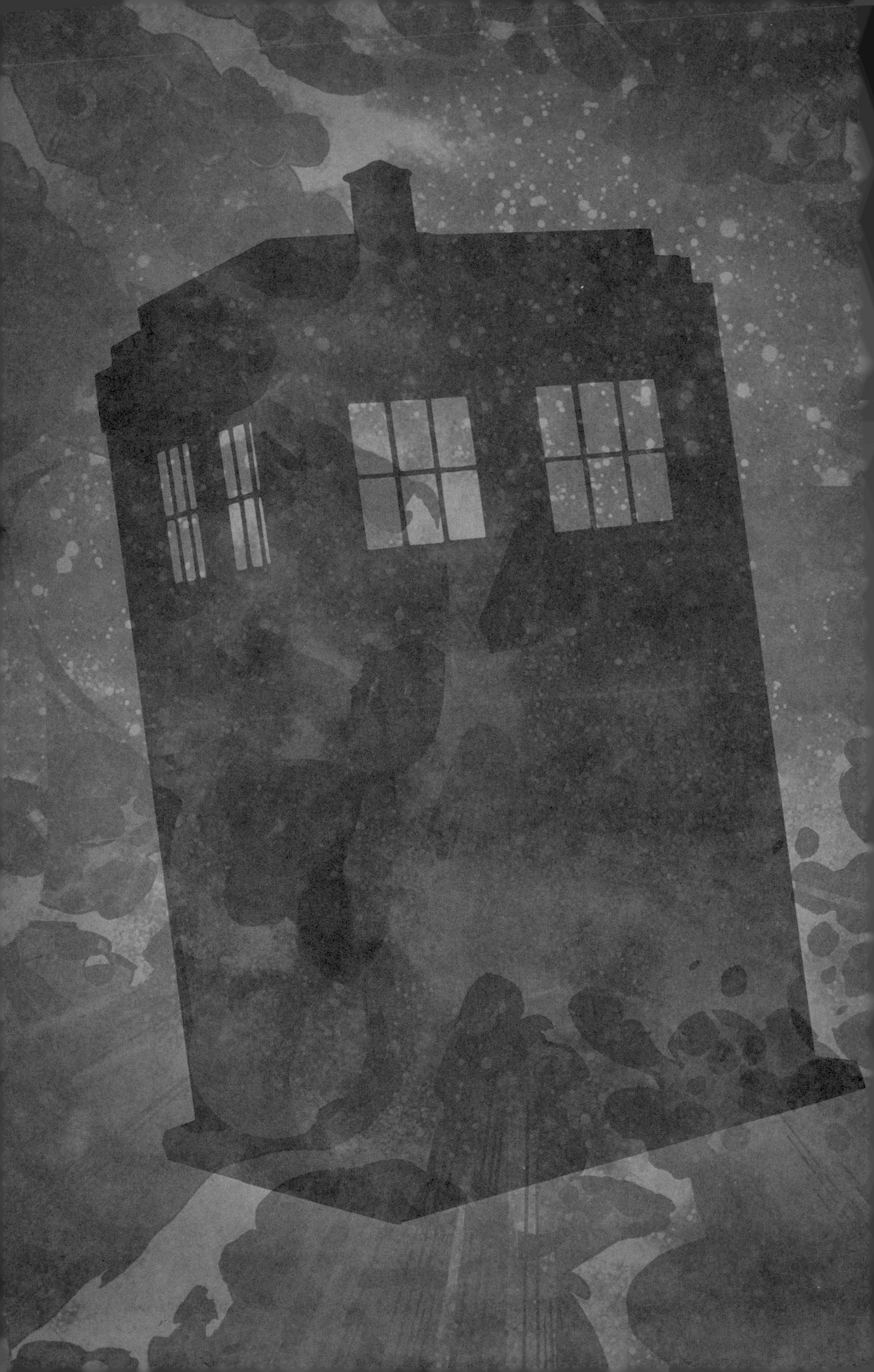

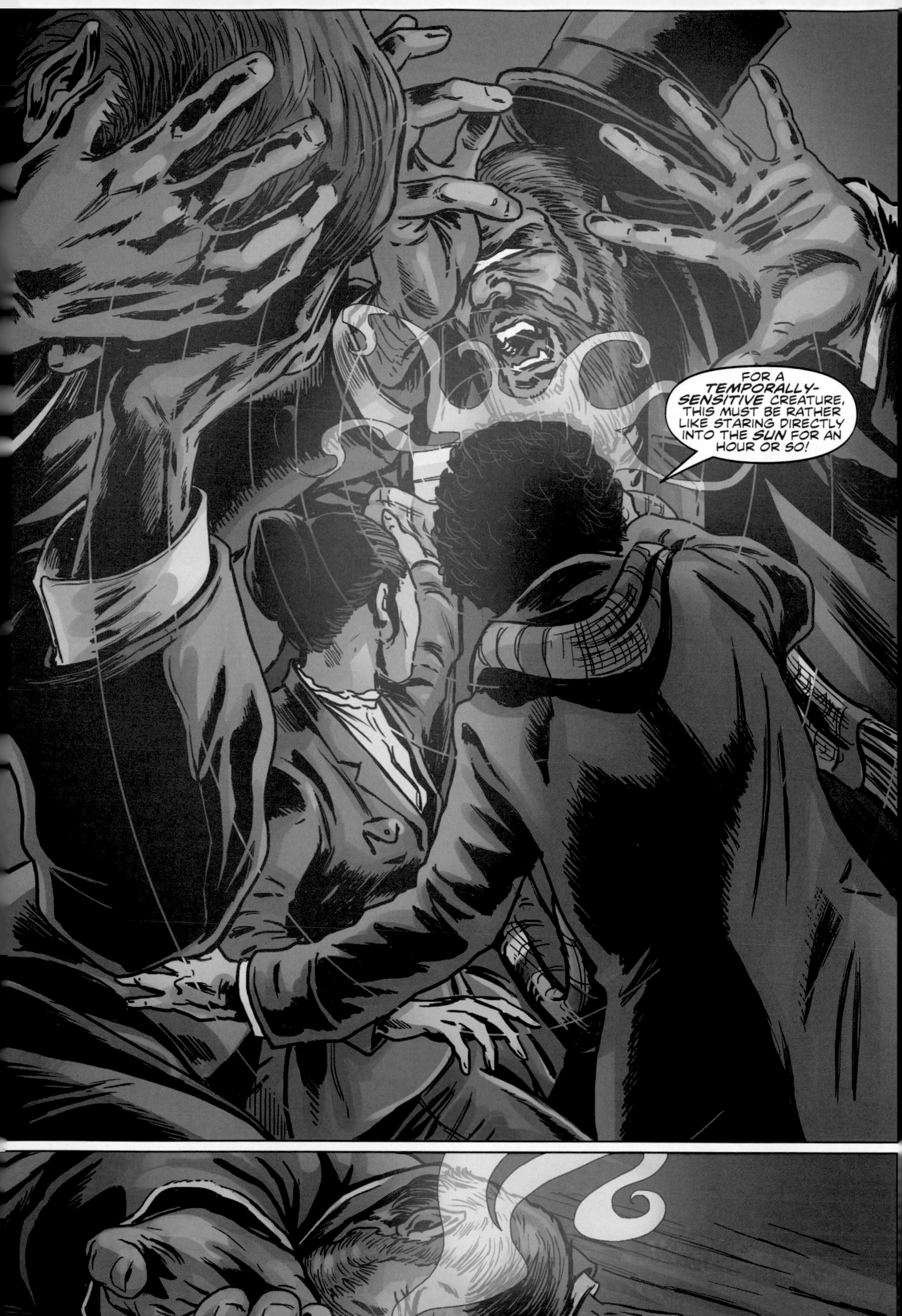
FOR A TEMPORALLY-SENSITIVE CREATURE, THIS MUST BE RATHER LIKE STARING DIRECTLY INTO THE SUN FOR AN HOUR OR SO!

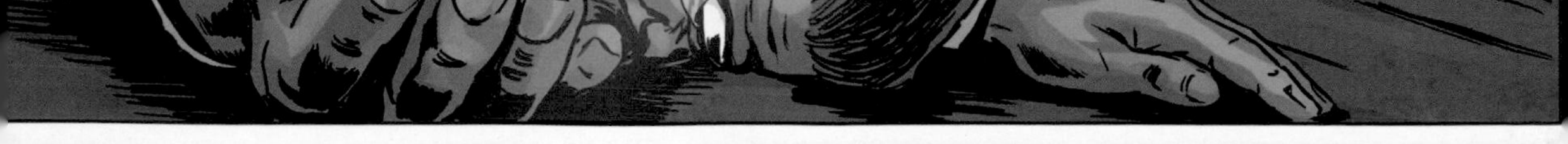

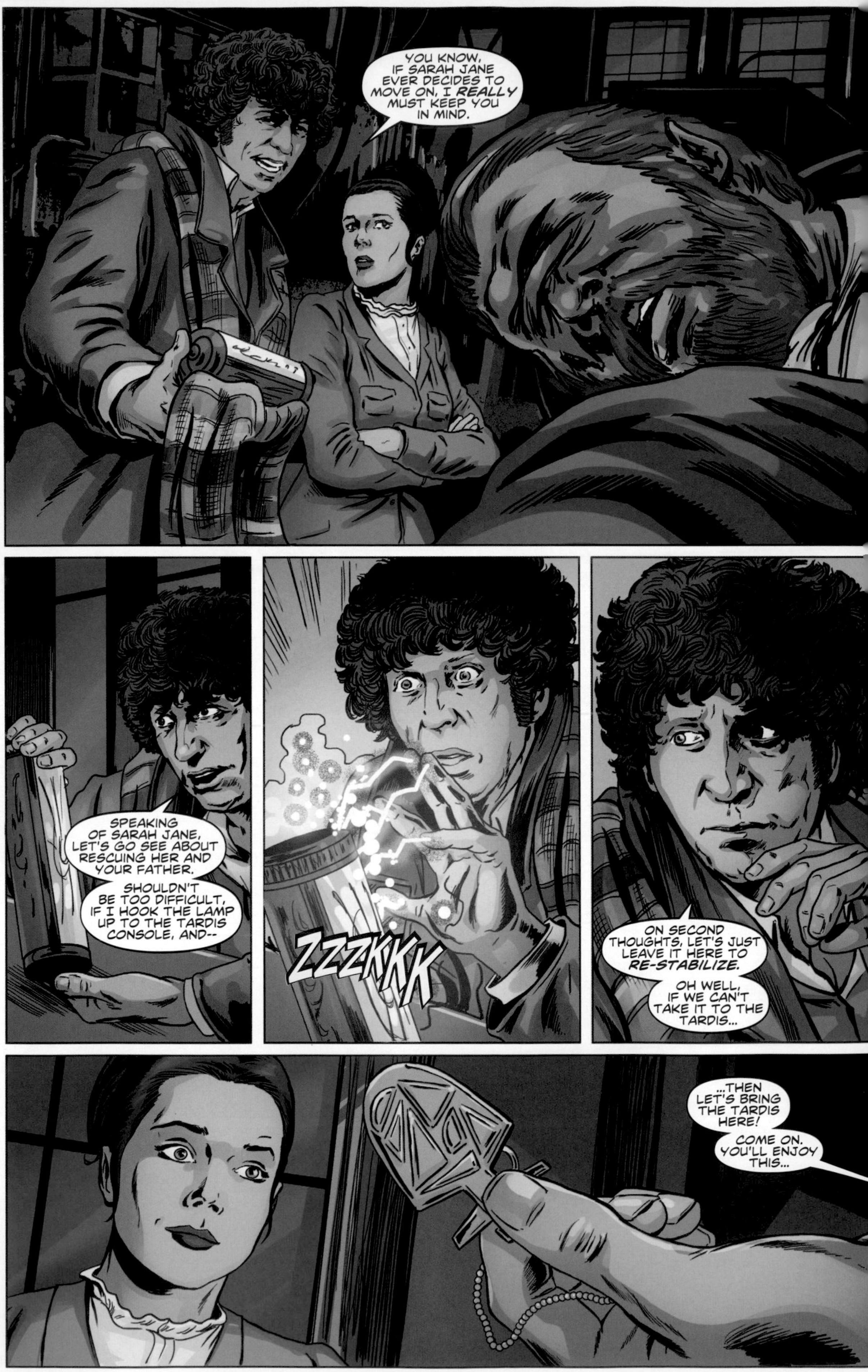
YOU KNOW, IF SARAH JANE EVER DECIDES TO MOVE ON, I *REALLY* MUST KEEP YOU IN MIND.
SPEAKING OF SARAH JANE, LET'S GO SEE ABOUT RESCUING HER AND YOUR FATHER.
SHOULDN'T BE TOO DIFFICULT, IF I HOOK THE LAMP UP TO THE TARDIS CONSOLE, AND--
ZZZKKK
ON SECOND THOUGHTS, LET'S JUST LEAVE IT HERE TO *RE-STABILIZE*.
OH WELL, IF WE CAN'T TAKE IT TO THE TARDIS...
...THEN LET'S BRING THE TARDIS HERE!
COME ON. YOU'LL ENJOY THIS...

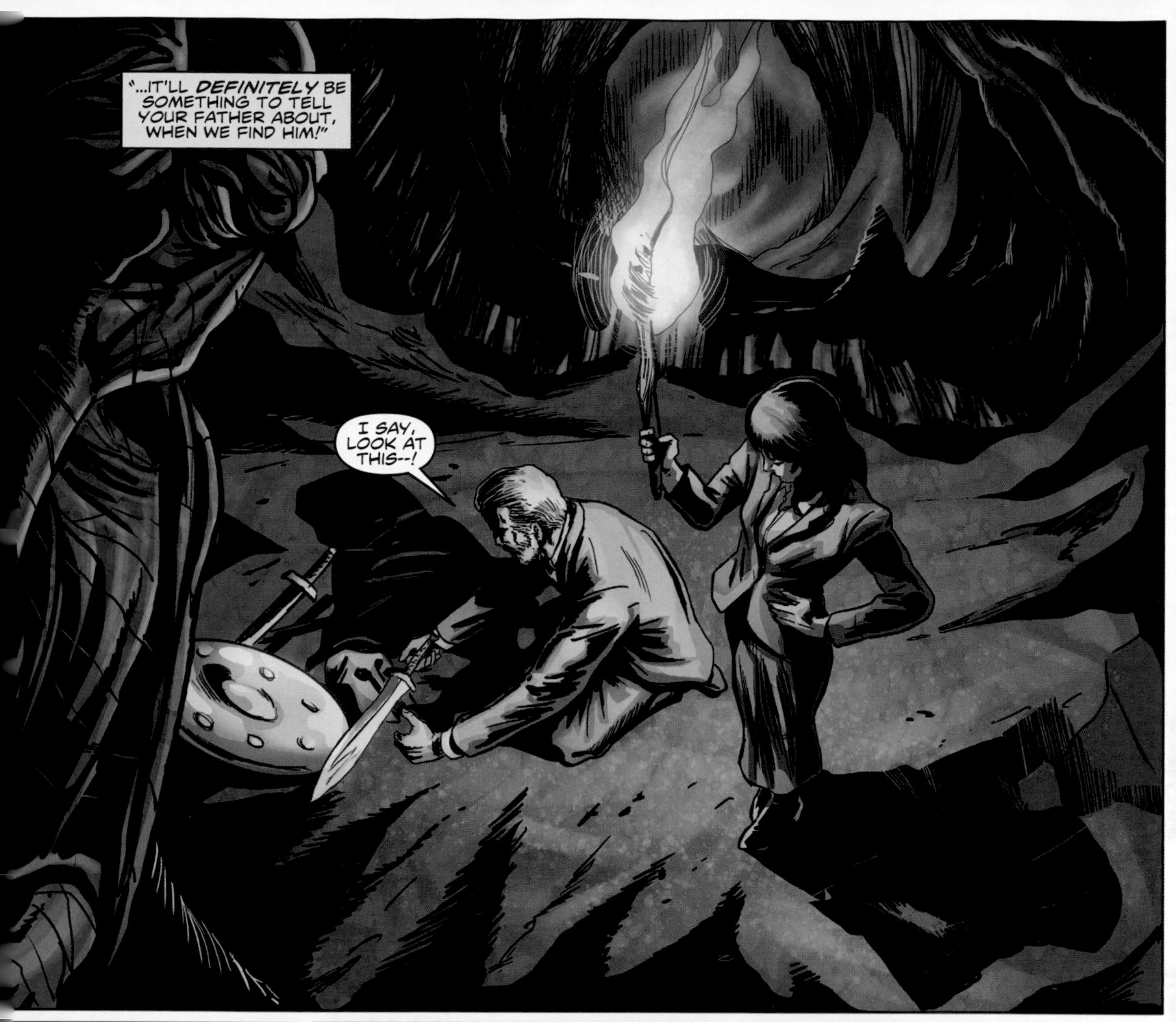
"...IT'LL *DEFINITELY* BE SOMETHING TO TELL YOUR FATHER ABOUT, WHEN WE FIND HIM!"
I SAY, LOOK AT THIS--!

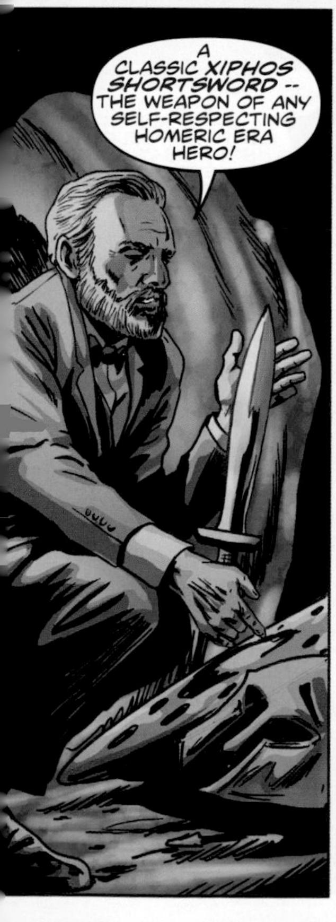
A CLASSIC *XIPHOS SHORTSWORD* -- THE WEAPON OF ANY SELF-RESPECTING HOMERIC ERA HERO!

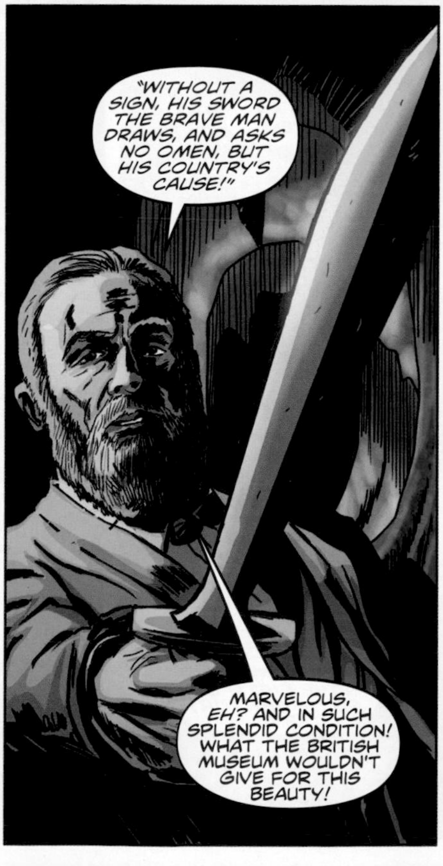
"WITHOUT A SIGN, HIS SWORD THE BRAVE MAN DRAWS, AND ASKS NO OMEN, BUT HIS COUNTRY'S CAUSE!"
MARVELOUS, EH? AND IN SUCH SPLENDID CONDITION! WHAT THE BRITISH MUSEUM WOULDN'T GIVE FOR THIS BEAUTY!

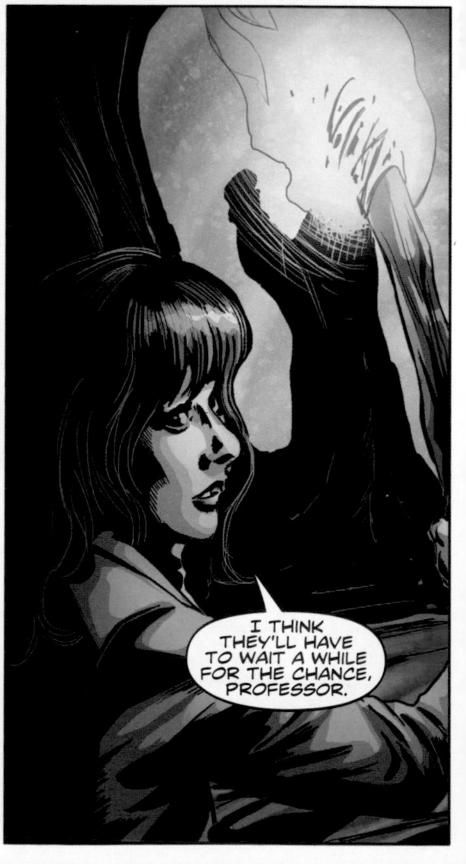
I THINK THEY'LL HAVE TO WAIT A WHILE FOR THE CHANCE, PROFESSOR.

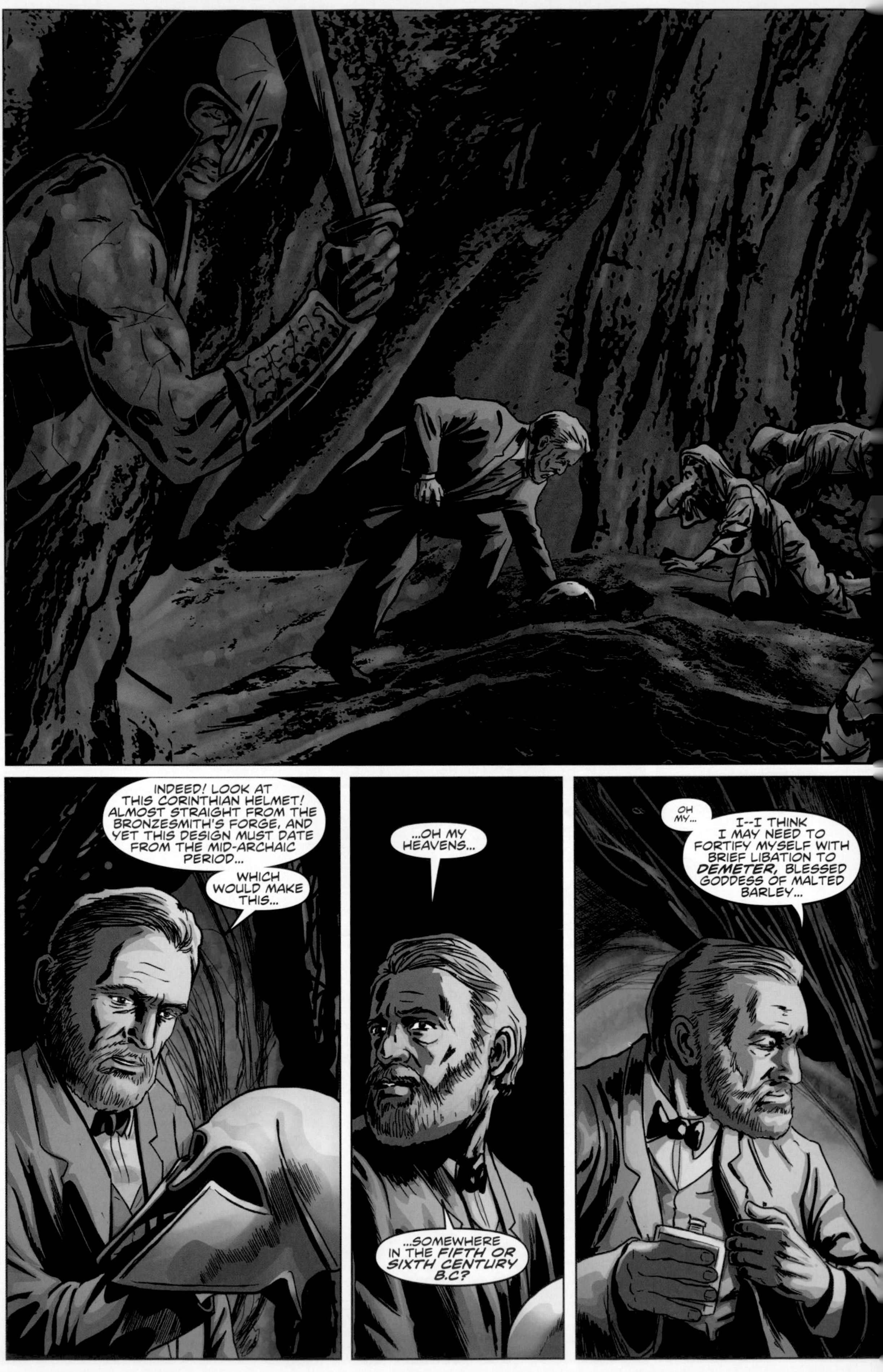
INDEED! LOOK AT THIS CORINTHIAN HELMET! ALMOST STRAIGHT FROM THE BRONZESMITH'S FORGE, AND YET THIS DESIGN MUST DATE FROM THE MID-ARCHAIC PERIOD...
WHICH WOULD MAKE THIS...
...OH MY HEAVENS...
...SOMEWHERE IN THE FIFTH OR SIXTH CENTURY B.C?
OH MY...
I--I THINK I MAY NEED TO FORTIFY MYSELF WITH BRIEF LIBATION TO DEMETER, BLESSED GODDESS OF MALTED BARLEY...

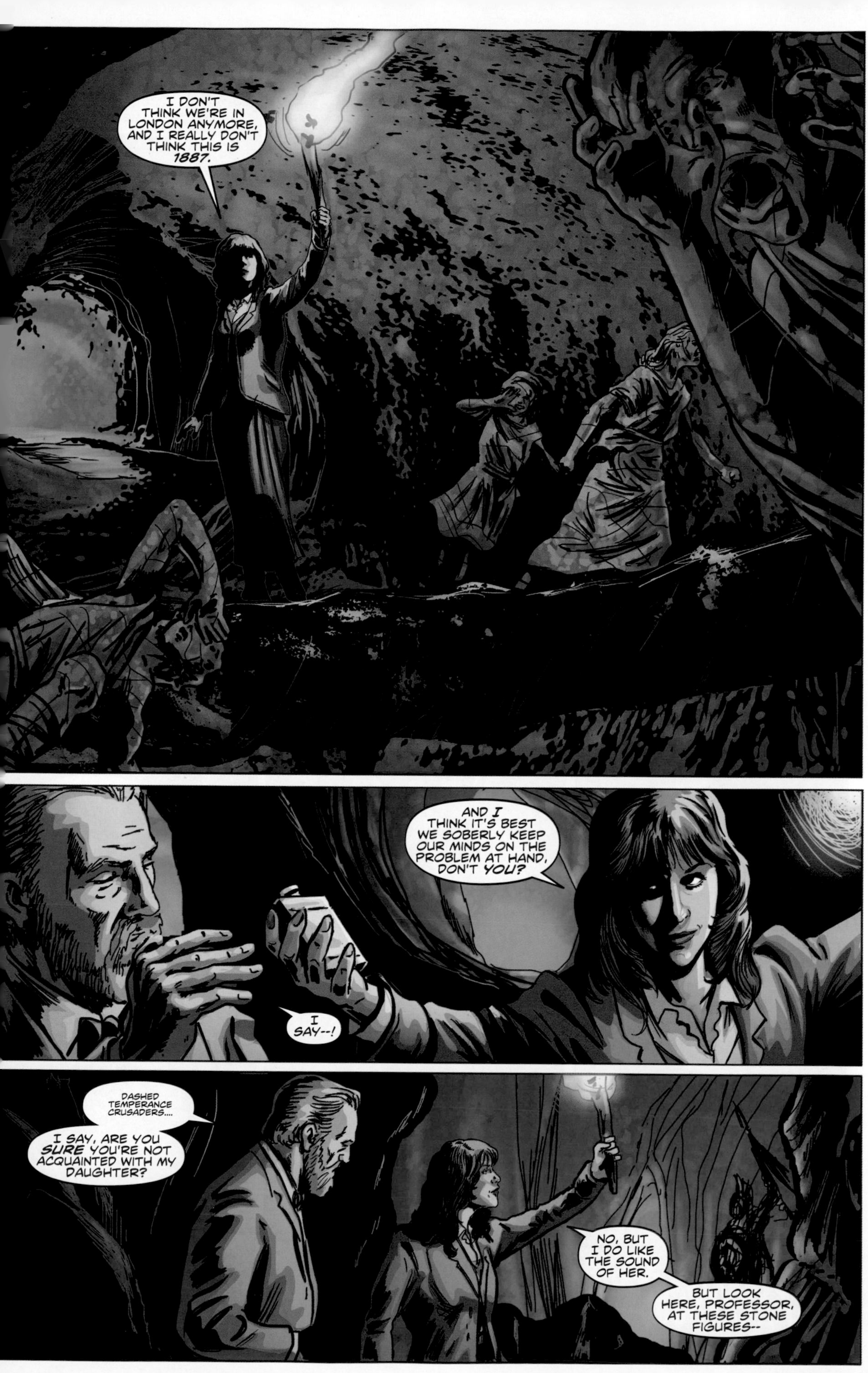
I DON'T THINK WE'RE IN LONDON ANYMORE, AND I REALLY DON'T THINK THIS IS 1887.
I SAY--!
AND I THINK IT'S BEST WE SOBERLY KEEP OUR MINDS ON THE PROBLEM AT HAND, DON'T YOU?
DASHED TEMPERANCE CRUSADERS....
I SAY, ARE YOU SURE YOU'RE NOT ACQUAINTED WITH MY DAUGHTER?
NO, BUT I DO LIKE THE SOUND OF HER.
BUT LOOK HERE, PROFESSOR, AT THESE STONE FIGURES--

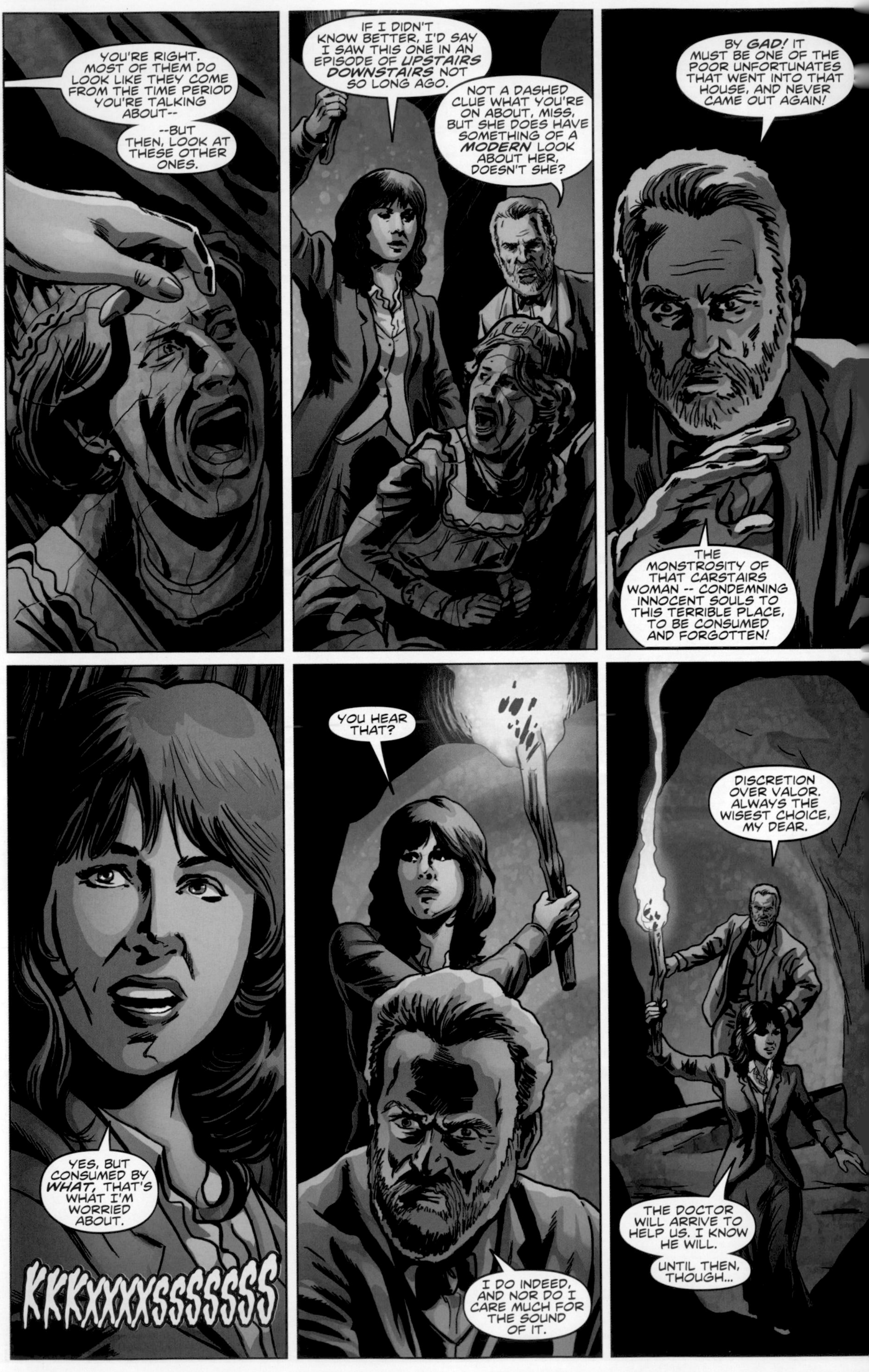

YOU'RE RIGHT. MOST OF THEM DO LOOK LIKE THEY COME FROM THE TIME PERIOD YOU'RE TALKING ABOUT--
--BUT THEN, LOOK AT THESE OTHER ONES.
IF I DIDN'T KNOW BETTER, I'D SAY I SAW THIS ONE IN AN EPISODE OF UPSTAIRS DOWNSTAIRS NOT SO LONG AGO.
NOT A DASHED CLUE WHAT YOU'RE ON ABOUT, MISS, BUT SHE DOES HAVE SOMETHING OF A MODERN LOOK ABOUT HER, DOESN'T SHE?
BY GAD! IT MUST BE ONE OF THE POOR UNFORTUNATES THAT WENT INTO THAT HOUSE, AND NEVER CAME OUT AGAIN!
THE MONSTROSITY OF THAT CARSTAIRS WOMAN -- CONDEMNING INNOCENT SOULS TO THIS TERRIBLE PLACE, TO BE CONSUMED AND FORGOTTEN!
YES, BUT CONSUMED BY WHAT, THAT'S WHAT I'M WORRIED ABOUT.
KKKXXXXSSSSSSS
YOU HEAR THAT?
I DO INDEED, AND NOR DO I CARE MUCH FOR THE SOUND OF IT.
DISCRETION OVER VALOR. ALWAYS THE WISEST CHOICE, MY DEAR.
THE DOCTOR WILL ARRIVE TO HELP US. I KNOW HE WILL.
UNTIL THEN, THOUGH...

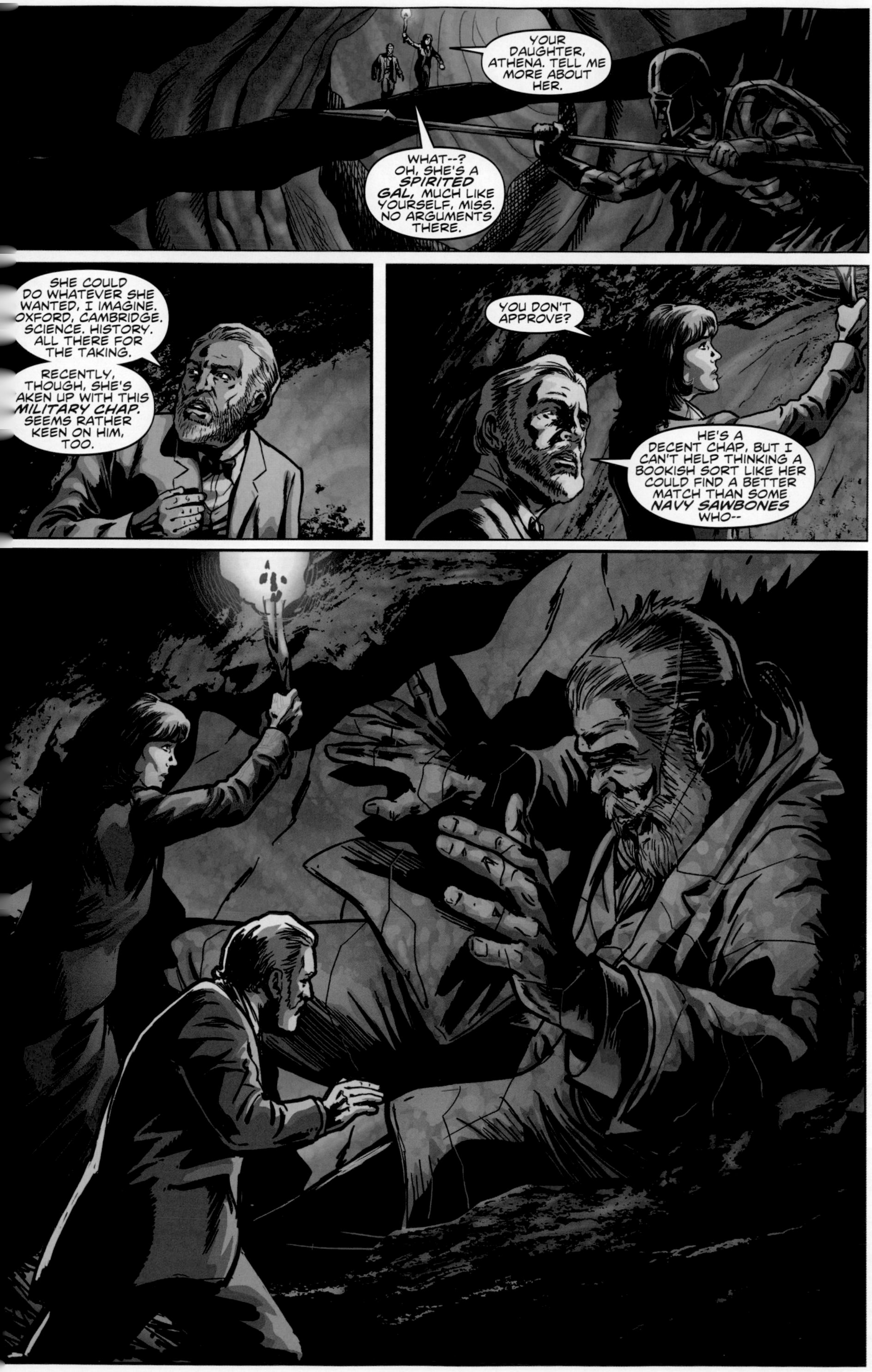
YOUR DAUGHTER, ATHENA. TELL ME MORE ABOUT HER.
WHAT--? OH, SHE'S A SPIRITED GAL, MUCH LIKE YOURSELF, MISS. NO ARGUMENTS THERE.
SHE COULD DO WHATEVER SHE WANTED, I IMAGINE. OXFORD, CAMBRIDGE. SCIENCE. HISTORY. ALL THERE FOR THE TAKING.
RECENTLY, THOUGH, SHE'S TAKEN UP WITH THIS MILITARY CHAP. SEEMS RATHER KEEN ON HIM, TOO.
YOU DON'T APPROVE?
HE'S A DECENT CHAP, BUT I CAN'T HELP THINKING A BOOKISH SORT LIKE HER COULD FIND A BETTER MATCH THAN SOME NAVY SAWBONES WHO--

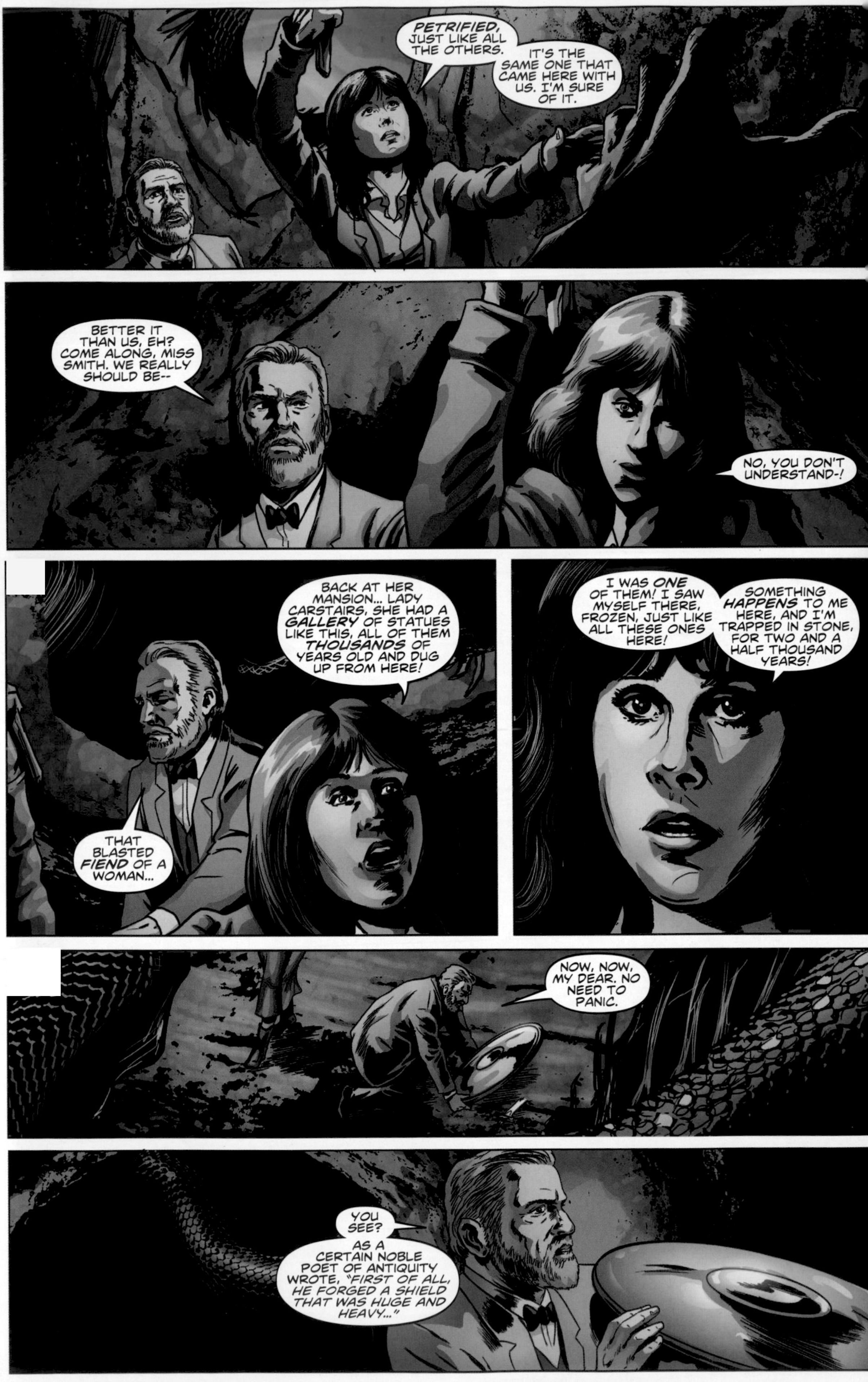
PETRIFIED, JUST LIKE ALL THE OTHERS.
IT'S THE SAME ONE THAT CAME HERE WITH US. I'M SURE OF IT.
BETTER IT THAN US, EH? COME ALONG, MISS SMITH. WE REALLY SHOULD BE--
NO, YOU DON'T UNDERSTAND-!
BACK AT HER MANSION... LADY CARSTAIRS, SHE HAD A GALLERY OF STATUES LIKE THIS, ALL OF THEM THOUSANDS OF YEARS OLD AND DUG UP FROM HERE!
THAT BLASTED FIEND OF A WOMAN...
I WAS ONE OF THEM! I SAW MYSELF THERE, FROZEN, JUST LIKE ALL THESE ONES HERE!
SOMETHING HAPPENS TO ME HERE, AND I'M TRAPPED IN STONE, FOR TWO AND A HALF THOUSAND YEARS!
NOW, NOW, MY DEAR. NO NEED TO PANIC.
YOU SEE?
AS A CERTAIN NOBLE POET OF ANTIQUITY WROTE, "FIRST OF ALL, HE FORGED A SHIELD THAT WAS HUGE AND HEAVY..."

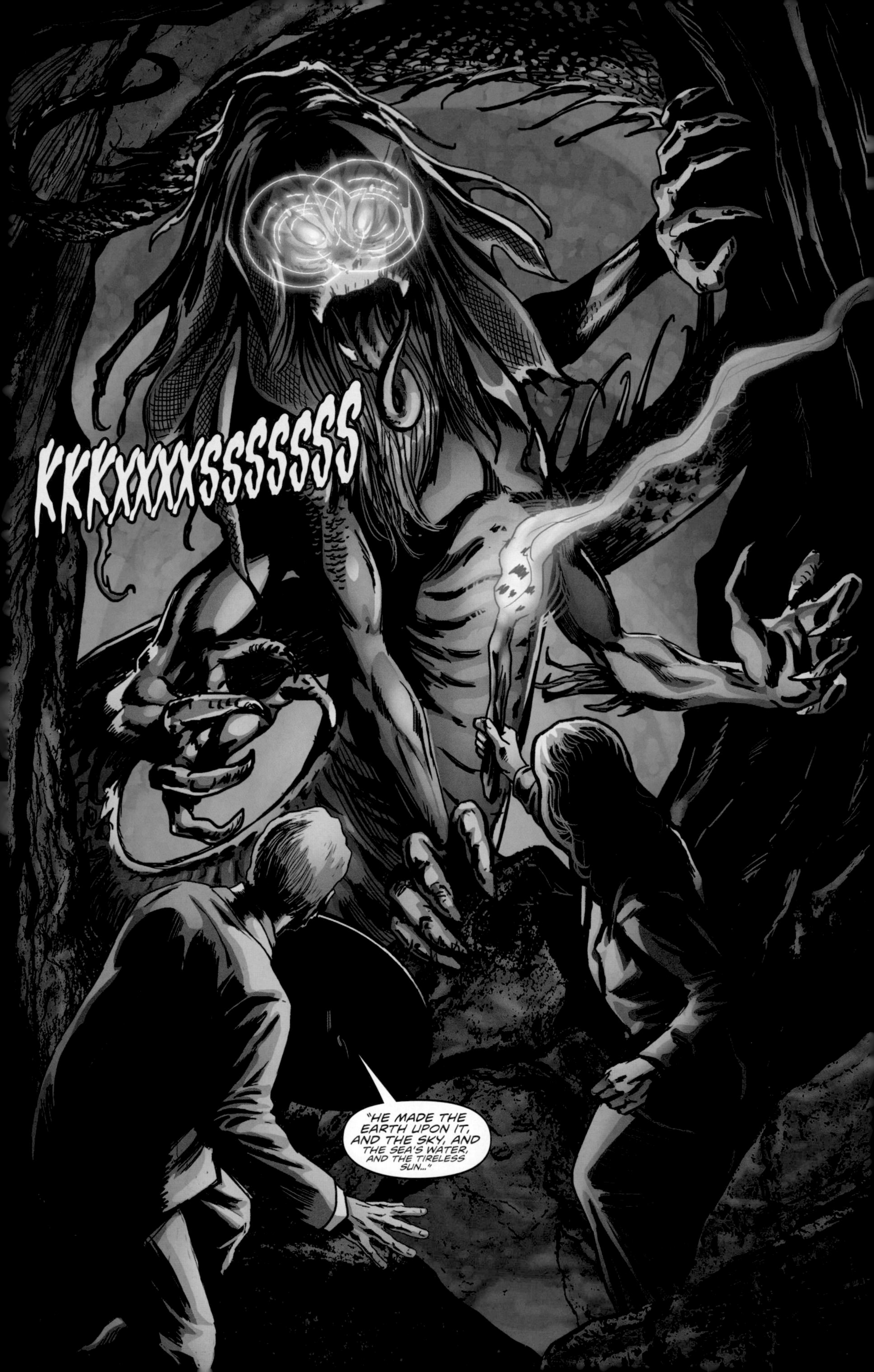
KKKXXXXSSSSSSS
"HE MADE THE EARTH UPON IT, AND THE SKY, AND THE SEA'S WATER, AND THE TIRELESS SUN..."

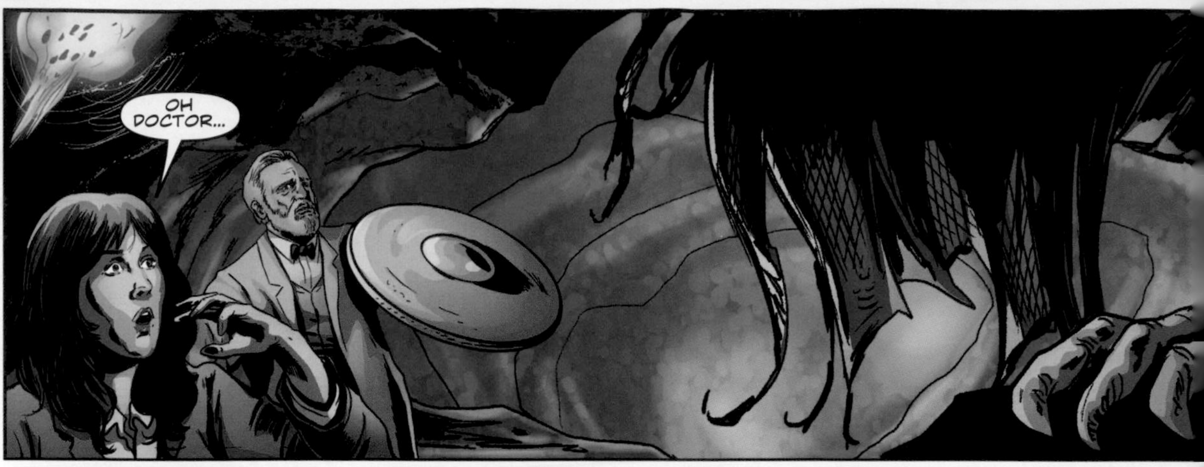
OH DOCTOR...

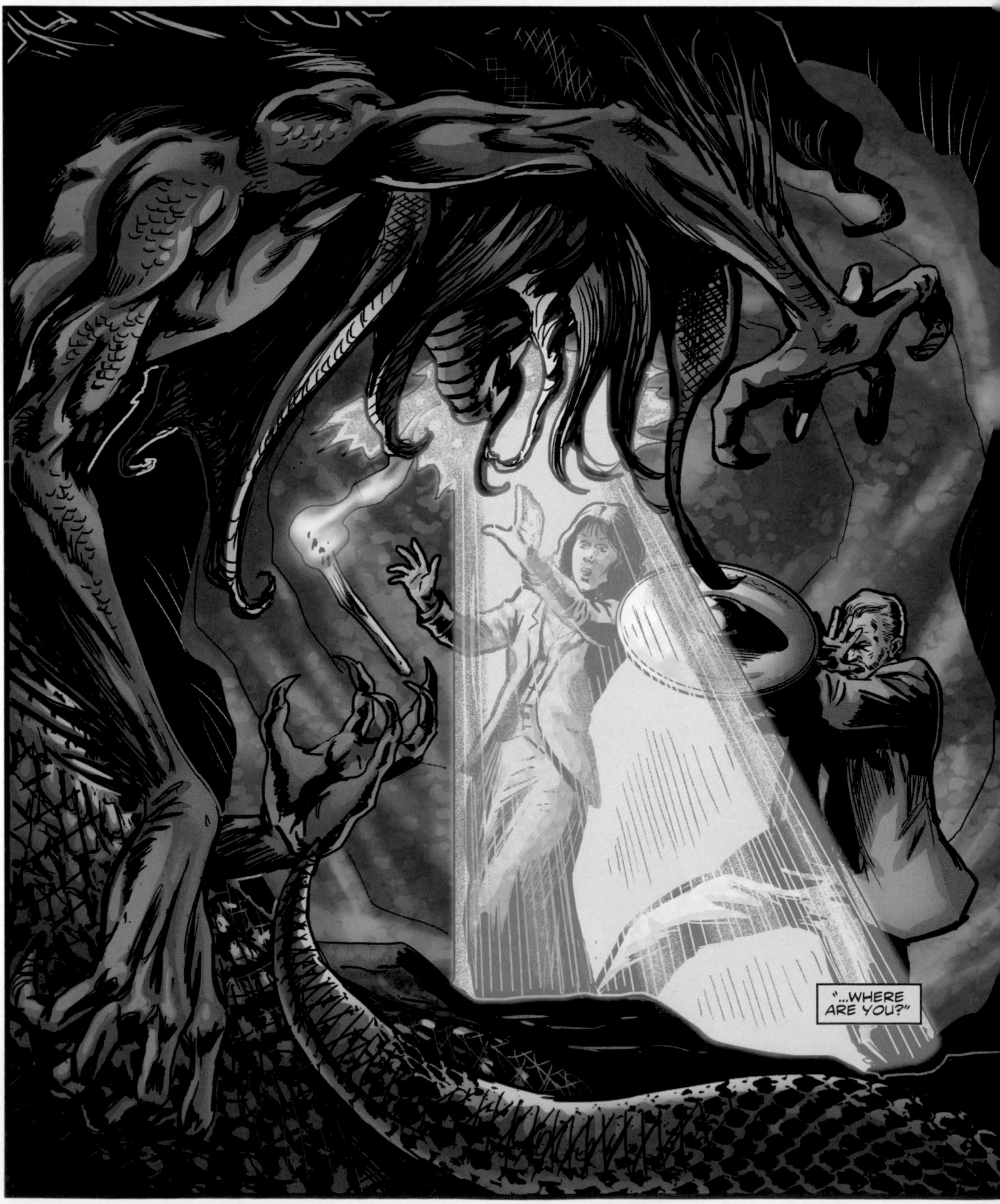
"...WHERE ARE YOU?"

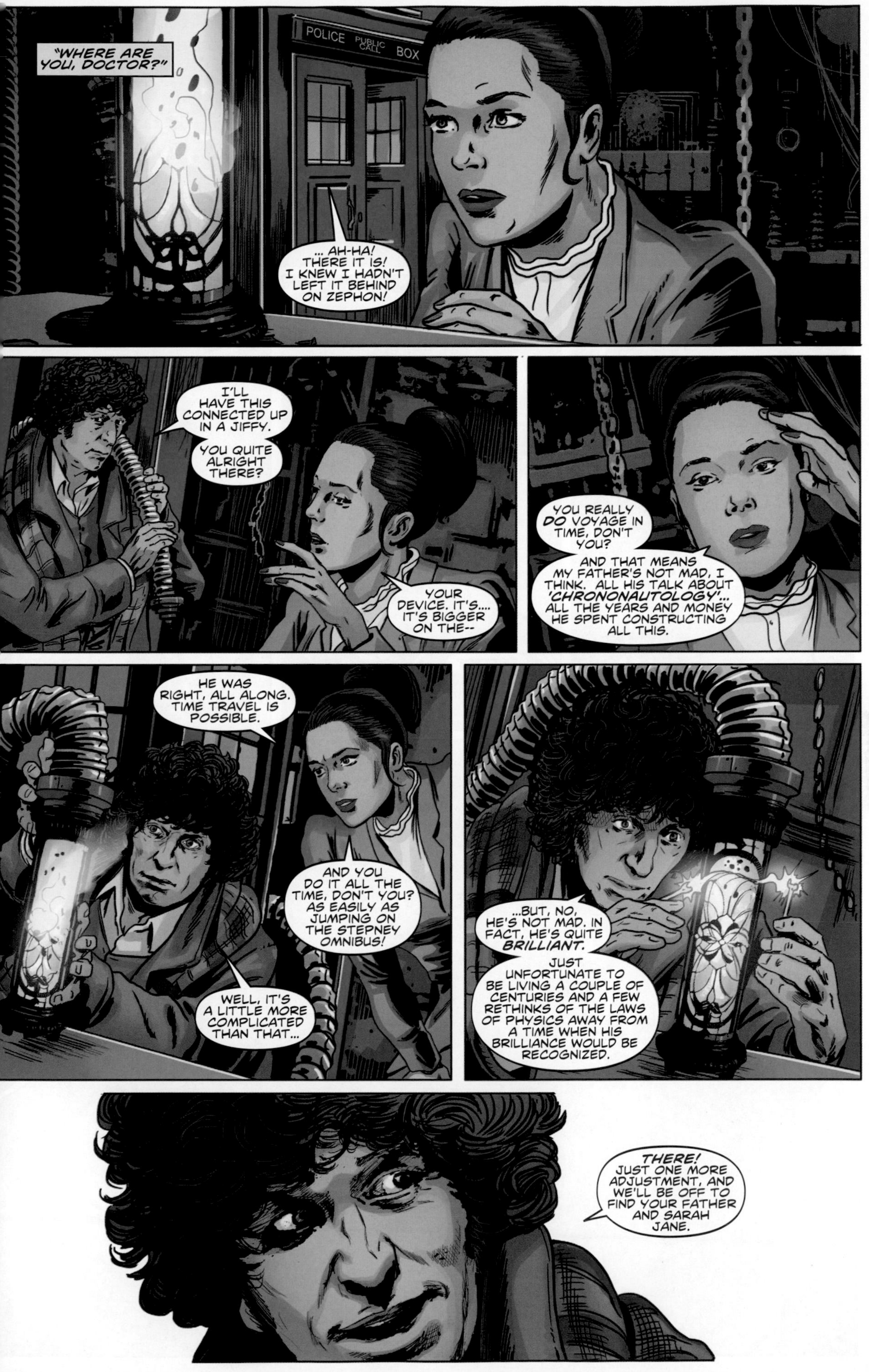

"WHERE ARE YOU, DOCTOR?"
POLICE PUBLIC CALL BOX
... AH-HA! THERE IT IS! I KNEW I HADN'T LEFT IT BEHIND ON ZEPHON!
I'LL HAVE THIS CONNECTED UP IN A JIFFY.
YOU QUITE ALRIGHT THERE?
YOUR DEVICE. IT'S.... IT'S BIGGER ON THE--
YOU REALLY DO VOYAGE IN TIME, DON'T YOU?
AND THAT MEANS MY FATHER'S NOT MAD, I THINK. ALL HIS TALK ABOUT 'CHRONONAUTOLOGY'... ALL THE YEARS AND MONEY HE SPENT CONSTRUCTING ALL THIS.
HE WAS RIGHT, ALL ALONG. TIME TRAVEL IS POSSIBLE.
AND YOU DO IT ALL THE TIME, DON'T YOU? AS EASILY AS JUMPING ON THE STEPNEY OMNIBUS!
WELL, IT'S A LITTLE MORE COMPLICATED THAN THAT...
...BUT, NO, HE'S NOT MAD. IN FACT, HE'S QUITE BRILLIANT.
JUST UNFORTUNATE TO BE LIVING A COUPLE OF CENTURIES AND A FEW RETHINKS OF THE LAWS OF PHYSICS AWAY FROM A TIME WHEN HIS BRILLIANCE WOULD BE RECOGNIZED.
THERE! JUST ONE MORE ADJUSTMENT, AND WE'LL BE OFF TO FIND YOUR FATHER AND SARAH JANE.

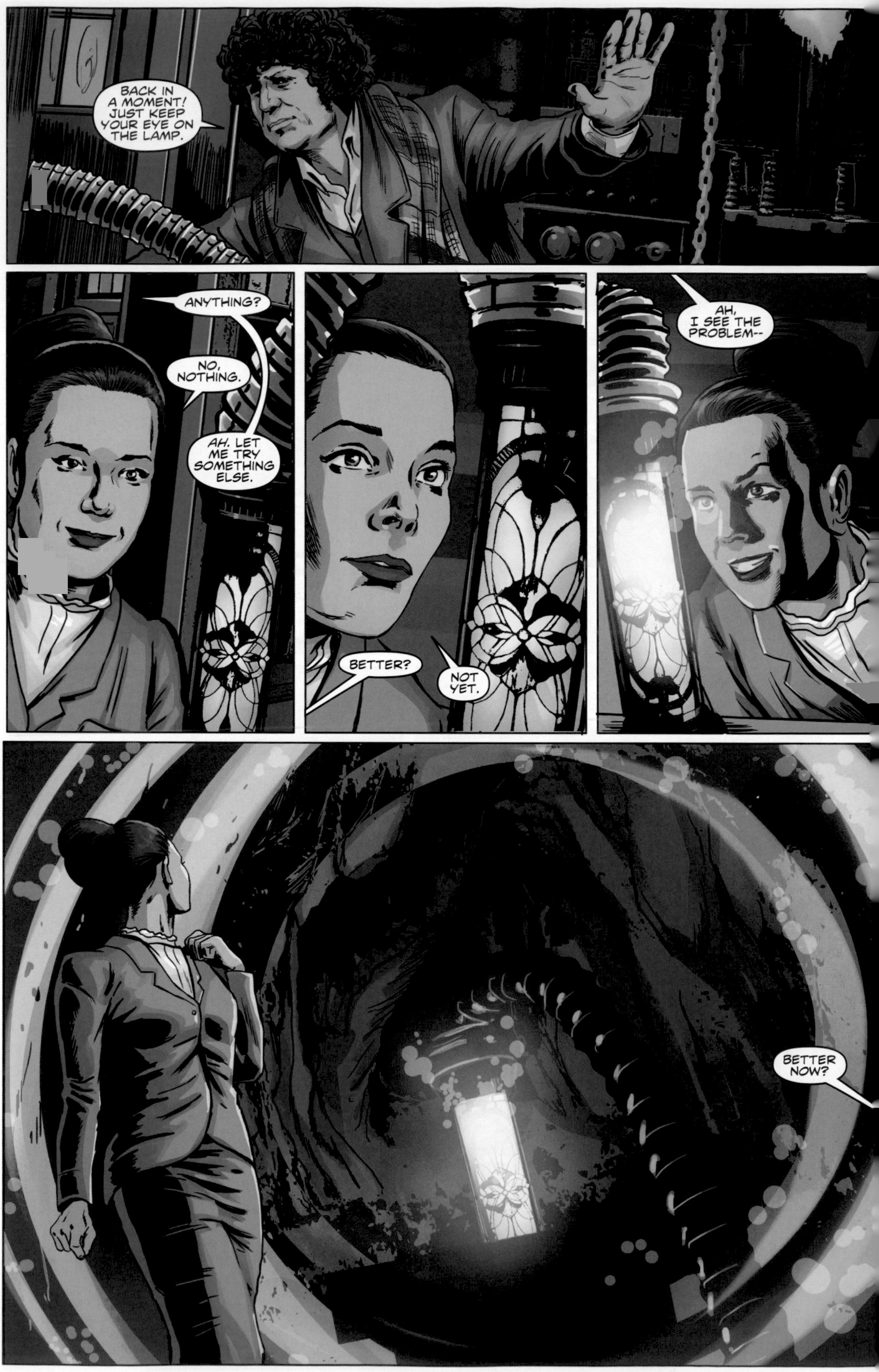
BACK IN A MOMENT! JUST KEEP YOUR EYE ON THE LAMP.
ANYTHING?
NO, NOTHING.
AH. LET ME TRY SOMETHING ELSE.
BETTER?
NOT YET.
AH, I SEE THE PROBLEM--
BETTER NOW?

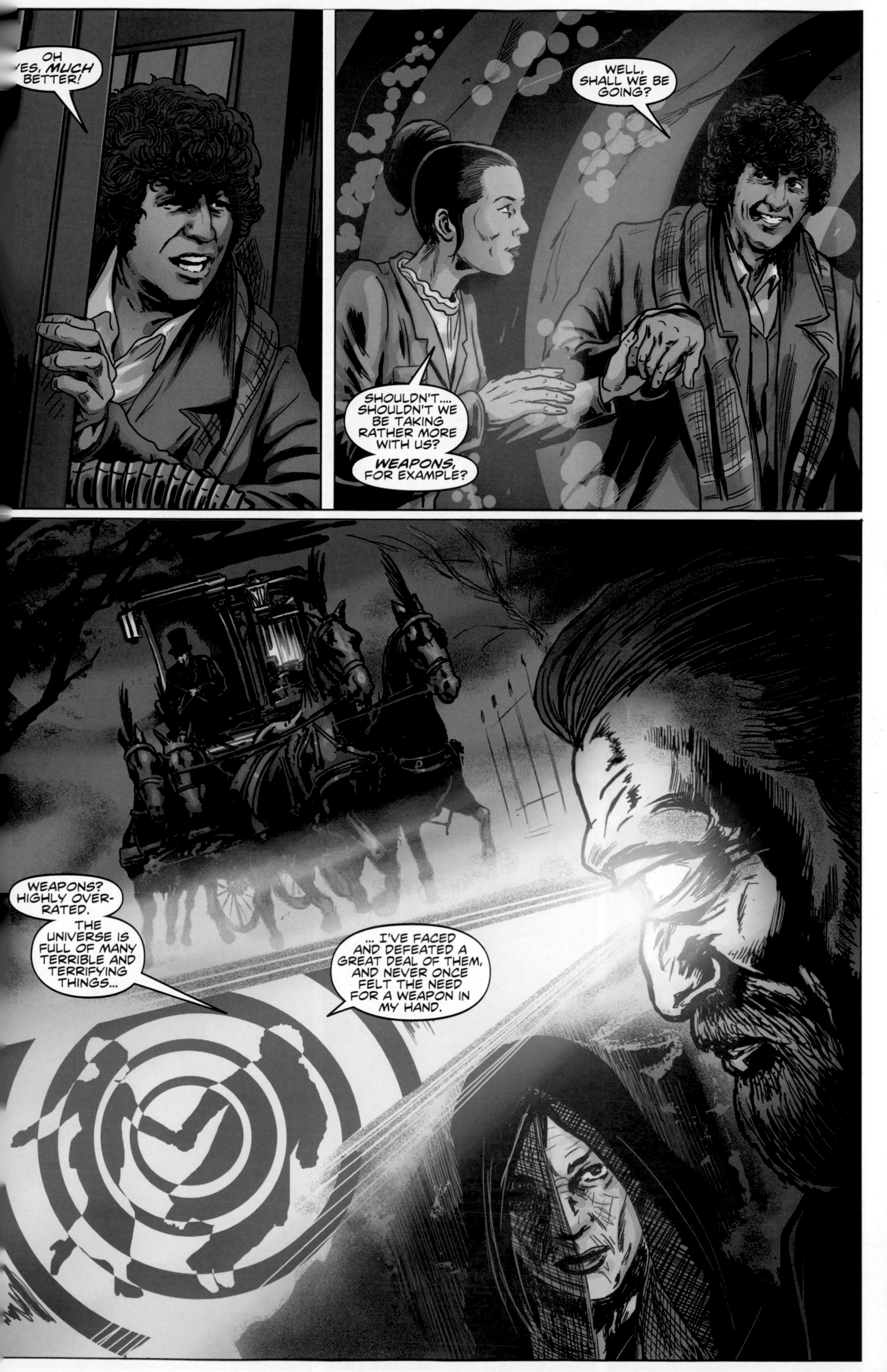
OH YES, MUCH BETTER!
WELL, SHALL WE BE GOING?
SHOULDN'T.... SHOULDN'T WE BE TAKING RATHER MORE WITH US?
WEAPONS, FOR EXAMPLE?
WEAPONS? HIGHLY OVER-RATED.
THE UNIVERSE IS FULL OF MANY TERRIBLE AND TERRIFYING THINGS...
... I'VE FACED AND DEFEATED A GREAT DEAL OF THEM, AND NEVER ONCE FELT THE NEED FOR A WEAPON IN MY HAND.

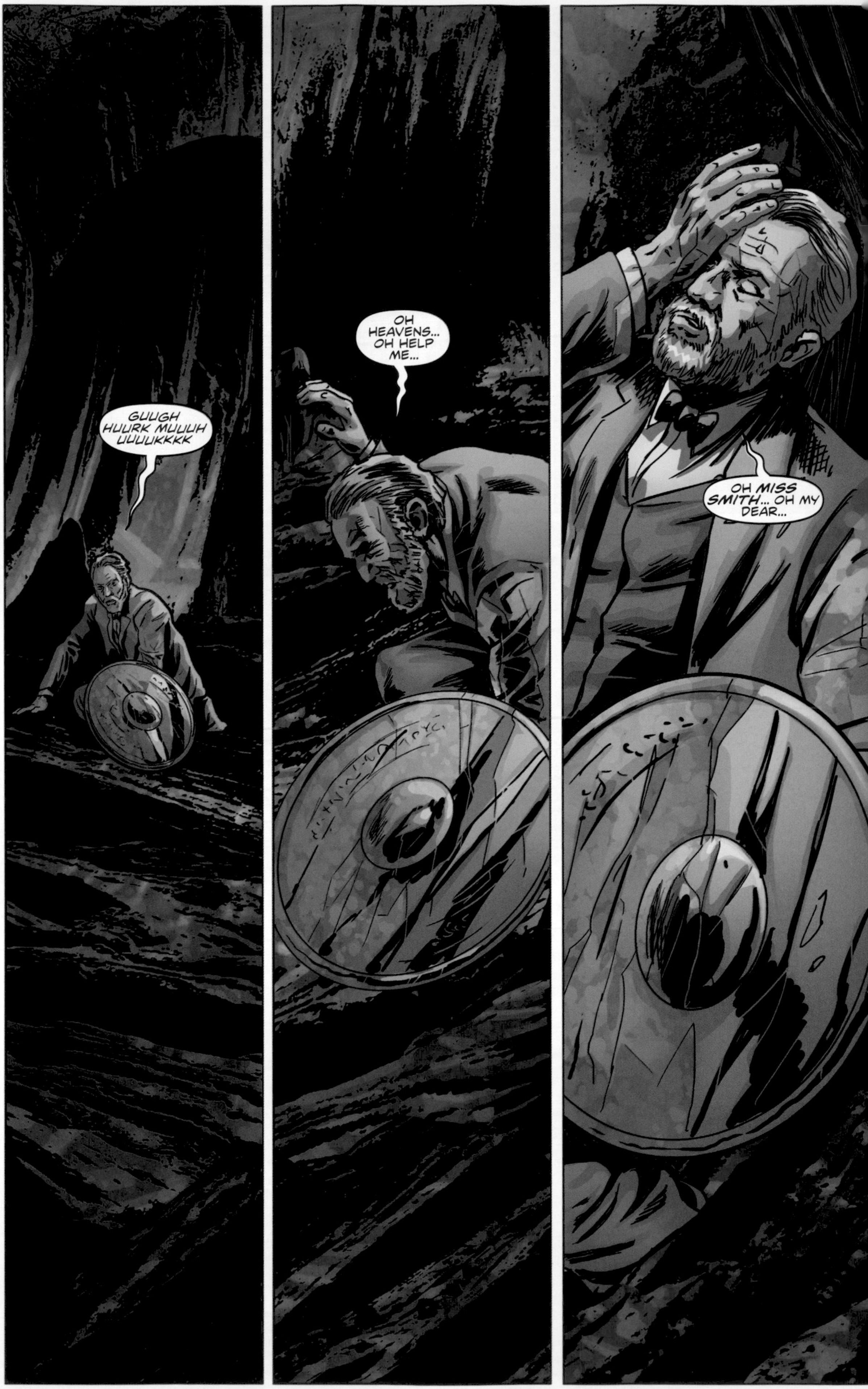
GUUGH HUURK MUUUH UUUUKKKK
OH HEAVENS... OH HELP ME...
OH MISS SMITH... OH MY DEAR...

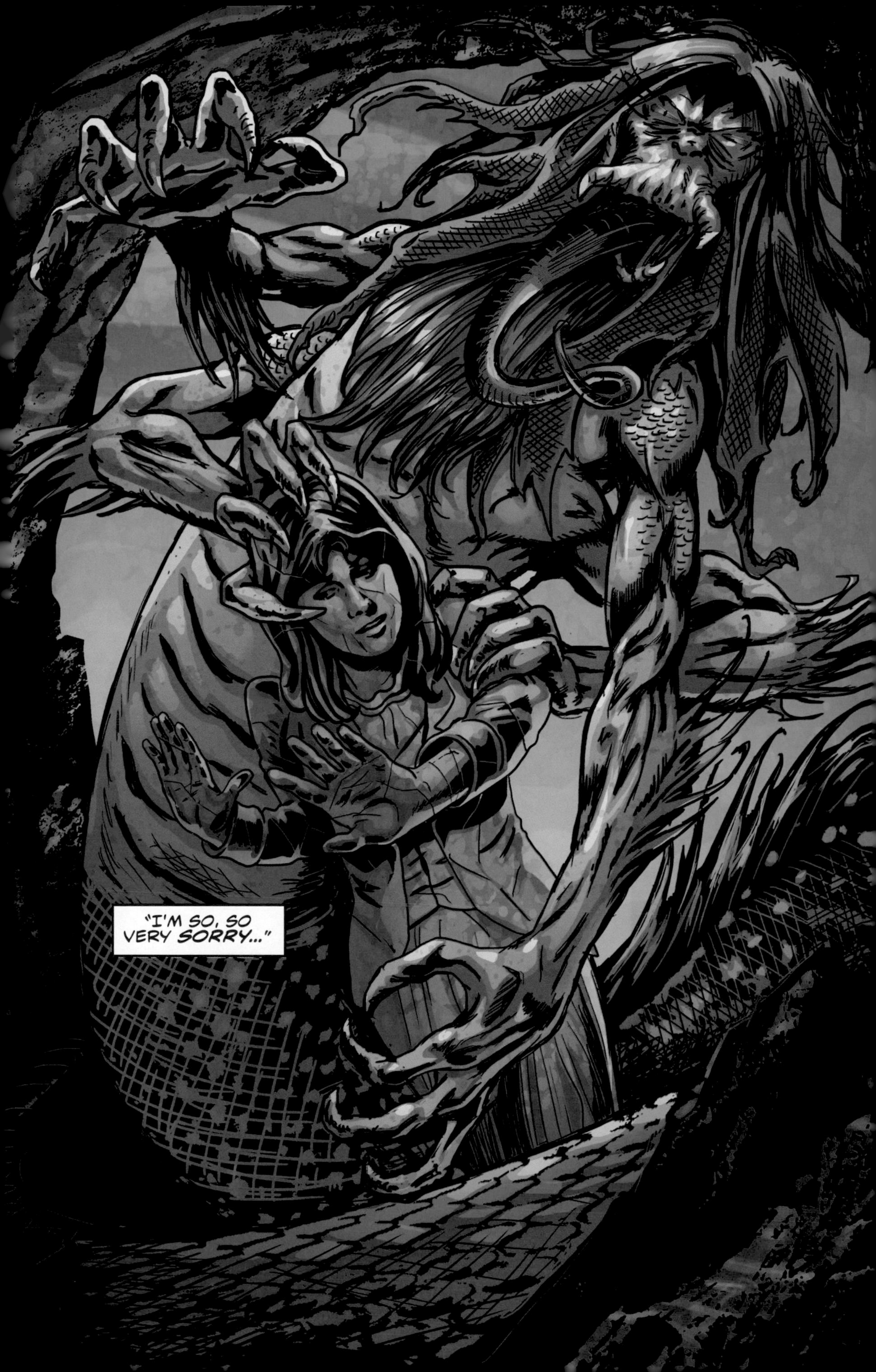
"I'M SO, SO VERY SORRY..."

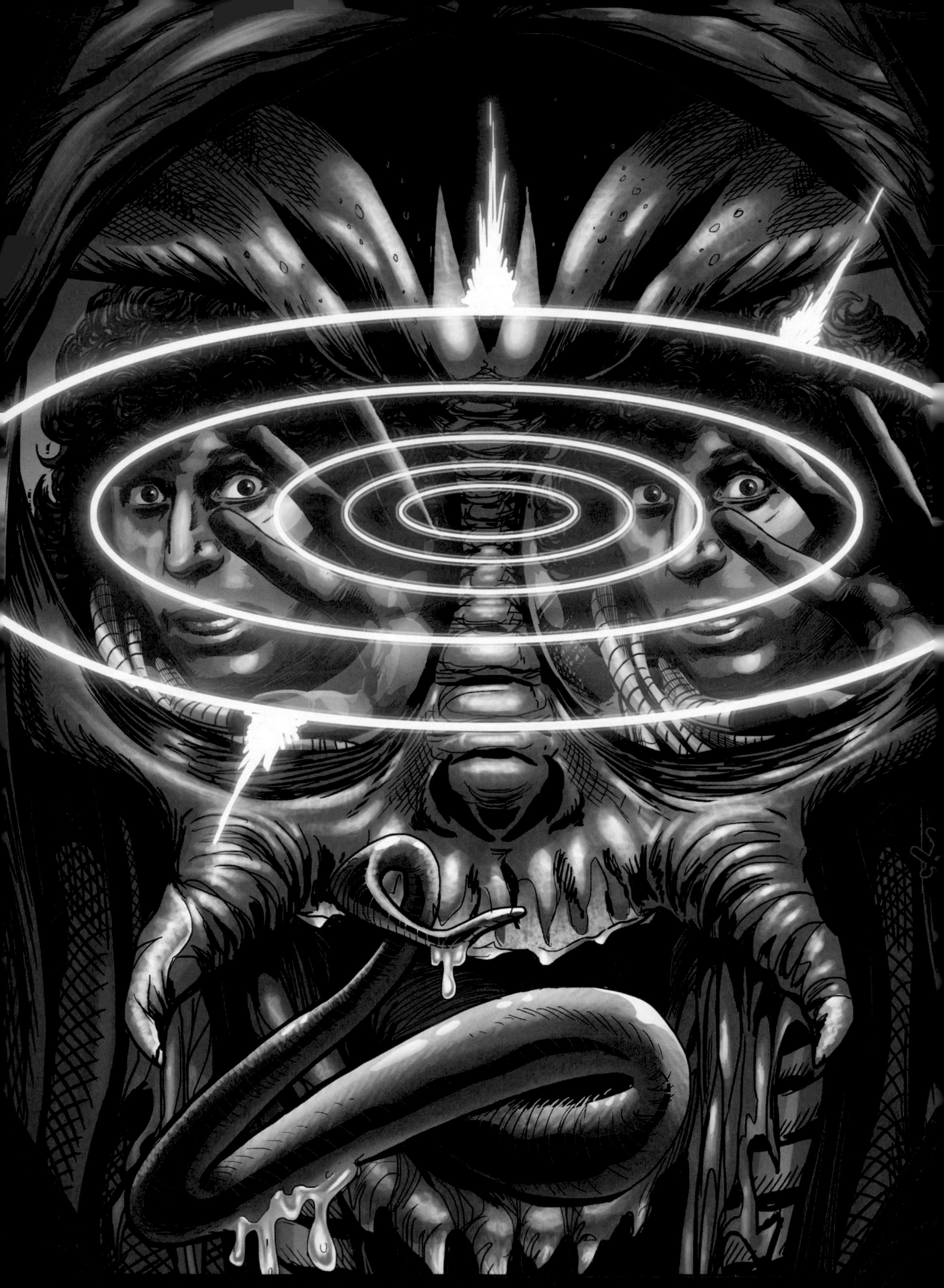

4D #4 Cover A: Brian Williamson & Hi Fi

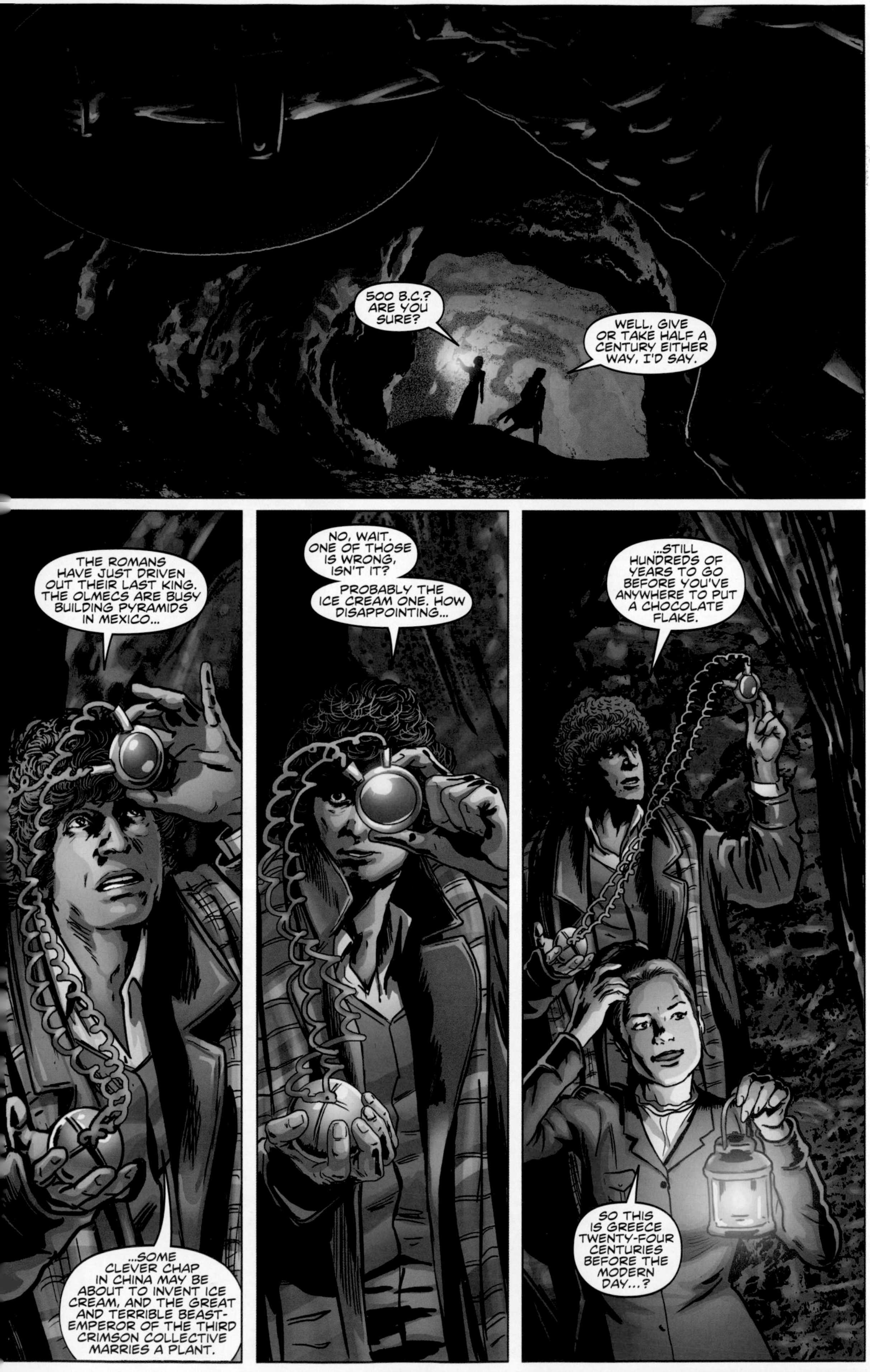
500 B.C.? ARE YOU SURE?
WELL, GIVE OR TAKE HALF A CENTURY EITHER WAY, I'D SAY.
THE ROMANS HAVE JUST DRIVEN OUT THEIR LAST KING. THE OLMECS ARE BUSY BUILDING PYRAMIDS IN MEXICO...
...SOME CLEVER CHAP IN CHINA MAY BE ABOUT TO INVENT ICE CREAM, AND THE GREAT AND TERRIBLE BEAST-EMPEROR OF THE THIRD CRIMSON COLLECTIVE MARRIES A PLANT.
NO, WAIT. ONE OF THOSE IS WRONG, ISN'T IT?
PROBABLY THE ICE CREAM ONE. HOW DISAPPOINTING...
...STILL HUNDREDS OF YEARS TO GO BEFORE YOU'VE ANYWHERE TO PUT A CHOCOLATE FLAKE.
SO THIS IS GREECE TWENTY-FOUR CENTURIES BEFORE THE MODERN DAY...?

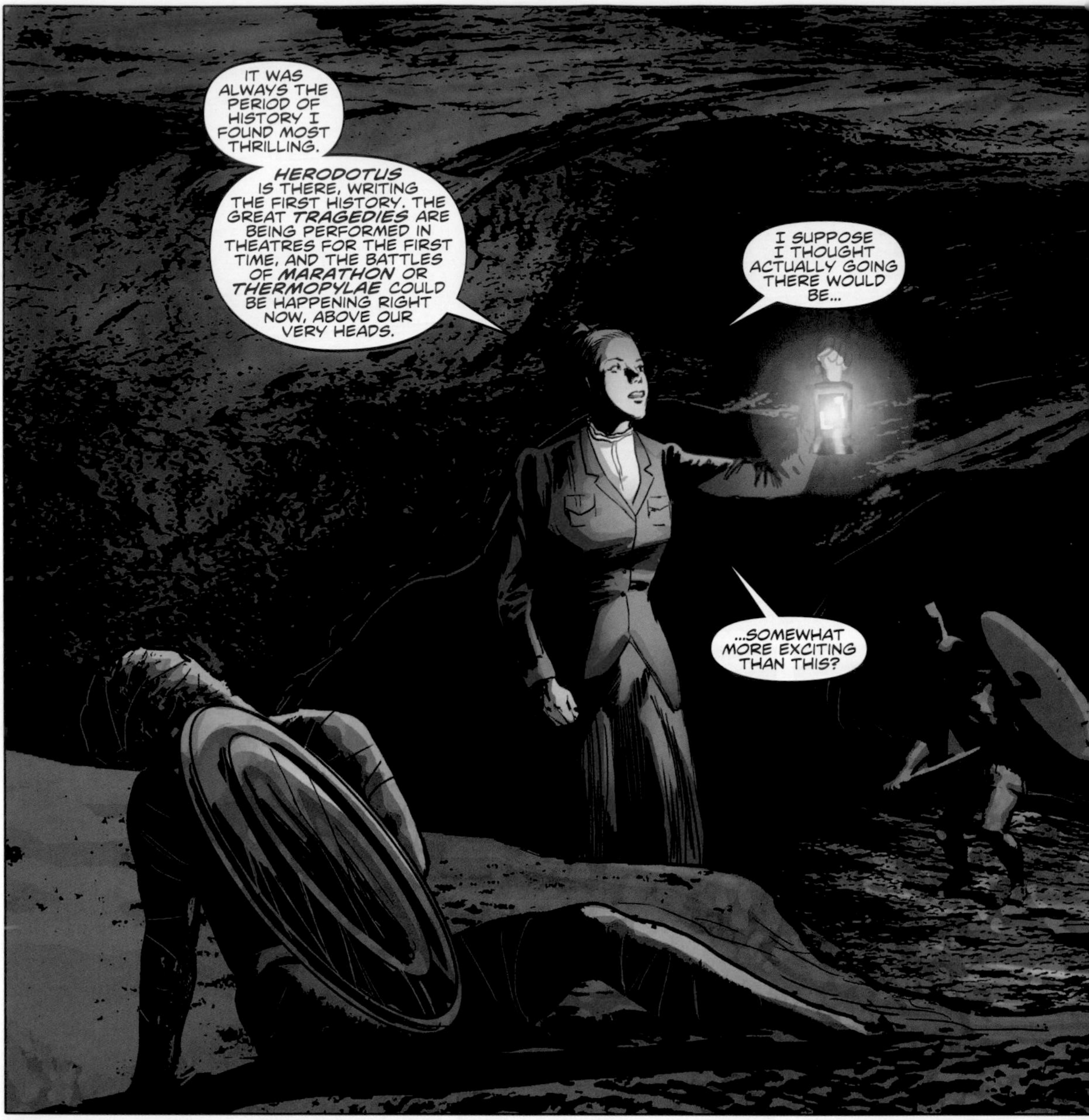
IT WAS ALWAYS THE PERIOD OF HISTORY I FOUND MOST THRILLING.
HERODOTUS IS THERE, WRITING THE FIRST HISTORY. THE GREAT TRAGEDIES ARE BEING PERFORMED IN THEATRES FOR THE FIRST TIME, AND THE BATTLES OF MARATHON OR THERMOPYLAE COULD BE HAPPENING RIGHT NOW, ABOVE OUR VERY HEADS.
I SUPPOSE I THOUGHT ACTUALLY GOING THERE WOULD BE...
...SOMEWHAT MORE EXCITING THAN THIS?

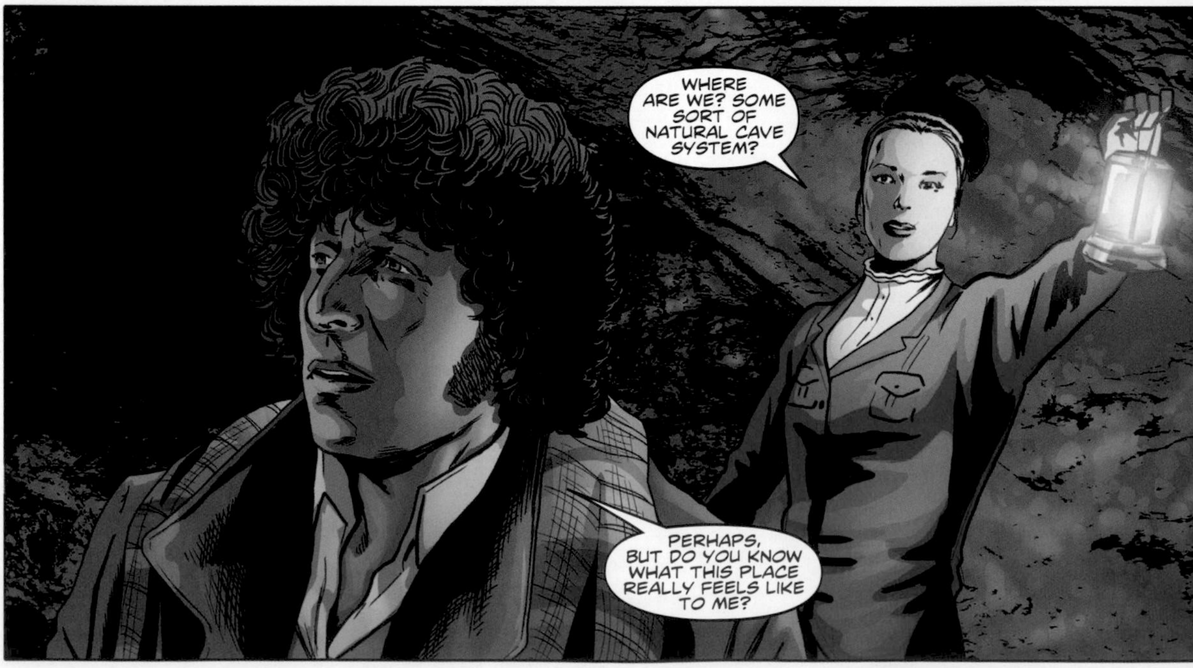
WHERE ARE WE? SOME SORT OF NATURAL CAVE SYSTEM?
PERHAPS, BUT DO YOU KNOW WHAT THIS PLACE REALLY FEELS LIKE TO ME?

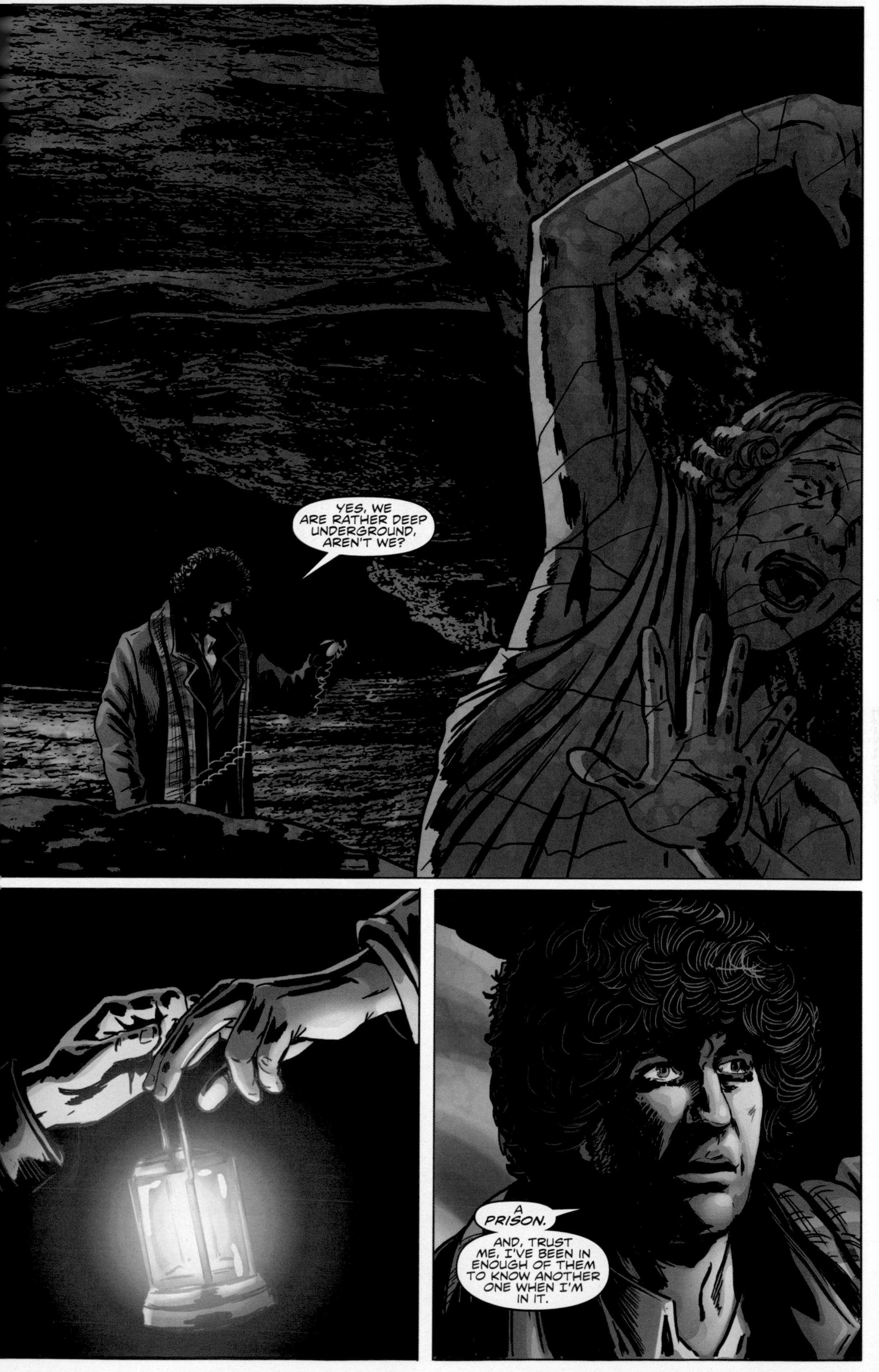
YES, WE ARE RATHER DEEP UNDERGROUND, AREN'T WE?
A PRISON.
AND, TRUST ME, I'VE BEEN IN ENOUGH OF THEM TO KNOW ANOTHER ONE WHEN I'M IN IT.

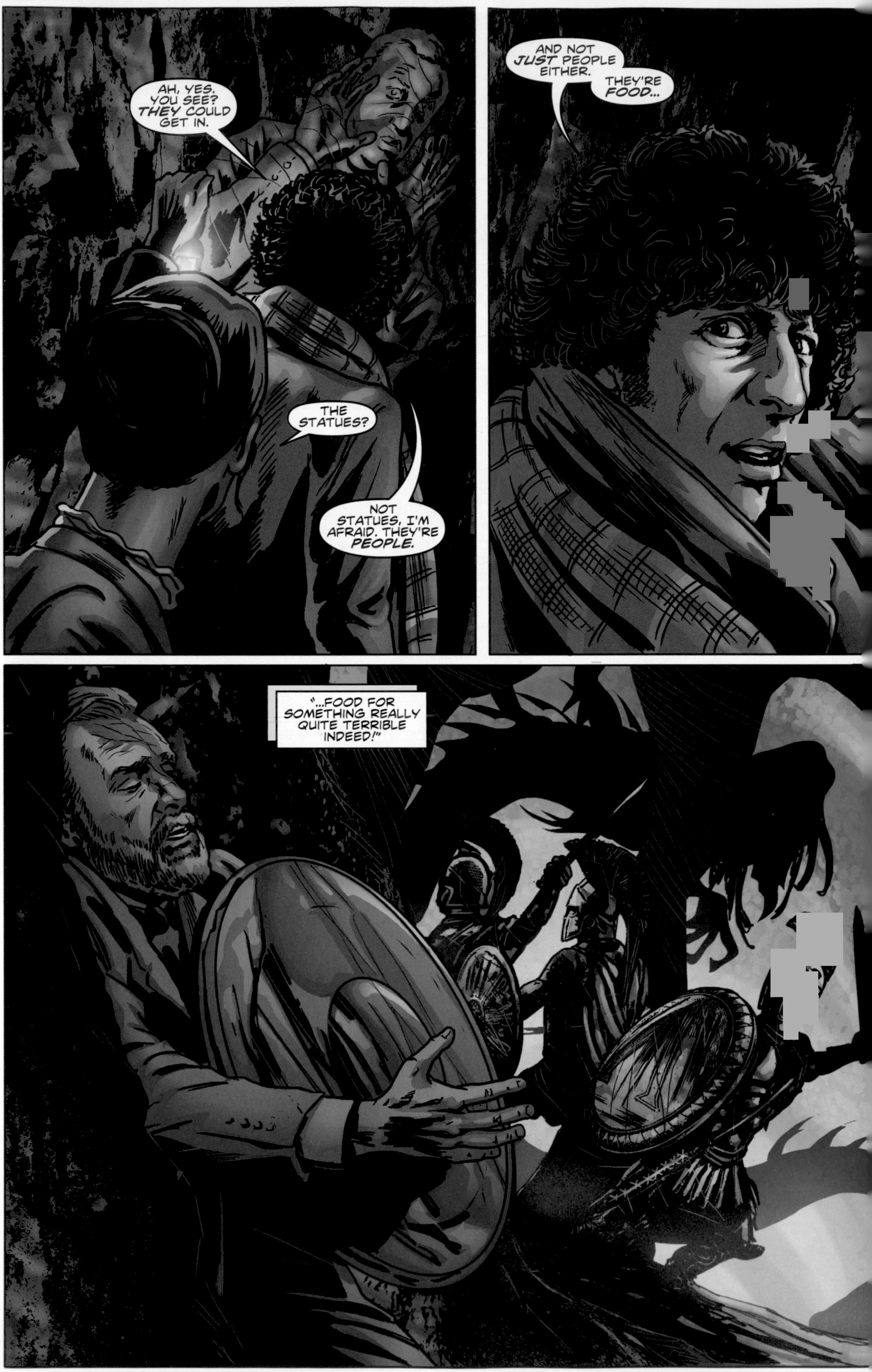
AH, YES. YOU SEE? *THEY* COULD GET IN.
THE STATUES?
NOT STATUES, I'M AFRAID. THEY'RE *PEOPLE.*
AND NOT *JUST* PEOPLE EITHER.
THEY'RE *FOOD*...
"...FOOD FOR SOMETHING REALLY QUITE TERRIBLE INDEED!"

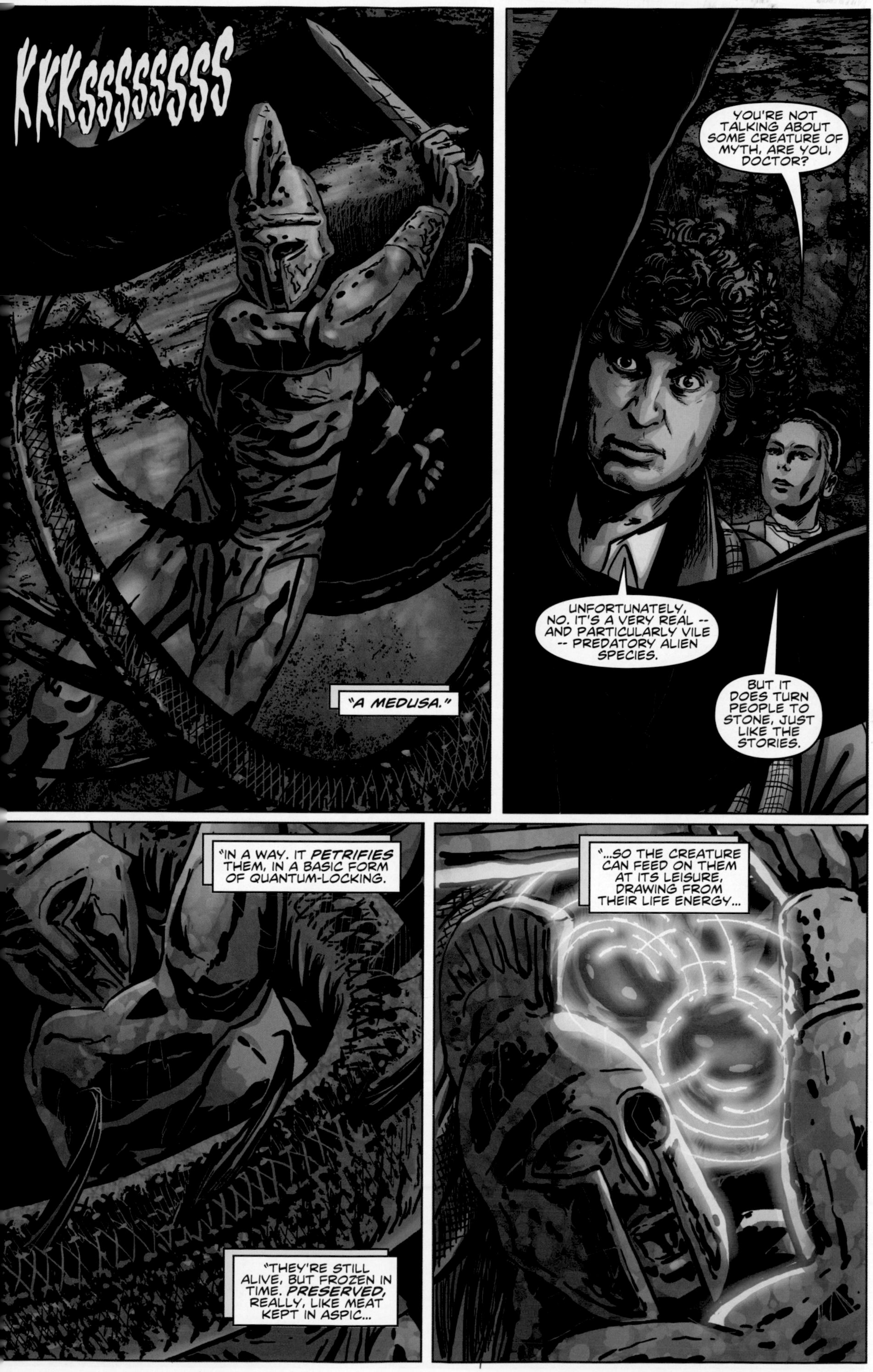
KKKSSSSSSSS
"A MEDUSA."
YOU'RE NOT TALKING ABOUT SOME CREATURE OF MYTH, ARE YOU, DOCTOR?
UNFORTUNATELY, NO. IT'S A VERY REAL -- AND PARTICULARLY VILE -- PREDATORY ALIEN SPECIES.
BUT IT DOES TURN PEOPLE TO STONE, JUST LIKE THE STORIES.
"IN A WAY. IT *PETRIFIES* THEM, IN A BASIC FORM OF QUANTUM-LOCKING.
"THEY'RE STILL ALIVE, BUT FROZEN IN TIME. *PRESERVED*, REALLY, LIKE MEAT KEPT IN ASPIC...
"...SO THE CREATURE CAN FEED ON THEM AT ITS LEISURE, DRAWING FROM THEIR LIFE ENERGY...

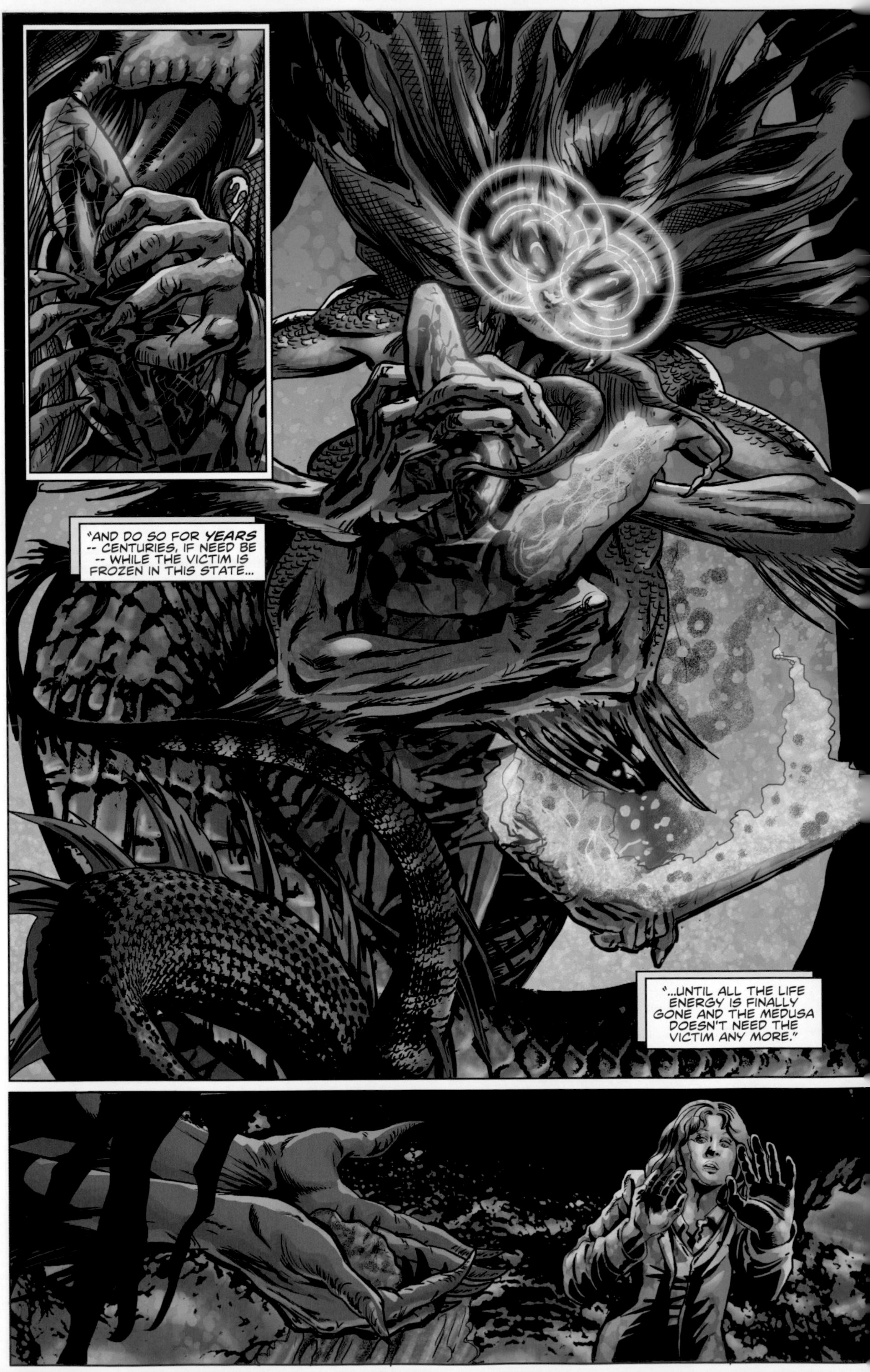
"AND DO SO FOR YEARS -- CENTURIES, IF NEED BE -- WHILE THE VICTIM IS FROZEN IN THIS STATE...
"...UNTIL ALL THE LIFE ENERGY IS FINALLY GONE AND THE MEDUSA DOESN'T NEED THE VICTIM ANY MORE."

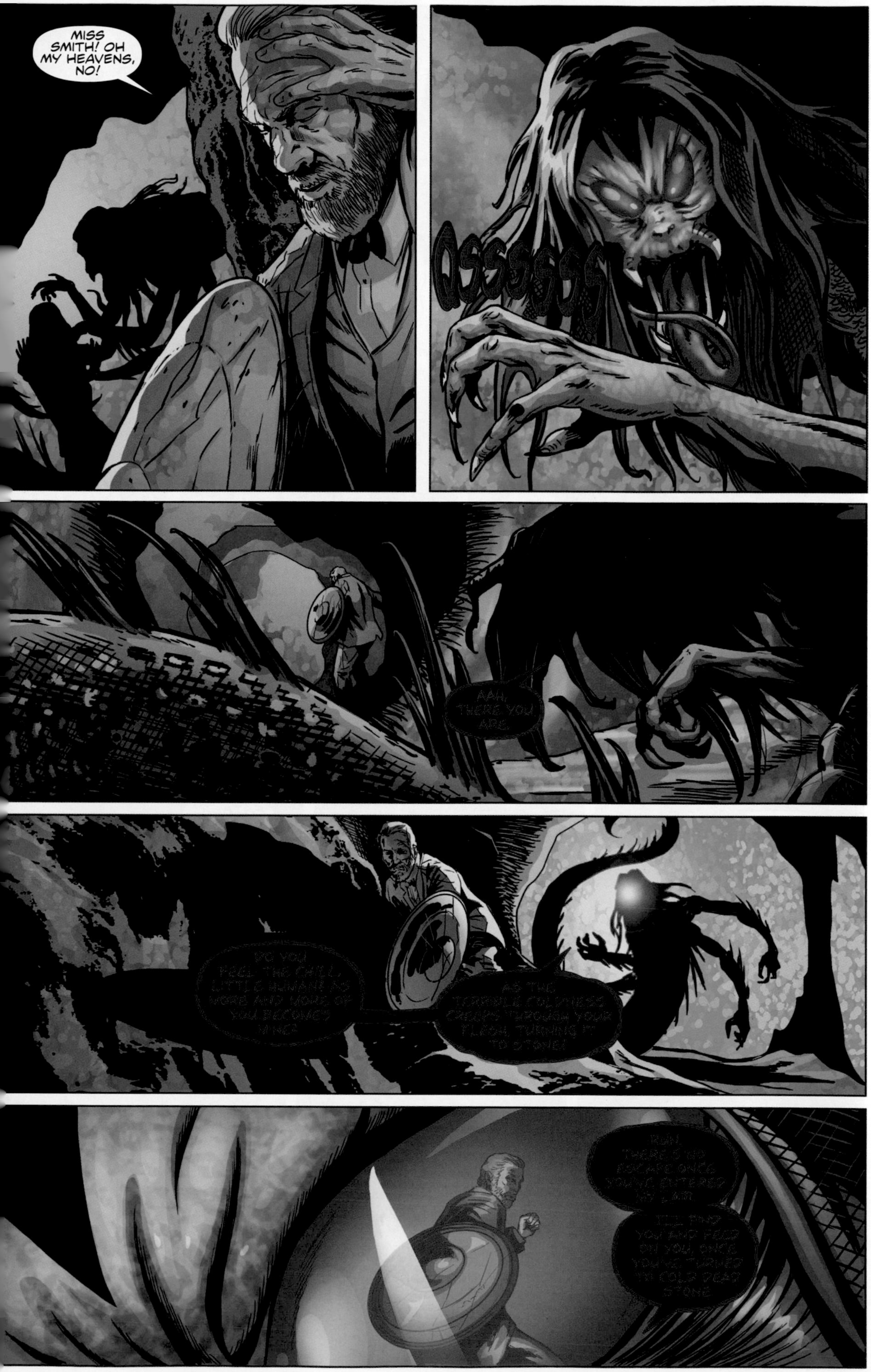
MISS SMITH! OH MY HEAVENS, NO!
QSSSSSS
AAH, THERE YOU ARE.
DO YOU FEEL THE CHILL, LITTLE HUMAN, AS MORE AND MORE OF YOU BECOMES MINE?
AS THE TERRIBLE COLDNESS CREEPS THROUGH YOUR FLESH, TURNING IT TO STONE!
RUN. THERE'S NO ESCAPE ONCE YOU'VE ENTERED MY LAIR.
I'LL FIND YOU AND FEED ON YOU, ONCE YOU'VE TURNED TO COLD DEAD STONE.

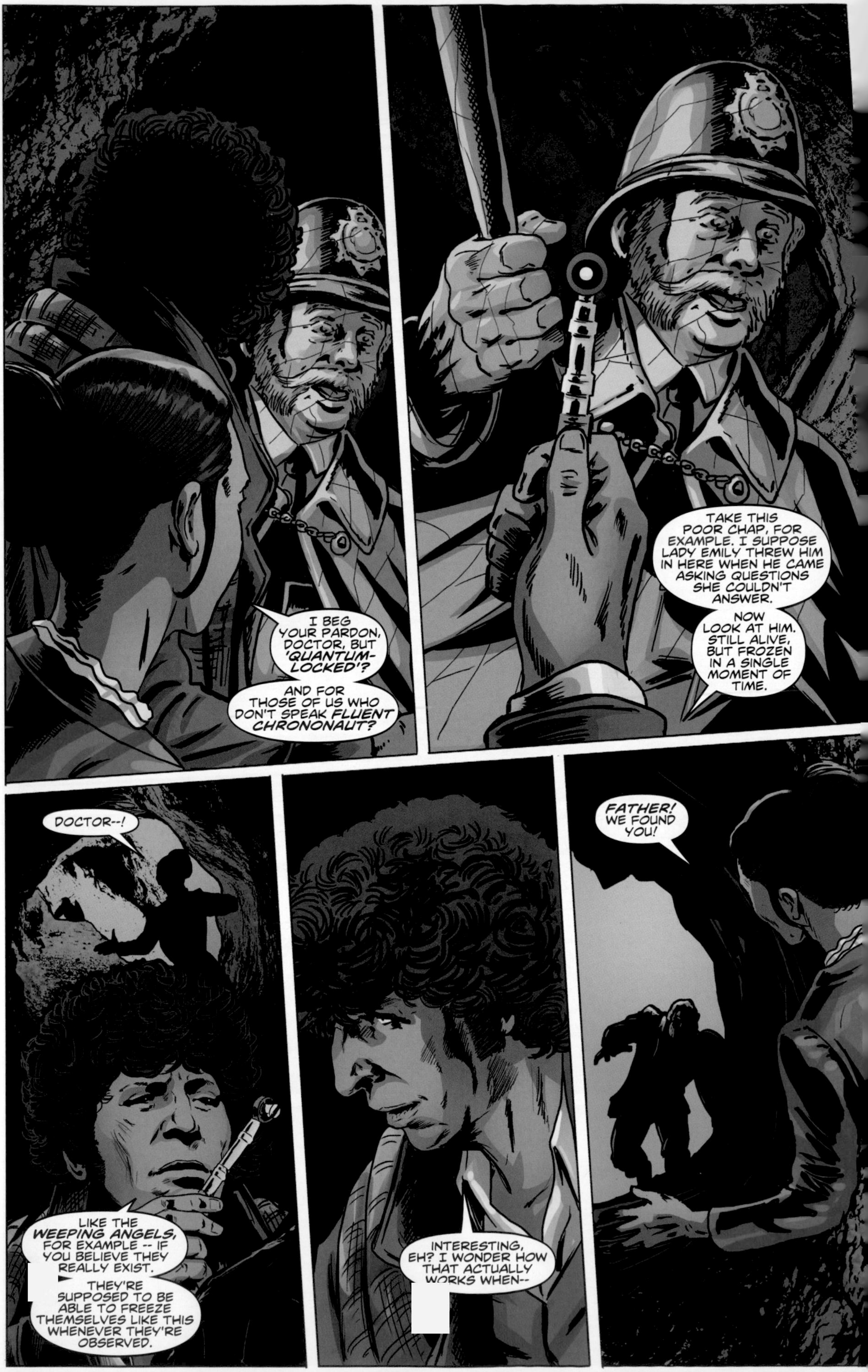
I BEG YOUR PARDON, DOCTOR, BUT 'QUANTUM-LOCKED'?
AND FOR THOSE OF US WHO DON'T SPEAK FLUENT CHRONONAUT?
TAKE THIS POOR CHAP, FOR EXAMPLE. I SUPPOSE LADY EMILY THREW HIM IN HERE WHEN HE CAME ASKING QUESTIONS SHE COULDN'T ANSWER.
NOW LOOK AT HIM. STILL ALIVE, BUT FROZEN IN A SINGLE MOMENT OF TIME.
DOCTOR--!
LIKE THE WEEPING ANGELS, FOR EXAMPLE -- IF YOU BELIEVE THEY REALLY EXIST.
THEY'RE SUPPOSED TO BE ABLE TO FREEZE THEMSELVES LIKE THIS WHENEVER THEY'RE OBSERVED.
INTERESTING, EH? I WONDER HOW THAT ACTUALLY WORKS WHEN--
FATHER! WE FOUND YOU!

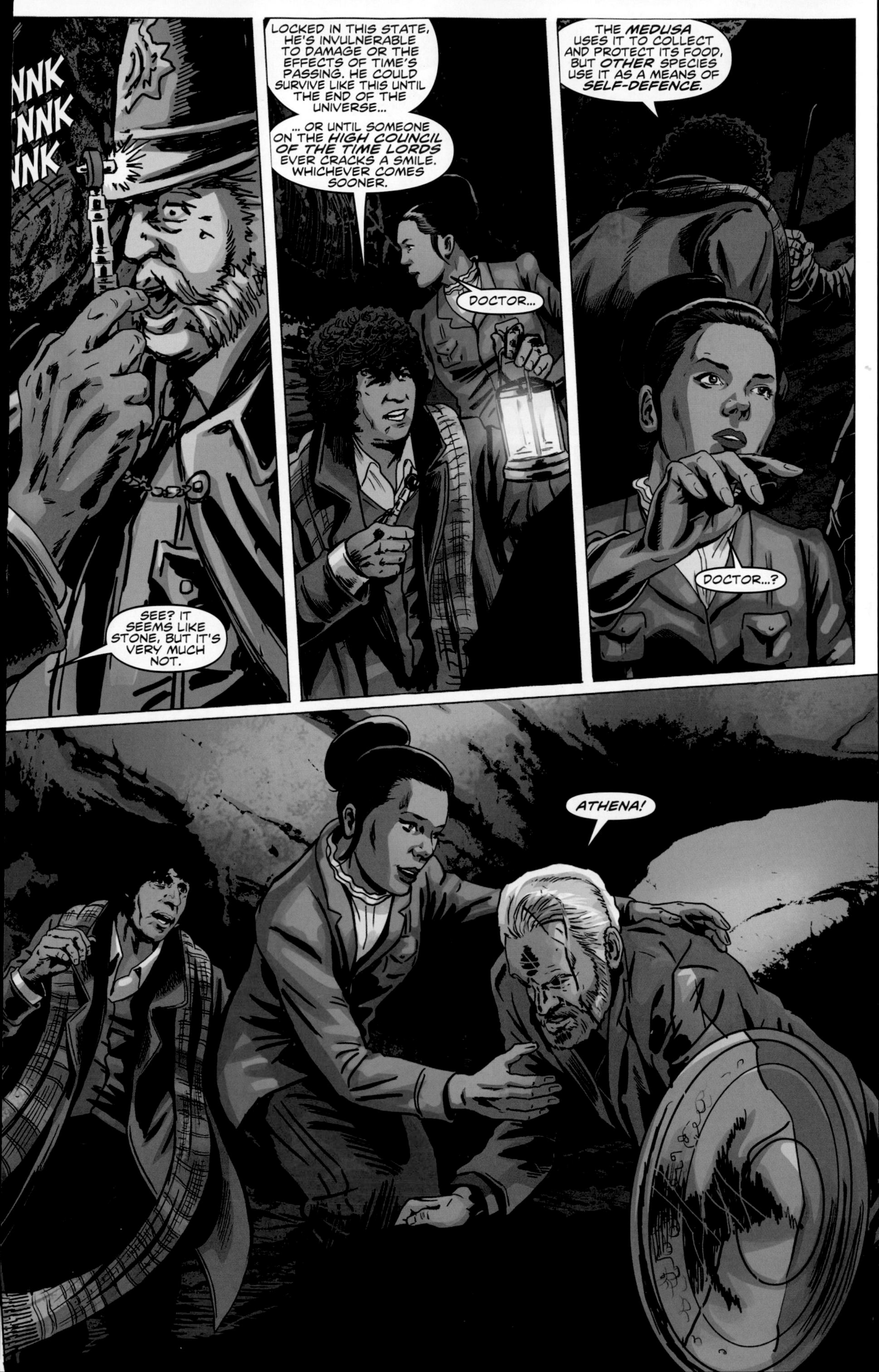
NNK
NNK
NNK
SEE? IT SEEMS LIKE STONE, BUT IT'S VERY MUCH NOT.
LOCKED IN THIS STATE, HE'S INVULNERABLE TO DAMAGE OR THE EFFECTS OF TIME'S PASSING. HE COULD SURVIVE LIKE THIS UNTIL THE END OF THE UNIVERSE...
...OR UNTIL SOMEONE ON THE HIGH COUNCIL OF THE TIME LORDS EVER CRACKS A SMILE. WHICHEVER COMES SOONER.
DOCTOR...
THE MEDUSA USES IT TO COLLECT AND PROTECT ITS FOOD, BUT OTHER SPECIES USE IT AS A MEANS OF SELF-DEFENCE.
DOCTOR...?
ATHENA!

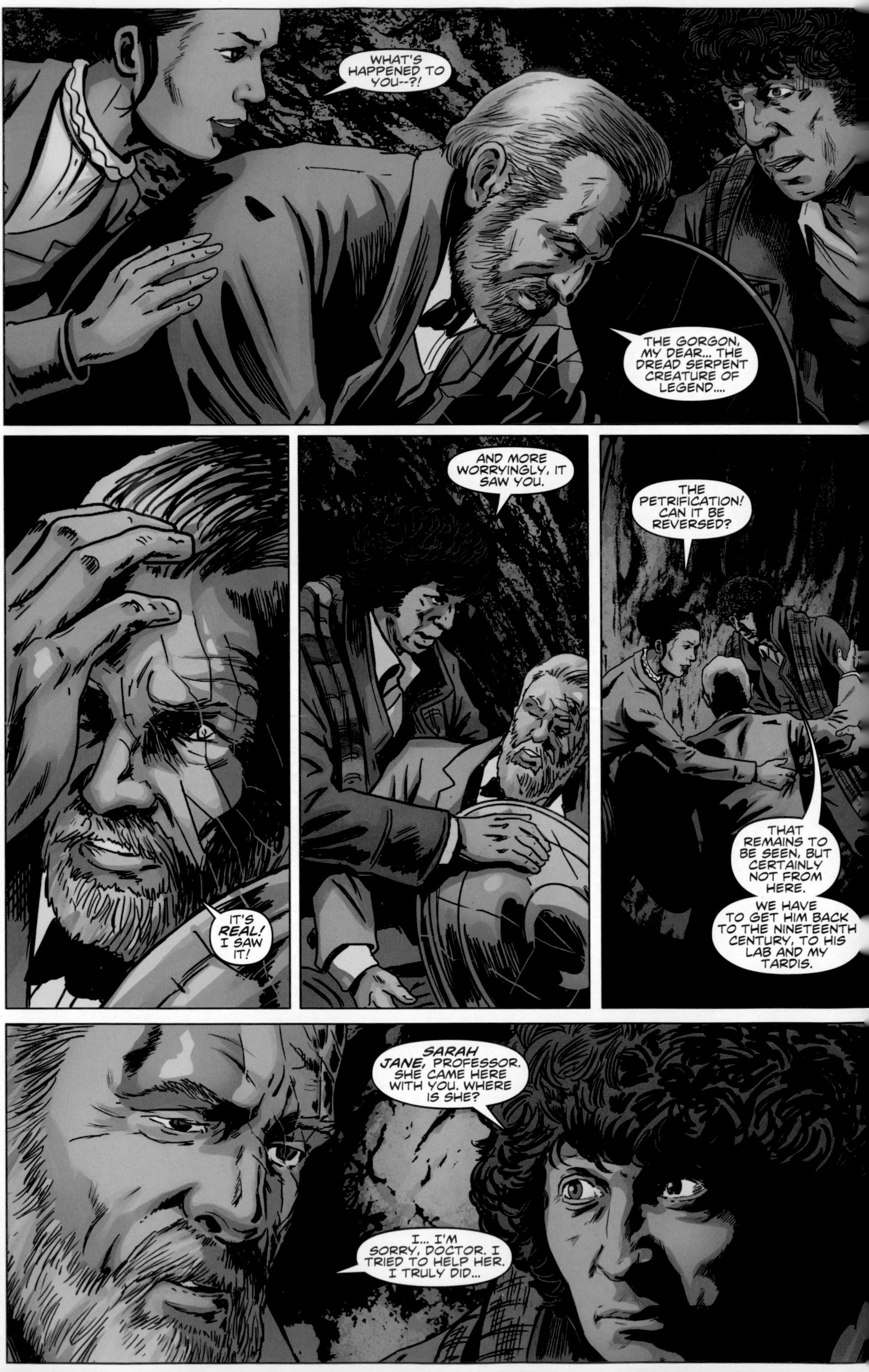
WHAT'S HAPPENED TO YOU--?!
THE GORGON, MY DEAR... THE DREAD SERPENT CREATURE OF LEGEND....
IT'S REAL! I SAW IT!
AND MORE WORRYINGLY, IT SAW YOU.
THE PETRIFICATION! CAN IT BE REVERSED?
THAT REMAINS TO BE SEEN, BUT CERTAINLY NOT FROM HERE.
WE HAVE TO GET HIM BACK TO THE NINETEENTH CENTURY, TO HIS LAB AND MY TARDIS.
SARAH JANE, PROFESSOR. SHE CAME HERE WITH YOU. WHERE IS SHE?
I... I'M SORRY, DOCTOR. I TRIED TO HELP HER. I TRULY DID...

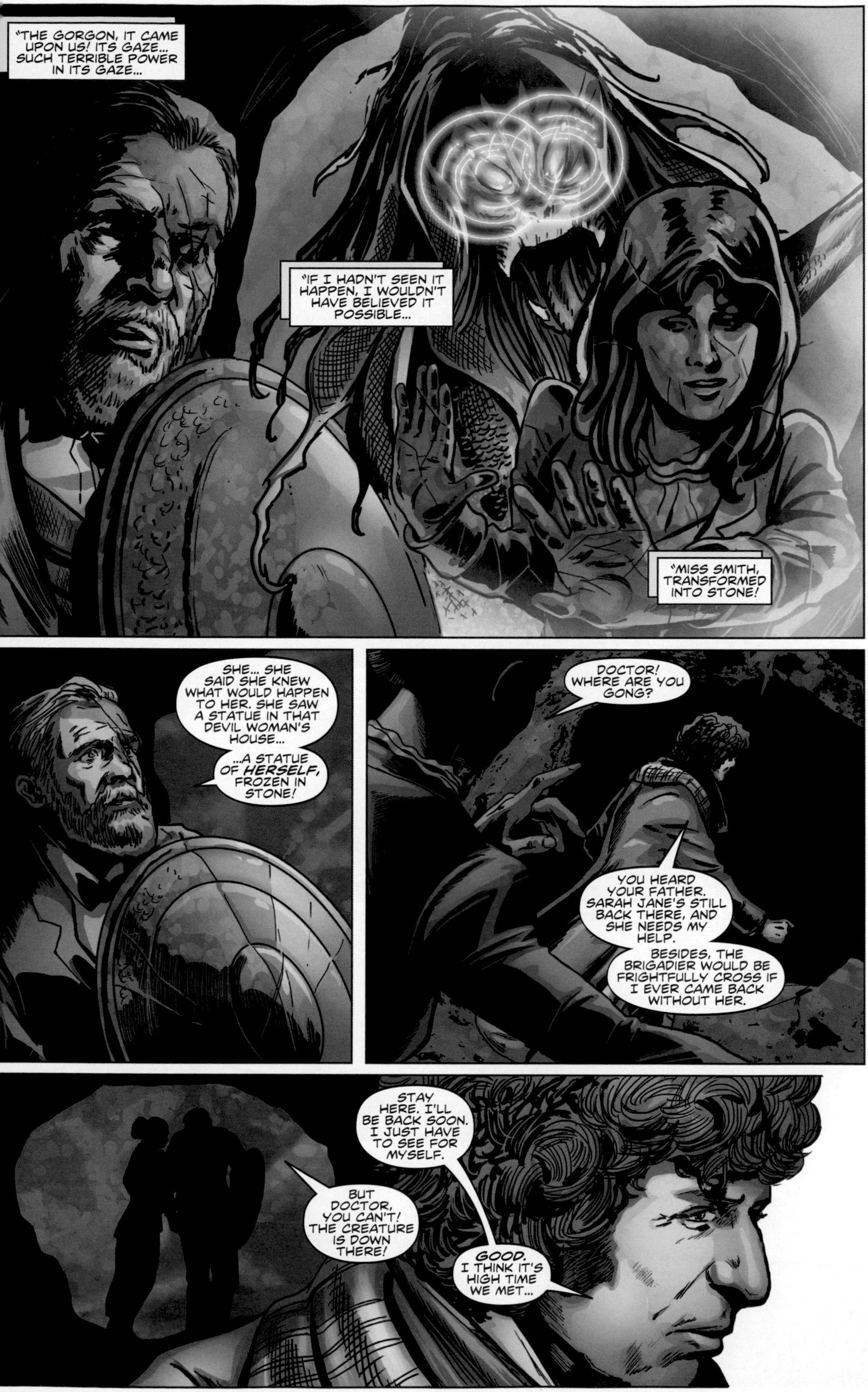
"THE GORGON, IT CAME UPON US! ITS GAZE... SUCH TERRIBLE POWER IN ITS GAZE...
"IF I HADN'T SEEN IT HAPPEN, I WOULDN'T HAVE BELIEVED IT POSSIBLE...
"MISS SMITH, TRANSFORMED INTO STONE!
SHE... SHE SAID SHE KNEW WHAT WOULD HAPPEN TO HER. SHE SAW A STATUE IN THAT DEVIL WOMAN'S HOUSE...
...A STATUE OF **HERSELF,** FROZEN IN STONE!
DOCTOR! WHERE ARE YOU GONG?
YOU HEARD YOUR FATHER. SARAH JANE'S STILL BACK THERE, AND SHE NEEDS MY HELP.
BESIDES, THE BRIGADIER WOULD BE FRIGHTFULLY CROSS IF I EVER CAME BACK WITHOUT HER.
STAY HERE. I'LL BE BACK SOON. I JUST HAVE TO SEE FOR MYSELF.
BUT DOCTOR, YOU CAN'T! THE CREATURE IS DOWN THERE!
GOOD. I THINK IT'S HIGH TIME WE MET...

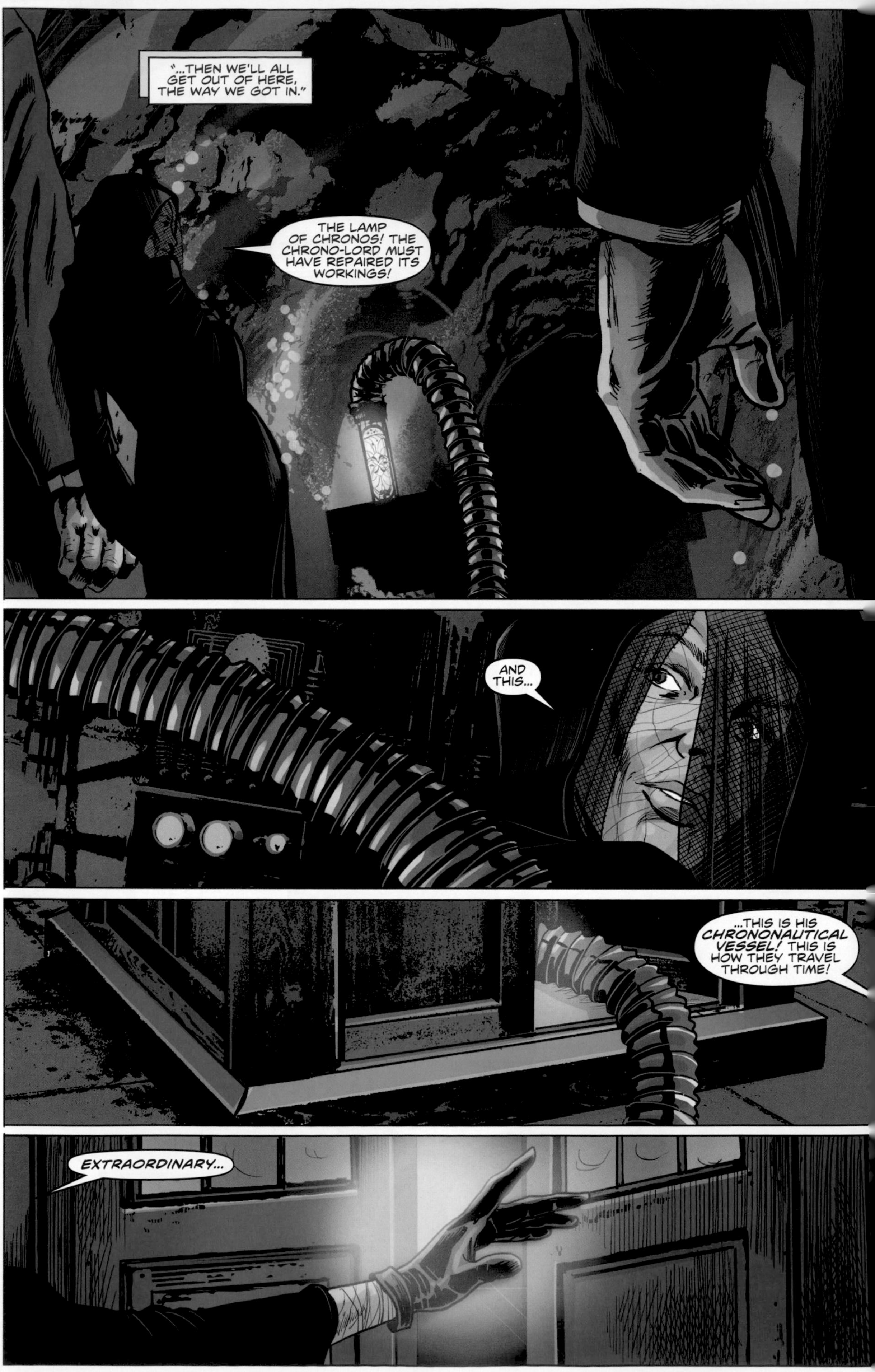
"...THEN WE'LL ALL GET OUT OF HERE, THE WAY WE GOT IN."
THE LAMP OF CHRONOS! THE CHRONO-LORD MUST HAVE REPAIRED ITS WORKINGS!
AND THIS...
...THIS IS HIS *CHRONONAUTICAL VESSEL!* THIS IS HOW THEY TRAVEL THROUGH TIME!
EXTRAORDINARY...

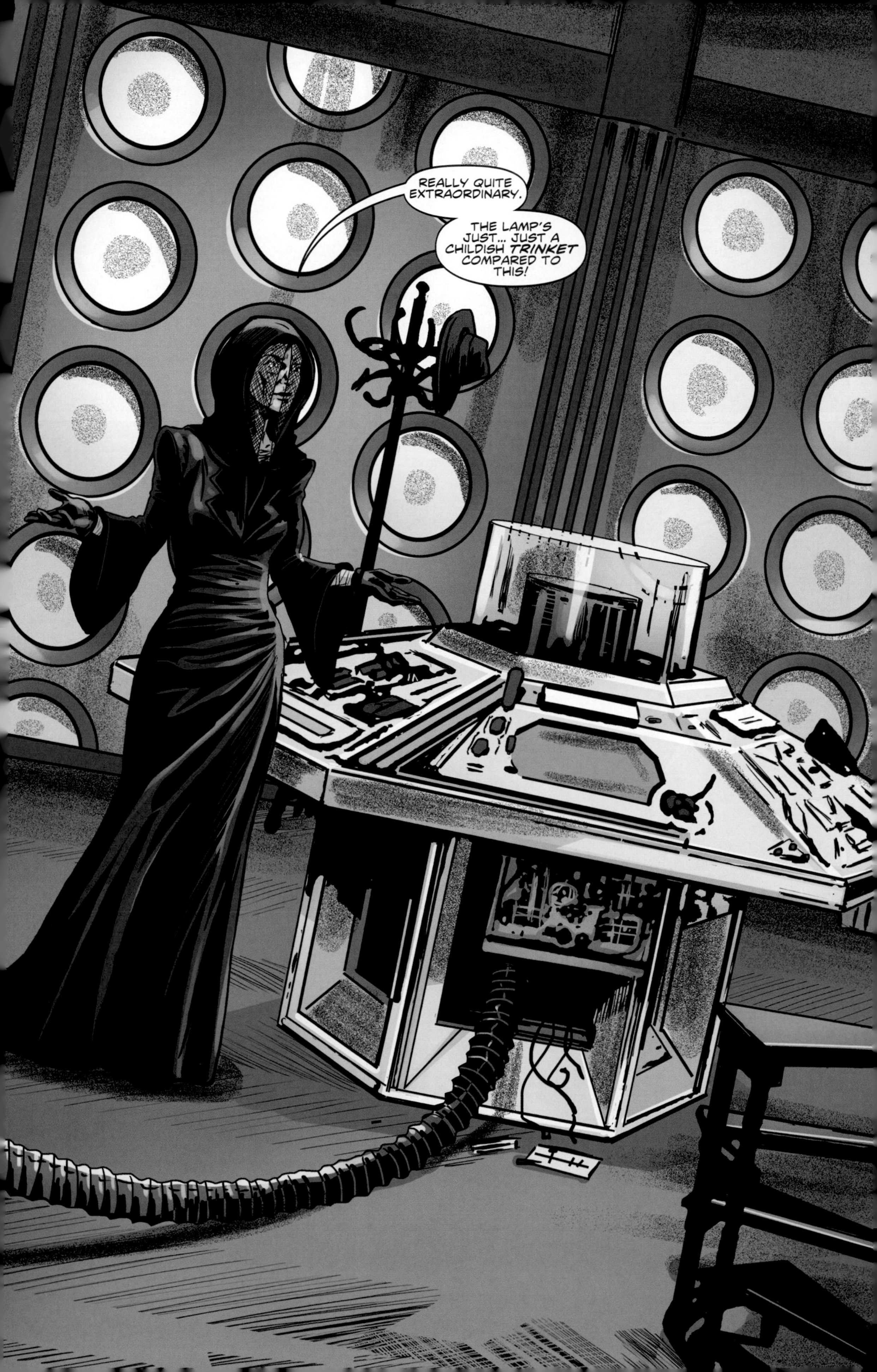
REALLY QUITE EXTRAORDINARY.
THE LAMP'S JUST... JUST A CHILDISH TRINKET COMPARED TO THIS!

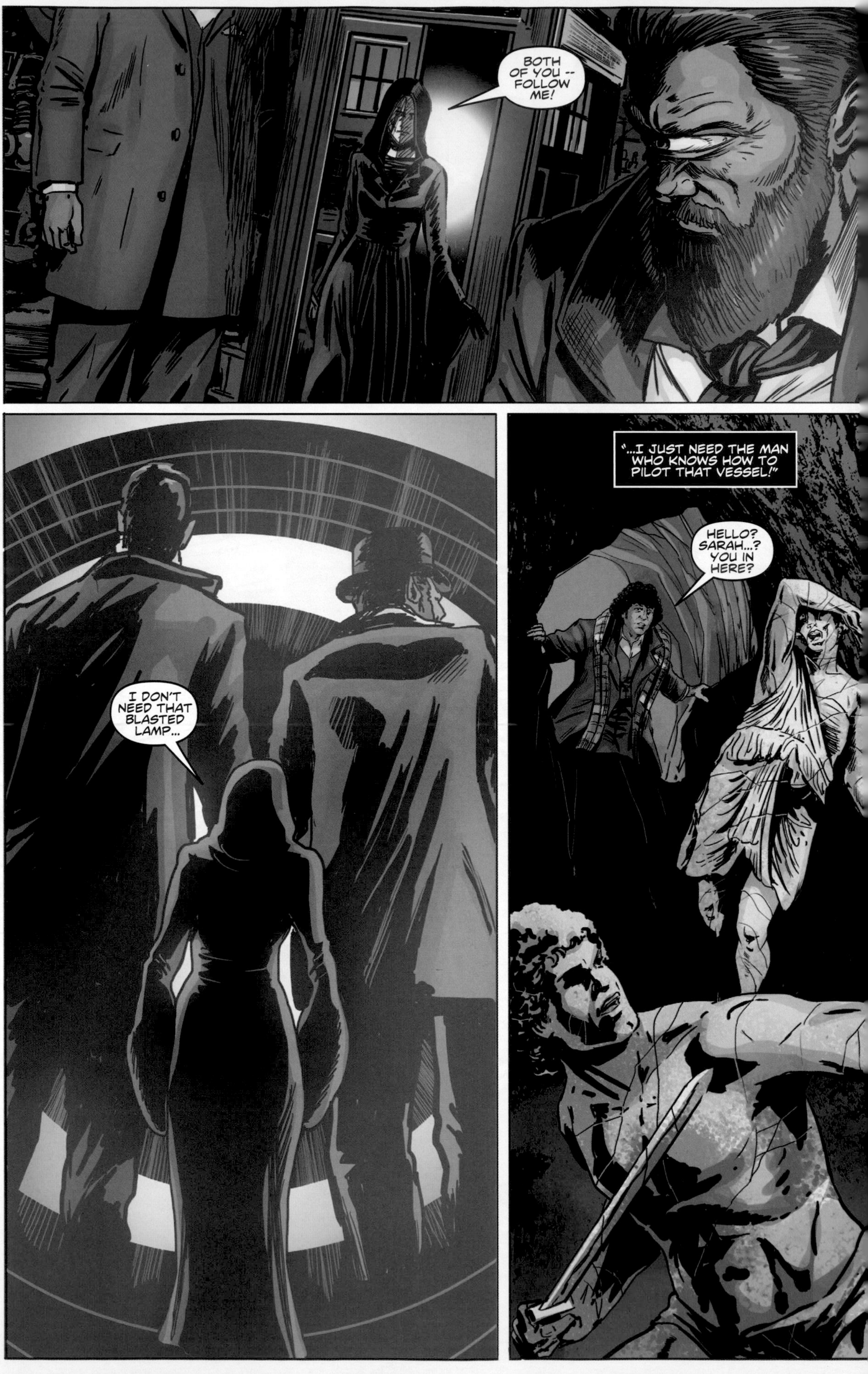
BOTH OF YOU -- FOLLOW ME!
I DON'T NEED THAT BLASTED LAMP...
"...I JUST NEED THE MAN WHO KNOWS HOW TO PILOT THAT VESSEL!"
HELLO? SARAH...? YOU IN HERE?

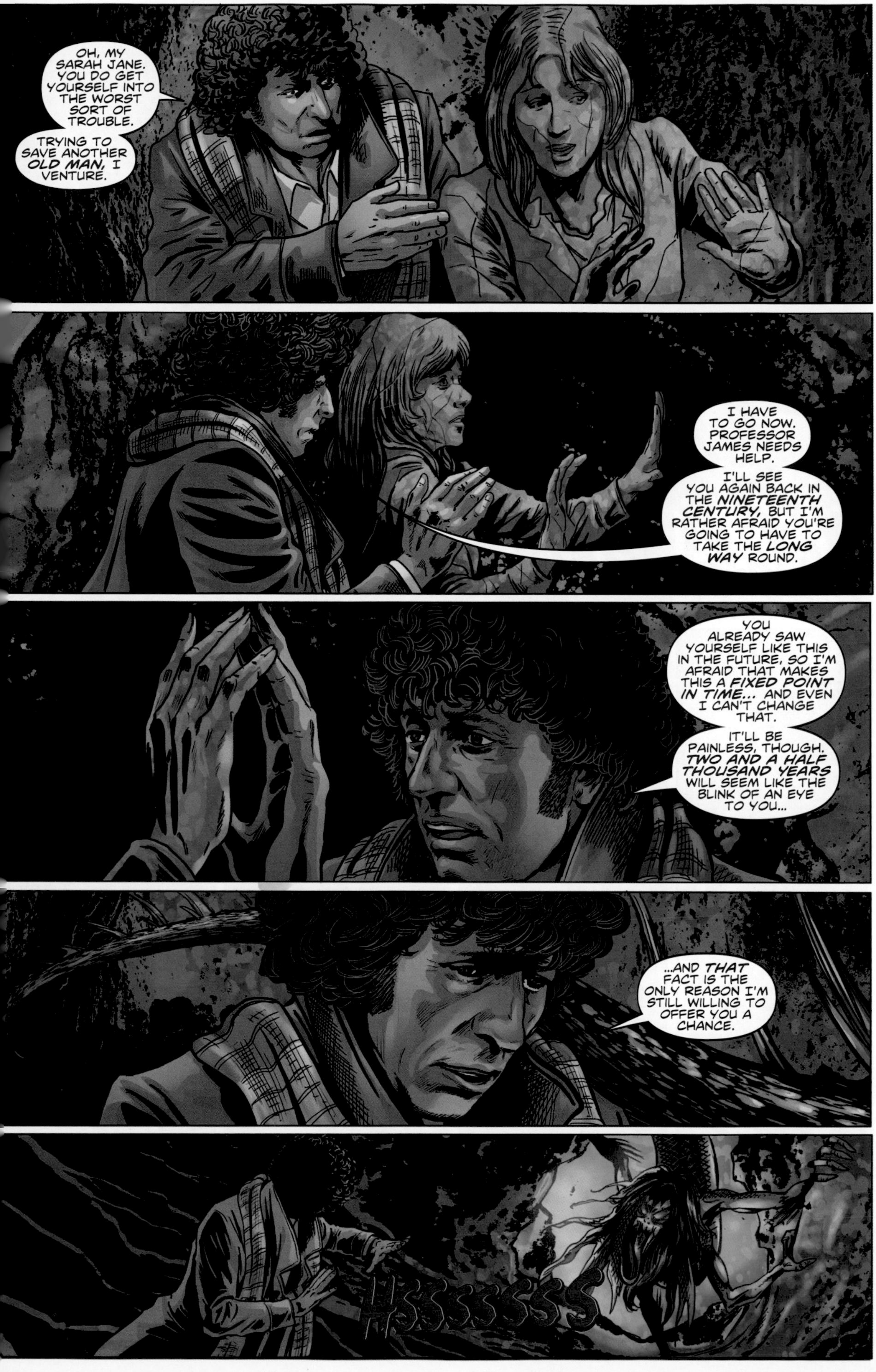
OH, MY SARAH JANE. YOU DO GET YOURSELF INTO THE WORST SORT OF TROUBLE.
TRYING TO SAVE ANOTHER OLD MAN, I VENTURE.
I HAVE TO GO NOW. PROFESSOR JAMES NEEDS HELP.
I'LL SEE YOU AGAIN BACK IN THE NINETEENTH CENTURY, BUT I'M RATHER AFRAID YOU'RE GOING TO HAVE TO TAKE THE LONG WAY ROUND.
YOU ALREADY SAW YOURSELF LIKE THIS IN THE FUTURE, SO I'M AFRAID THAT MAKES THIS A FIXED POINT IN TIME... AND EVEN I CAN'T CHANGE THAT.
IT'LL BE PAINLESS, THOUGH. TWO AND A HALF THOUSAND YEARS WILL SEEM LIKE THE BLINK OF AN EYE TO YOU...
...AND THAT FACT IS THE ONLY REASON I'M STILL WILLING TO OFFER YOU A CHANCE.
HSSSSSSS

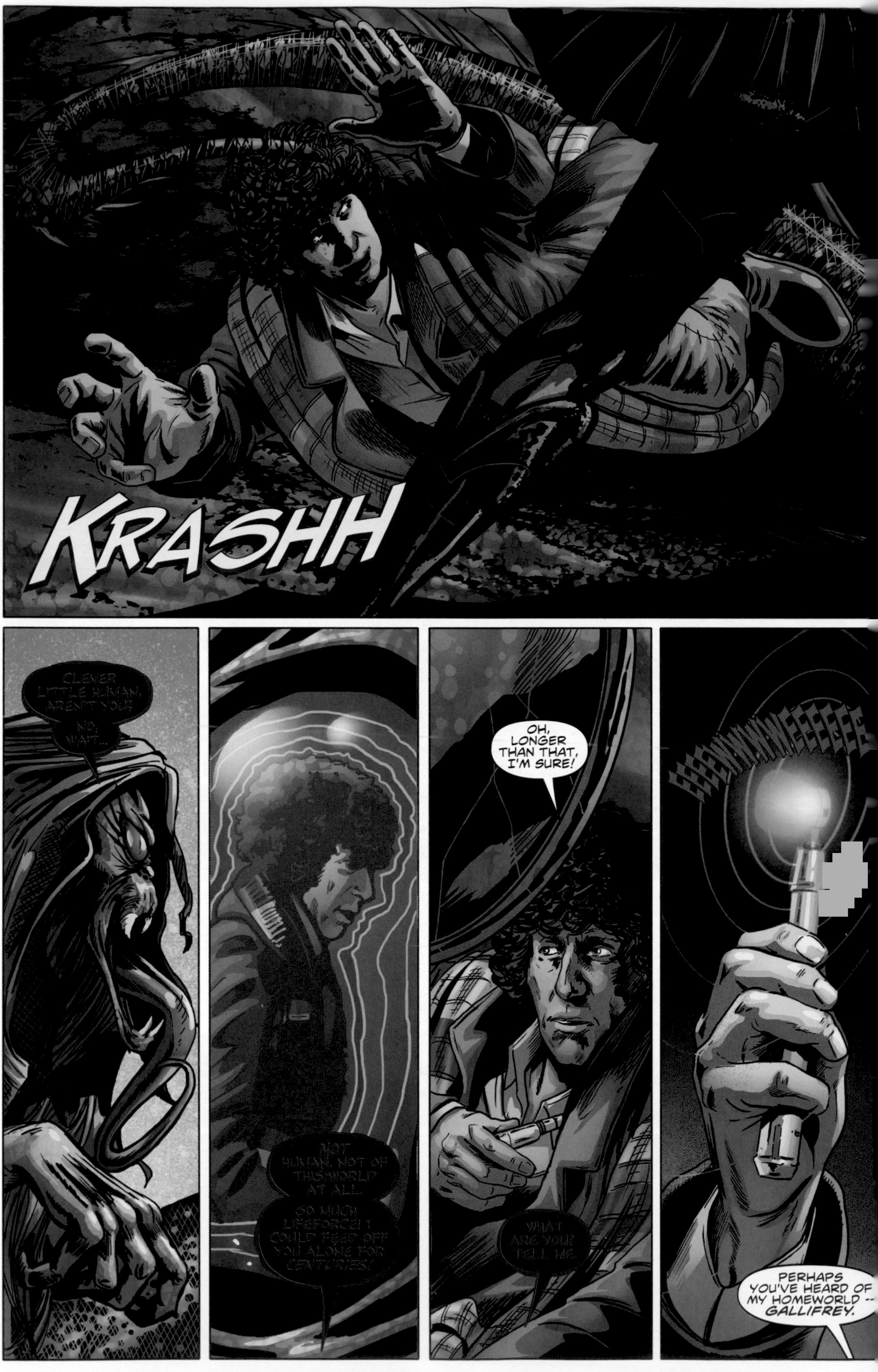
KRASHH
CLEVER LITTLE HUMAN, AREN'T YOU?
NO, WAIT...
NOT HUMAN. NOT OF THIS WORLD AT ALL.
SO MUCH LIFEFORCE! I COULD FEED OFF YOU ALONE FOR CENTURIES!
OH, LONGER THAN THAT, I'M SURE!
WHAT ARE YOU? TELL ME.
EEEENNNNNWEEEEEE
PERHAPS YOU'VE HEARD OF MY HOMEWORLD -- GALLIFREY.

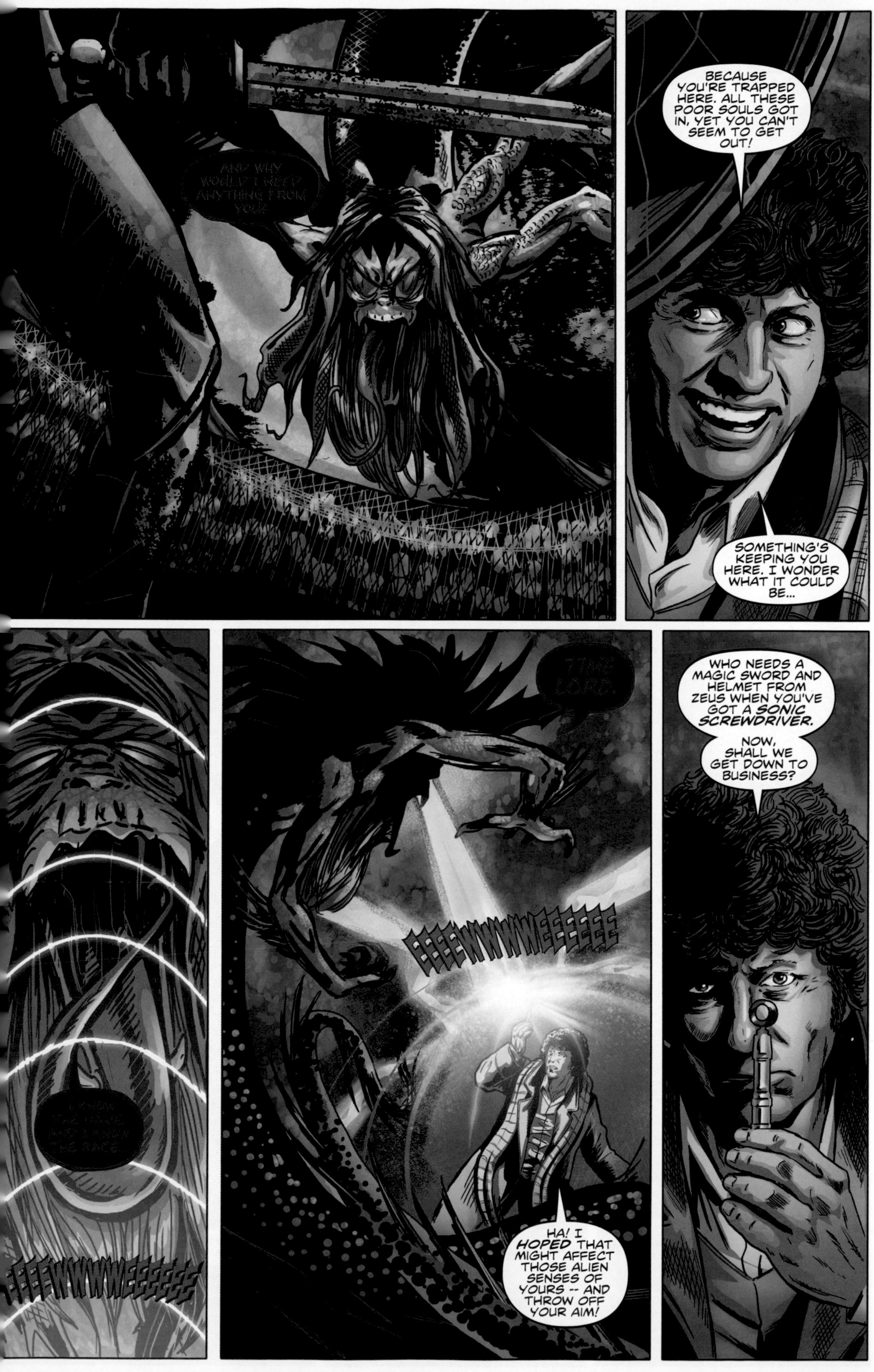
AND WHY WOULD I NEED ANYTHING FROM YOU?
BECAUSE YOU'RE TRAPPED HERE. ALL THESE POOR SOULS GOT IN, YET YOU CAN'T SEEM TO GET OUT!
SOMETHING'S KEEPING YOU HERE. I WONDER WHAT IT COULD BE...
EEEEWWWWEEEEEE!
THE LORD.
EEEEWWWWEEEEEE
HA! I *HOPED* THAT MIGHT AFFECT THOSE ALIEN SENSES OF YOURS -- AND THROW OFF YOUR AIM!
WHO NEEDS A MAGIC SWORD AND HELMET FROM ZEUS WHEN YOU'VE GOT A ***SONIC SCREWDRIVER.***
NOW, SHALL WE GET DOWN TO BUSINESS?

L-LISTEN, MY DEAR. I--I KNOW I'VE BEEN A DASHED POOR FATHER TO YOU AT TIMES...

DON'T -- DON'T TALK LIKE THIS, FATHER. THE DOCTOR SAID HE COULD *REVERSE* WHAT'S BEEN DONE TO YOU.

THAT YOUNG MILITARY MAN YOU'VE TAKEN UP WITH... I KNOW I PRETEND TO DISAPPROVE, BUT HE SEEMS A DECENT SORT REALLY.

WHAT I'M TRYING TO SAY, MY DEAR, IS THAT IF YOU AND HE WANT TO--

HUSH, PLEASE--!

SOMEONE'S COMING!

THERE. THAT OLD FOOL AND HIS DAUGHTER. BRING THEM HERE.

RUN, ATHENA! FIND THE DOCTOR!

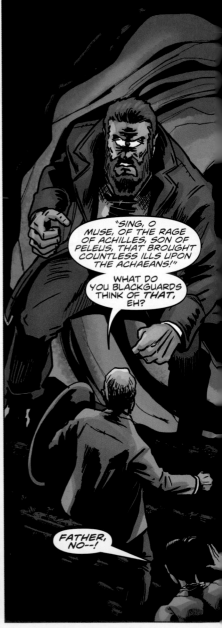

"SING, O MUSE, OF THE RAGE OF ACHILLES, SON OF PELEUS, THAT BROUGHT COUNTLESS ILLS UPON THE ACHAEANS!"

WHAT DO YOU BLACKGUARDS THINK OF *THAT*, EH?

FATHER, NO--!

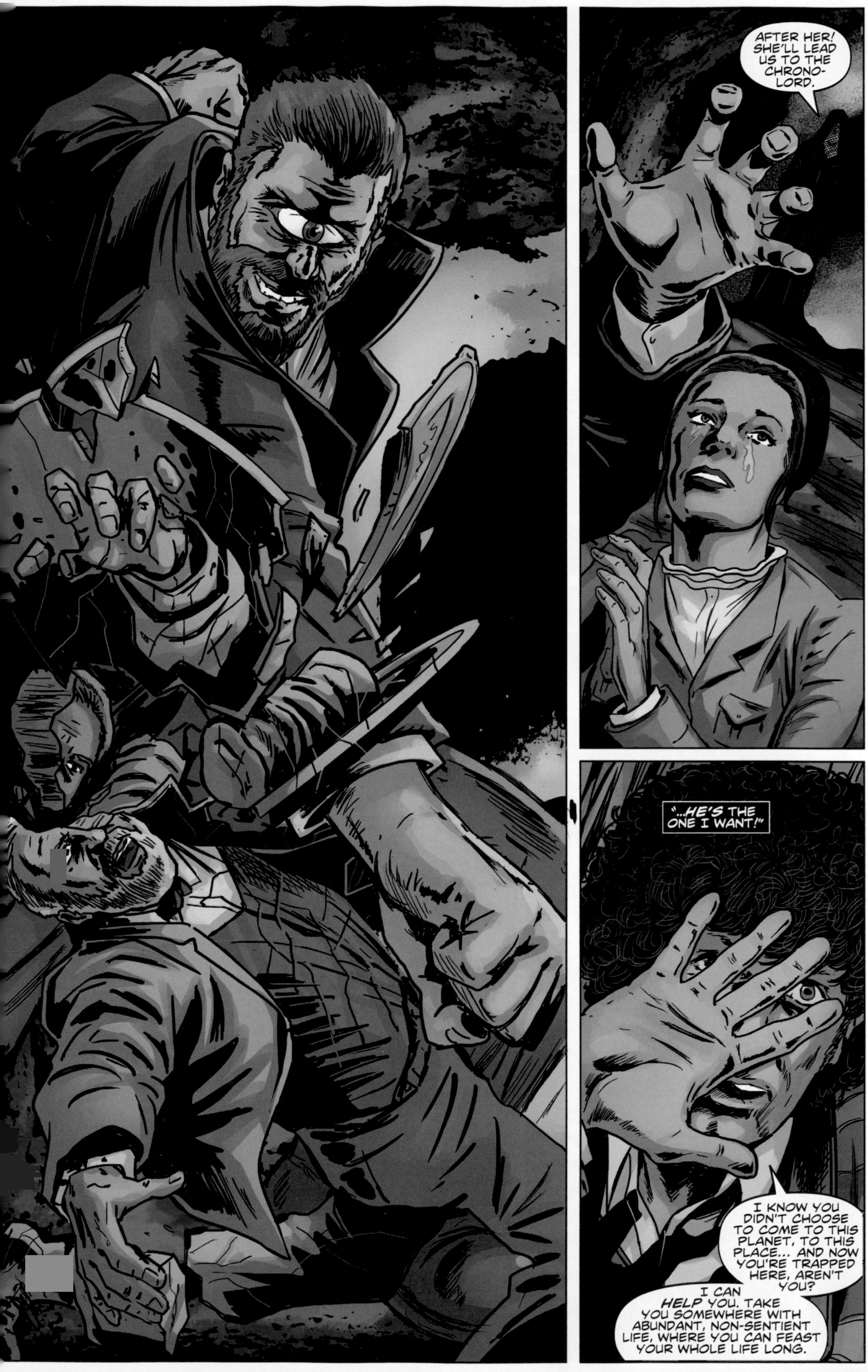
AFTER HER! SHE'LL LEAD US TO THE CHRONO-LORD.
"...HE'S THE ONE I WANT!"
I KNOW YOU DIDN'T CHOOSE TO COME TO THIS PLANET, TO THIS PLACE... AND NOW YOU'RE TRAPPED HERE, AREN'T YOU?
I CAN HELP YOU. TAKE YOU SOMEWHERE WITH ABUNDANT, NON-SENTIENT LIFE, WHERE YOU CAN FEAST YOUR WHOLE LIFE LONG.

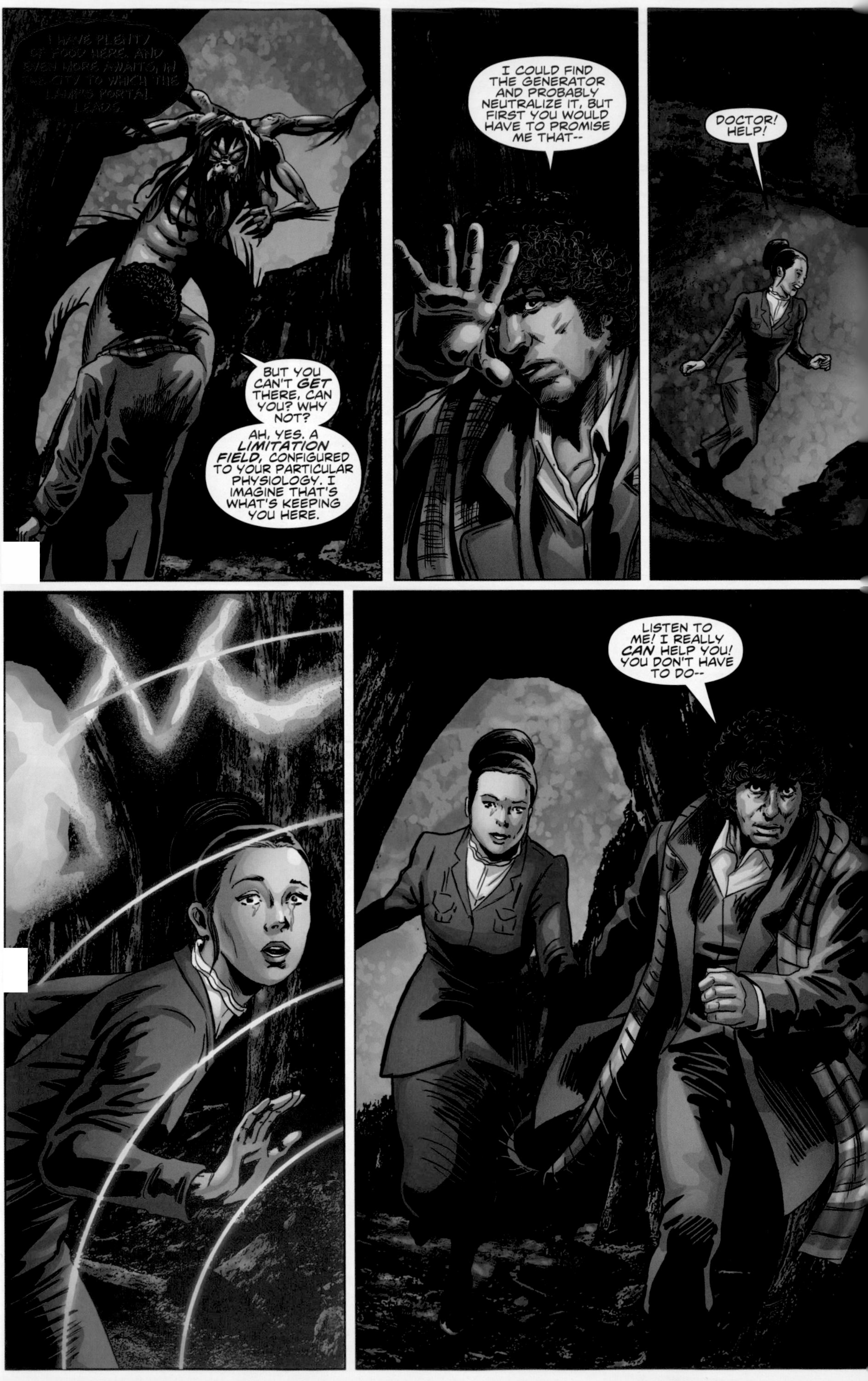
I HAVE PLENTY OF FOOD HERE, AND EVEN MORE AWAITS, IN THE CITY TO WHICH THE LAMP'S PORTAL LEADS.
BUT YOU CAN'T GET THERE, CAN YOU? WHY NOT?
AH, YES. A LIMITATION FIELD, CONFIGURED TO YOUR PARTICULAR PHYSIOLOGY. I IMAGINE THAT'S WHAT'S KEEPING YOU HERE.
I COULD FIND THE GENERATOR AND PROBABLY NEUTRALIZE IT, BUT FIRST YOU WOULD HAVE TO PROMISE ME THAT--
DOCTOR! HELP!
LISTEN TO ME! I REALLY CAN HELP YOU! YOU DON'T HAVE TO DO--

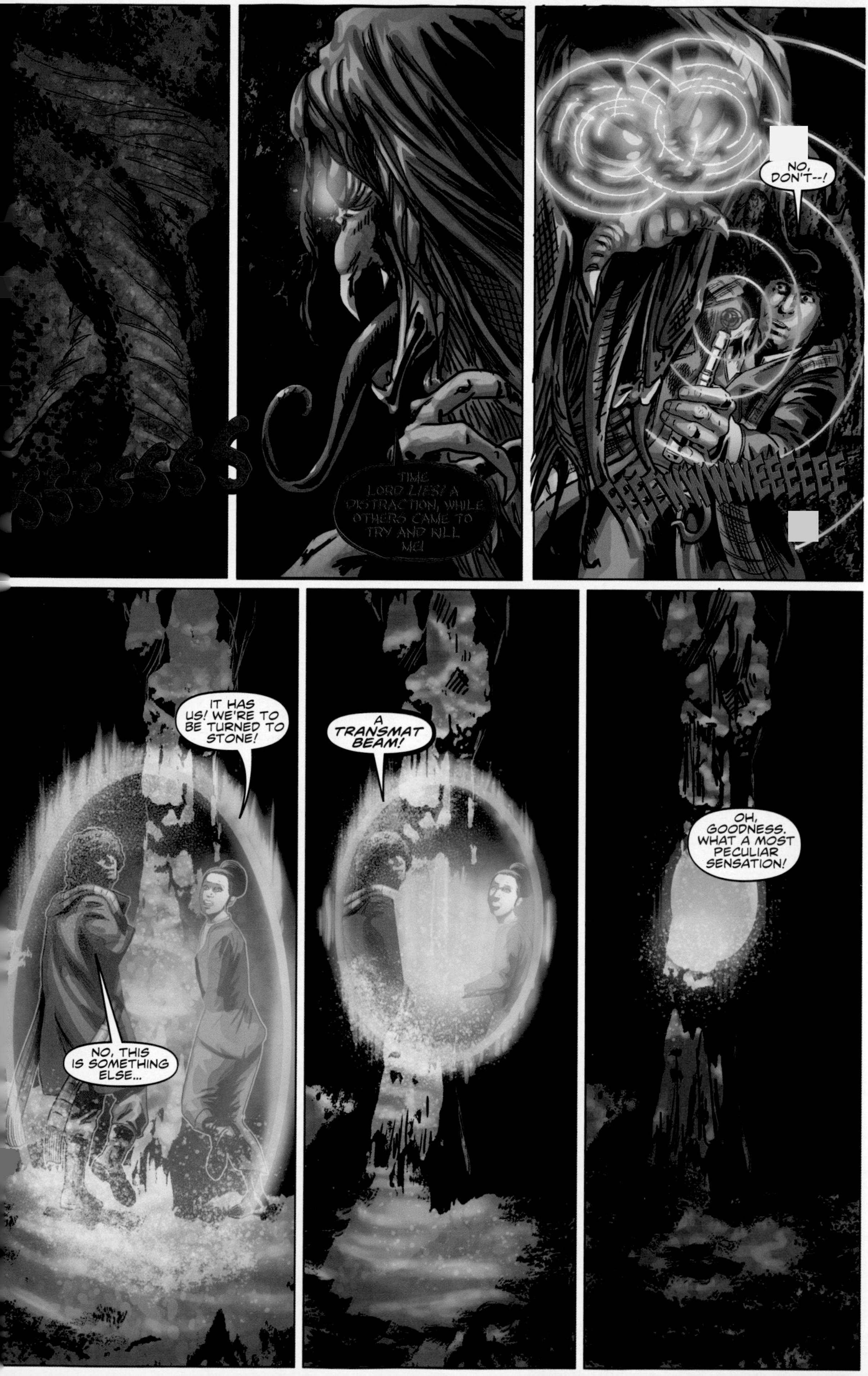
TIME LORD LIES! A DISTRACTION, WHILE OTHERS CAME TO TRY AND KILL ME!
NO, DON'T--!
IT HAS US! WE'RE TO BE TURNED TO STONE!
NO, THIS IS SOMETHING ELSE...
A TRANSMAT BEAM!
OH, GOODNESS. WHAT A MOST PECULIAR SENSATION!

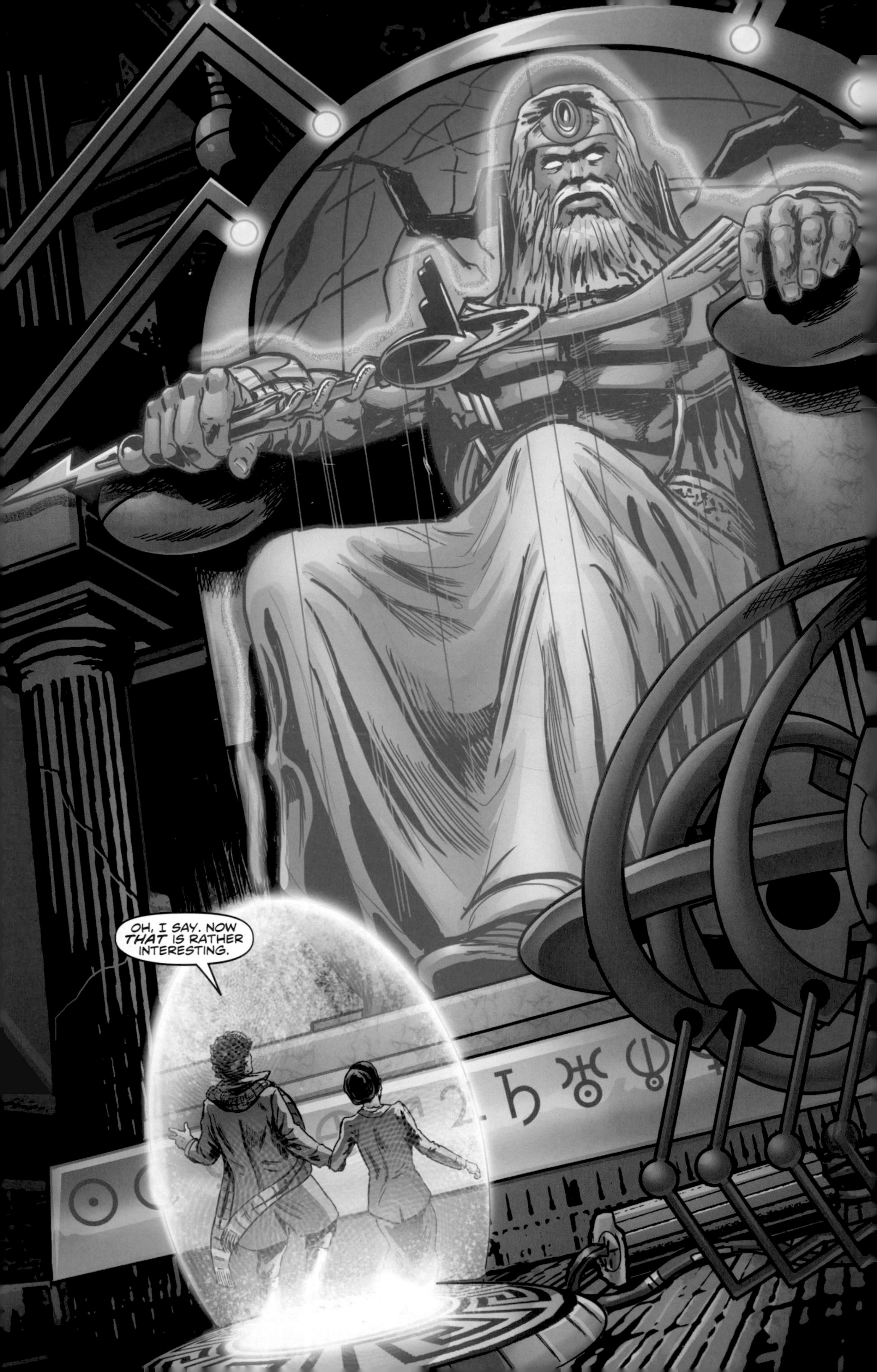
OH, I SAY. NOW *THAT* IS RATHER INTERESTING.

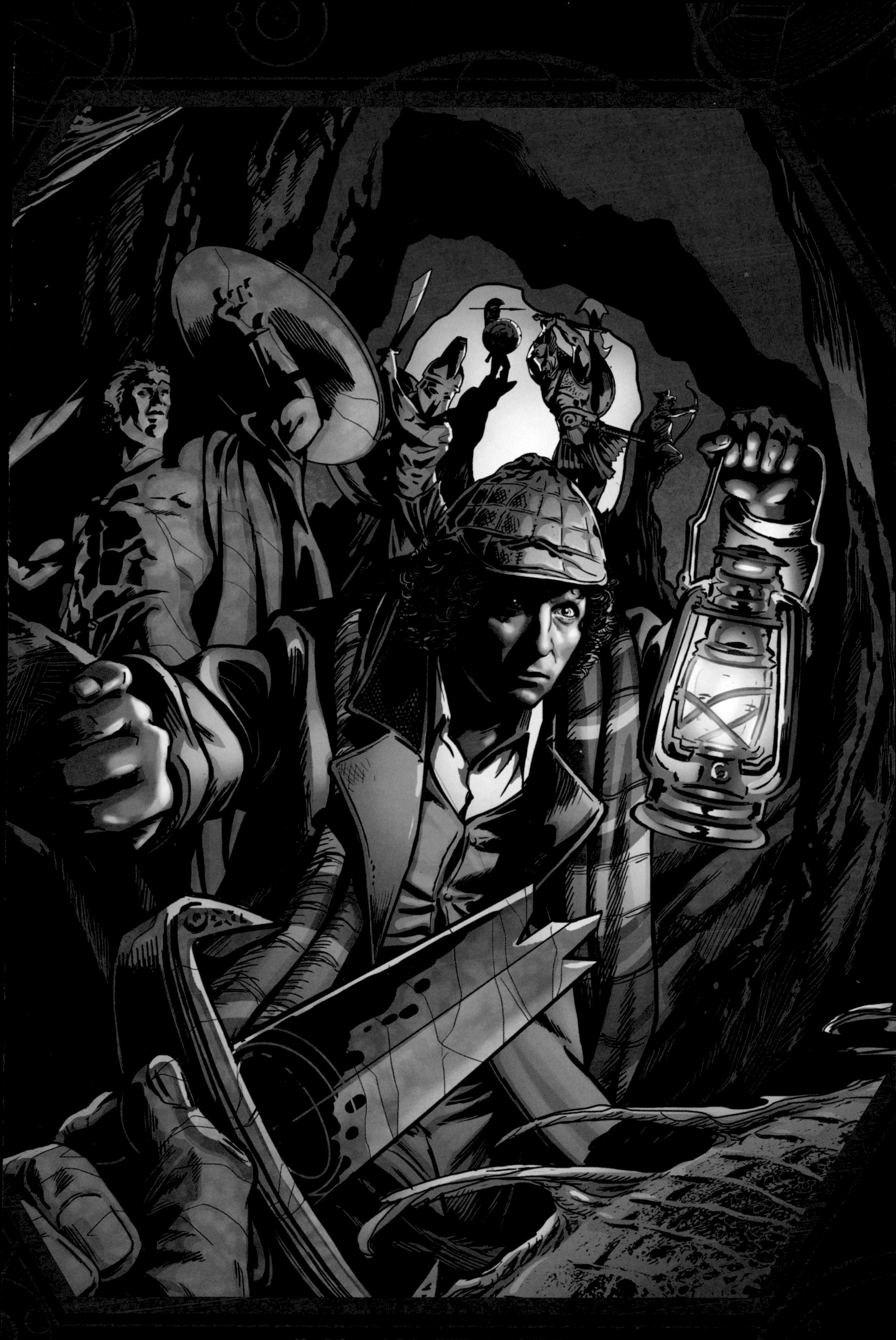

4D #5 Cover A: Brian Williamson & Hi Fi

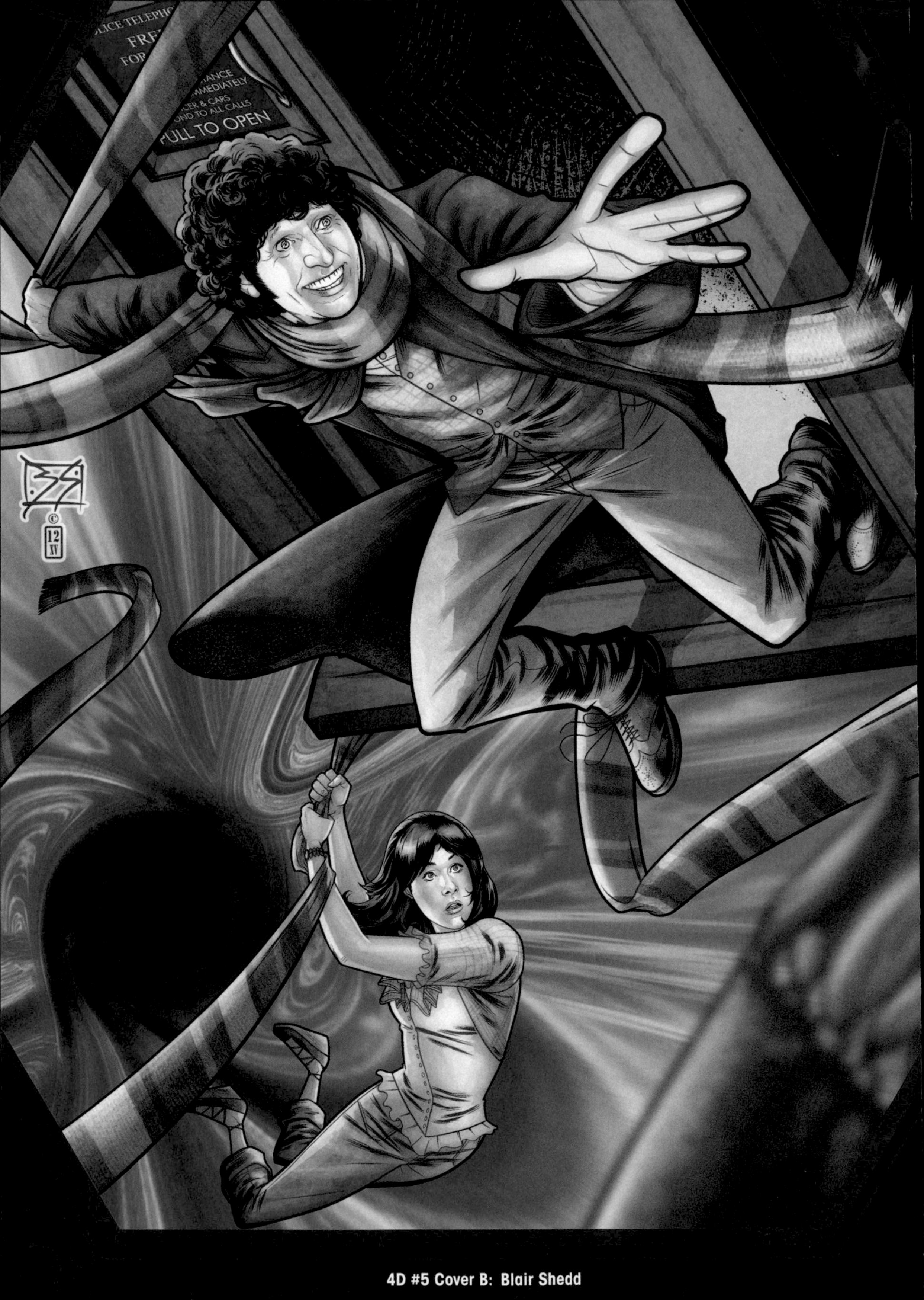
PULL TO OPEN

4D #5 Cover B: Blair Shedd

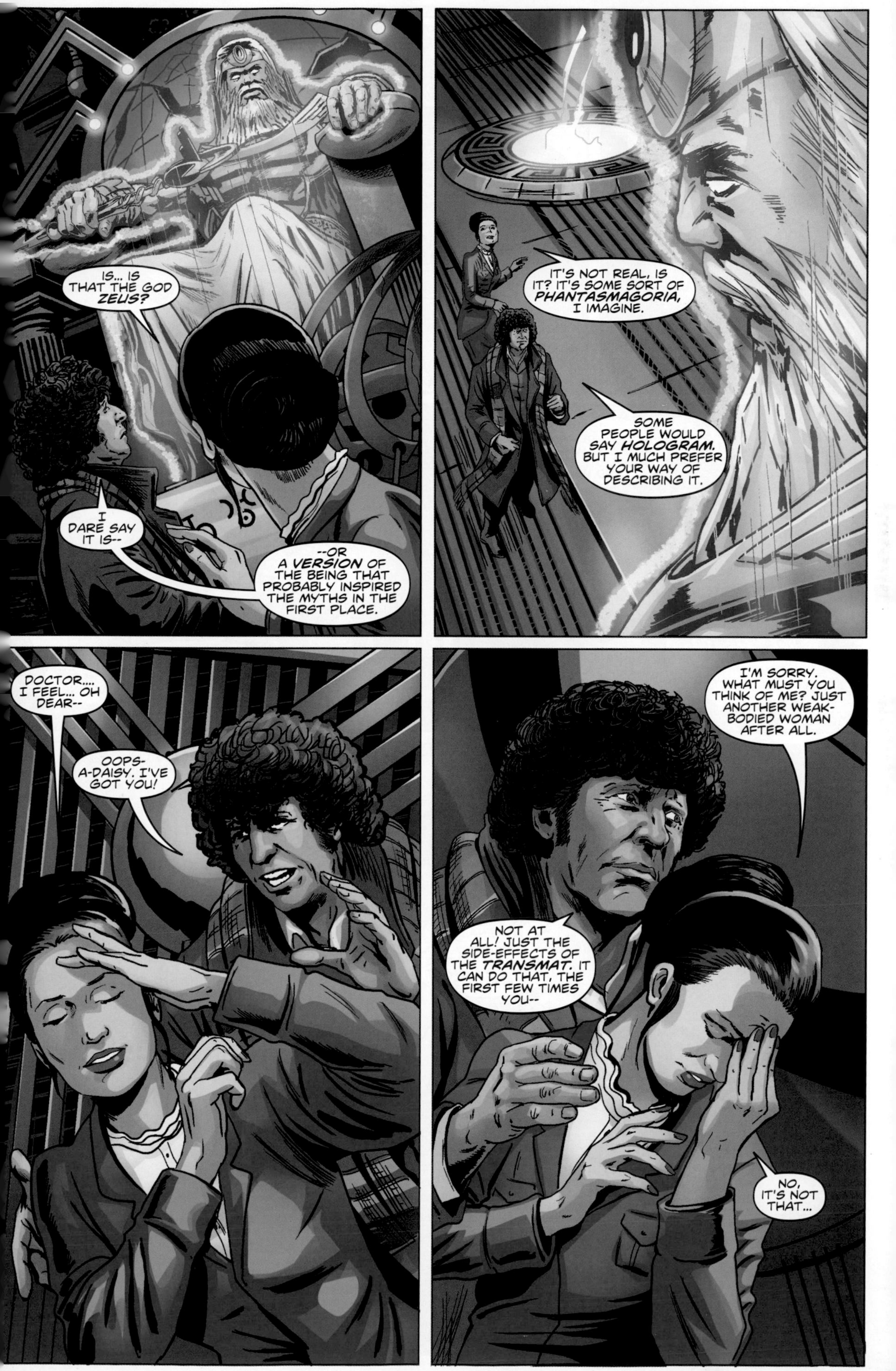

IS... IS THAT THE GOD ZEUS?
I DARE SAY IT IS--
--OR A VERSION OF THE BEING THAT PROBABLY INSPIRED THE MYTHS IN THE FIRST PLACE.
IT'S NOT REAL, IS IT? IT'S SOME SORT OF PHANTASMAGORIA, I IMAGINE.
SOME PEOPLE WOULD SAY HOLOGRAM. BUT I MUCH PREFER YOUR WAY OF DESCRIBING IT.
DOCTOR.... I FEEL... OH DEAR--
OOPS-A-DAISY. I'VE GOT YOU!
I'M SORRY. WHAT MUST YOU THINK OF ME? JUST ANOTHER WEAK-BODIED WOMAN AFTER ALL.
NOT AT ALL! JUST THE SIDE-EFFECTS OF THE TRANSMAT. IT CAN DO THAT, THE FIRST FEW TIMES YOU--
NO, IT'S NOT THAT...

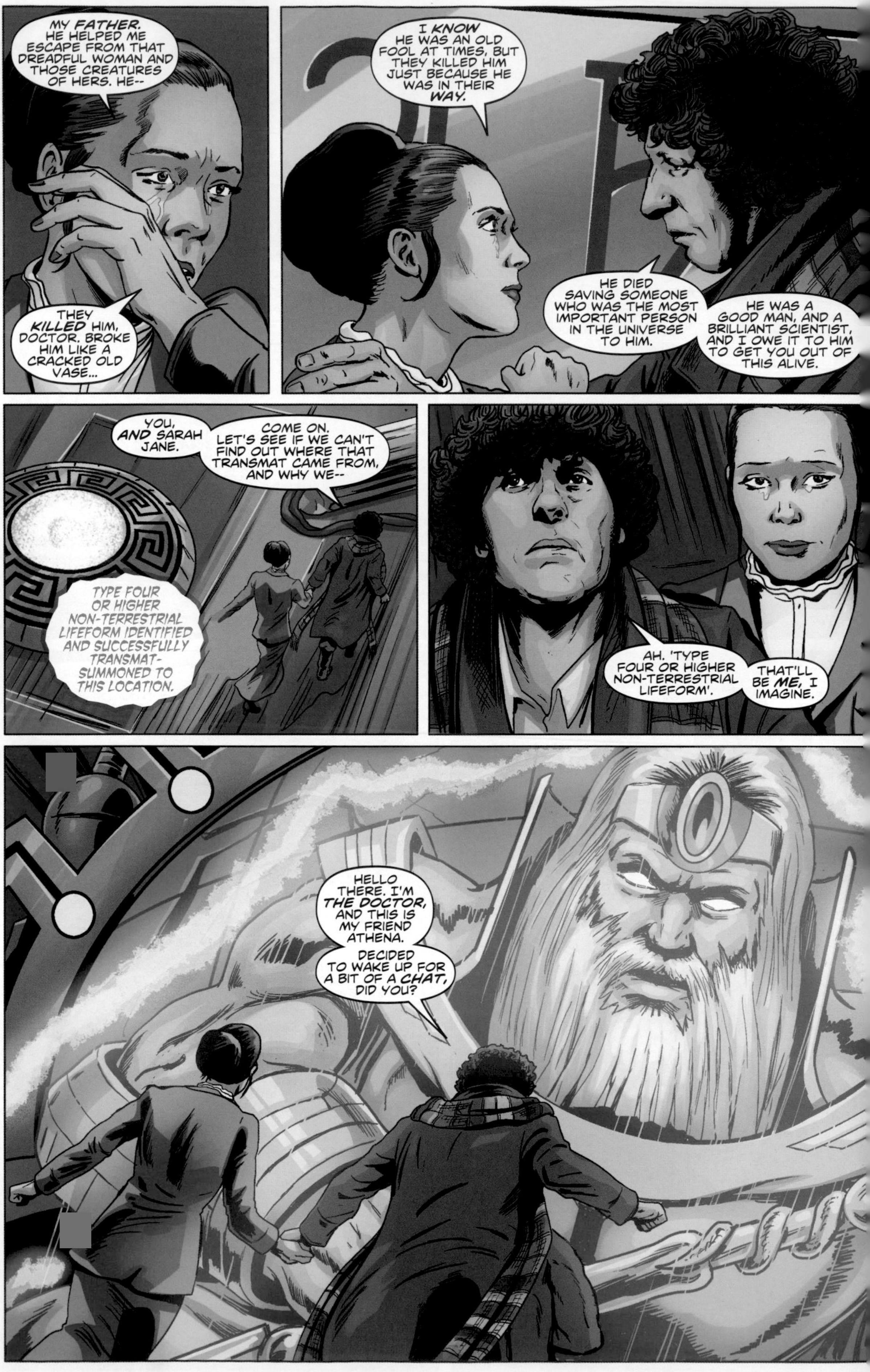
MY FATHER. HE HELPED ME ESCAPE FROM THAT DREADFUL WOMAN AND THOSE CREATURES OF HERS. HE--
THEY KILLED HIM, DOCTOR. BROKE HIM LIKE A CRACKED OLD VASE...
I KNOW HE WAS AN OLD FOOL AT TIMES, BUT THEY KILLED HIM JUST BECAUSE HE WAS IN THEIR WAY.
HE DIED SAVING SOMEONE WHO WAS THE MOST IMPORTANT PERSON IN THE UNIVERSE TO HIM.
HE WAS A GOOD MAN, AND A BRILLIANT SCIENTIST, AND I OWE IT TO HIM TO GET YOU OUT OF THIS ALIVE.
YOU, AND SARAH JANE.
COME ON. LET'S SEE IF WE CAN'T FIND OUT WHERE THAT TRANSMAT CAME FROM, AND WHY WE--
TYPE FOUR OR HIGHER NON-TERRESTRIAL LIFEFORM IDENTIFIED AND SUCCESSFULLY TRANSMAT-SUMMONED TO THIS LOCATION.
AH. 'TYPE FOUR OR HIGHER NON-TERRESTRIAL LIFEFORM'.
THAT'LL BE ME, I IMAGINE.
HELLO THERE. I'M THE DOCTOR, AND THIS IS MY FRIEND ATHENA.
DECIDED TO WAKE UP FOR A BIT OF A CHAT, DID YOU?

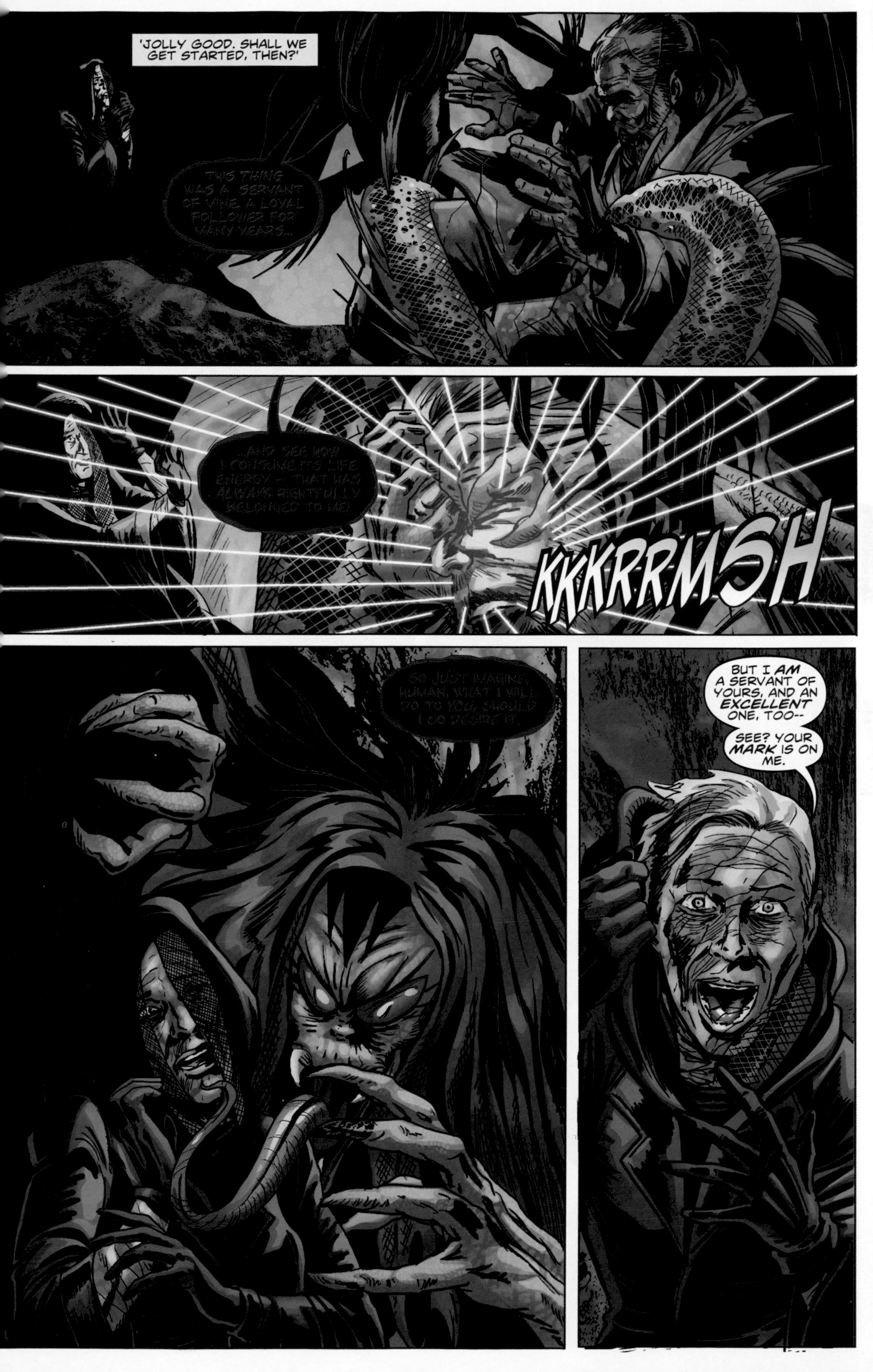
'JOLLY GOOD. SHALL WE GET STARTED, THEN?'
THIS THING WAS A SERVANT OF MINE, A LOYAL FOLLOWER FOR MANY YEARS...
...AND SEE HOW I CONSUME ITS LIFE ENERGY -- THAT HAS ALWAYS RIGHTFULLY BELONGED TO ME!
KKKRRMSH
SO JUST IMAGINE, HUMAN, WHAT I WILL DO TO YOU, SHOULD I SO DESIRE IT.
BUT I AM A SERVANT OF YOURS, AND AN EXCELLENT ONE, TOO--
SEE? YOUR MARK IS ON ME.

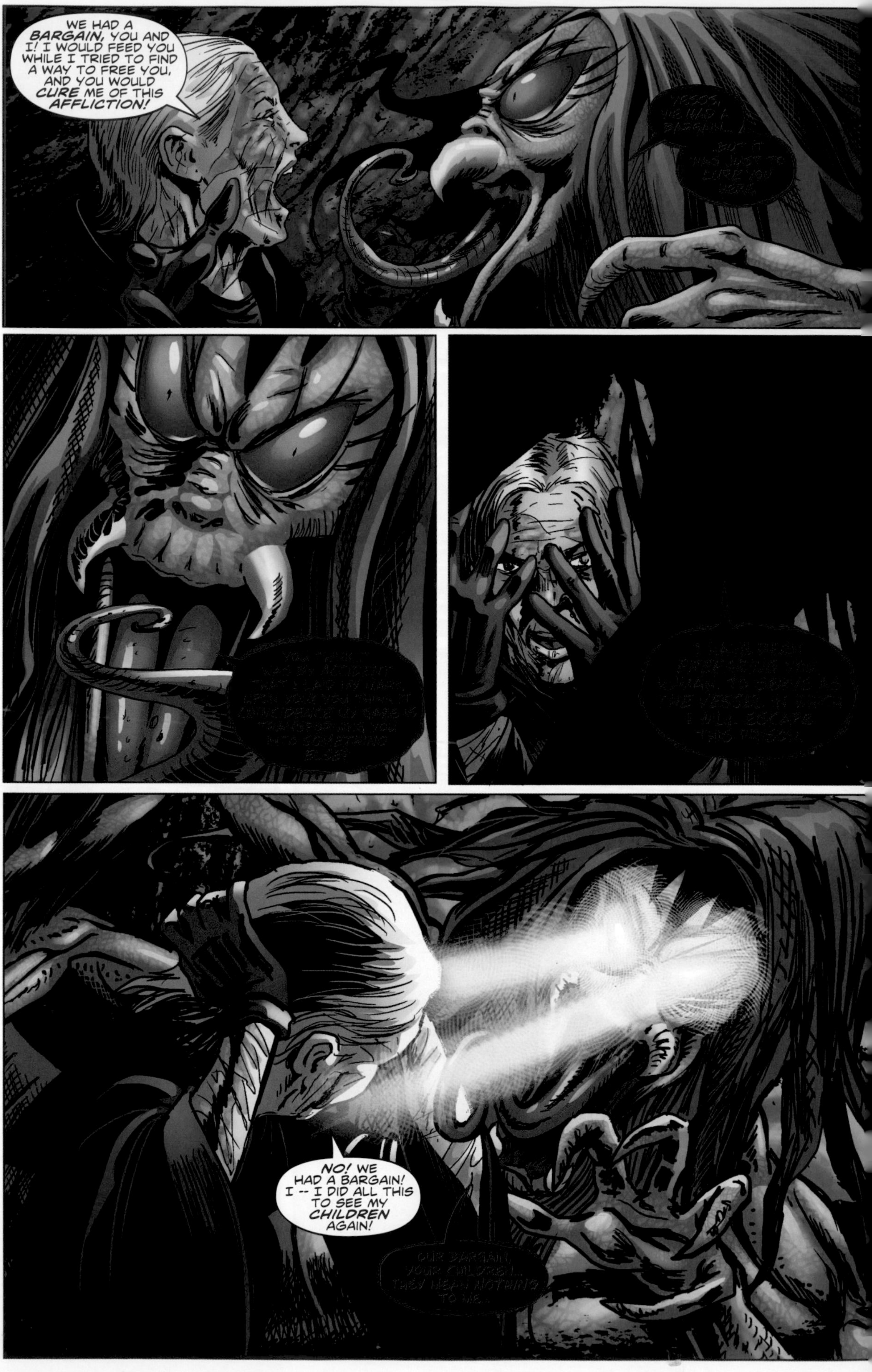
WE HAD A BARGAIN, YOU AND I! I WOULD FEED YOU WHILE I TRIED TO FIND A WAY TO FREE YOU, AND YOU WOULD CURE ME OF THIS AFFLICTION!
NO! WE HAD A BARGAIN! I -- I DID ALL THIS TO SEE MY CHILDREN AGAIN!

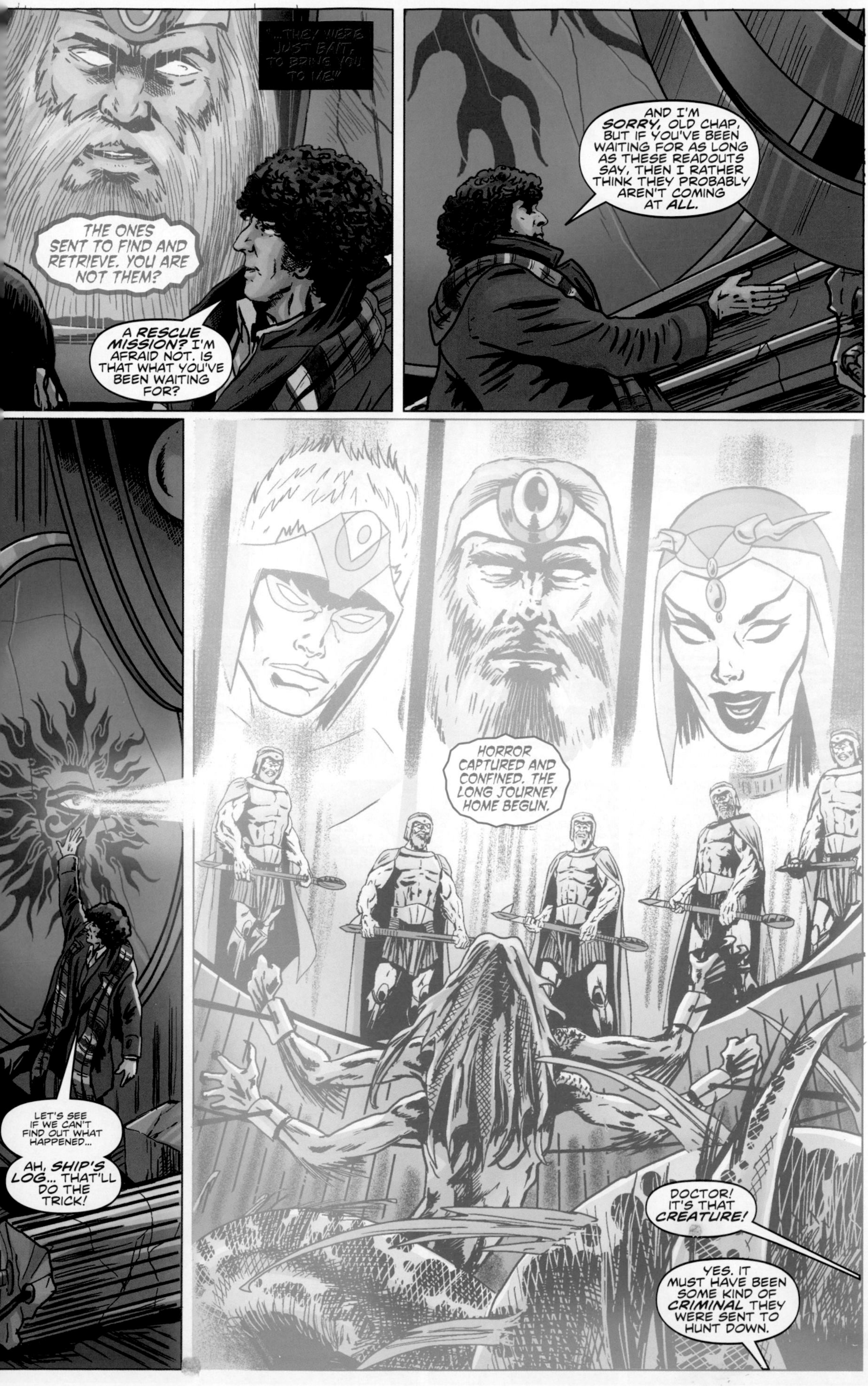
"...THEY WERE JUST BAIT, TO BRING YOU TO ME!"
THE ONES SENT TO FIND AND RETRIEVE. YOU ARE NOT THEM?
A RESCUE MISSION? I'M AFRAID NOT. IS THAT WHAT YOU'VE BEEN WAITING FOR?
AND I'M SORRY, OLD CHAP, BUT IF YOU'VE BEEN WAITING FOR AS LONG AS THESE READOUTS SAY, THEN I RATHER THINK THEY PROBABLY AREN'T COMING AT ALL.
LET'S SEE IF WE CAN'T FIND OUT WHAT HAPPENED...
AH, SHIP'S LOG... THAT'LL DO THE TRICK!
HORROR CAPTURED AND CONFINED. THE LONG JOURNEY HOME BEGUN.
DOCTOR! IT'S THAT CREATURE!
YES. IT MUST HAVE BEEN SOME KIND OF CRIMINAL THEY WERE SENT TO HUNT DOWN.

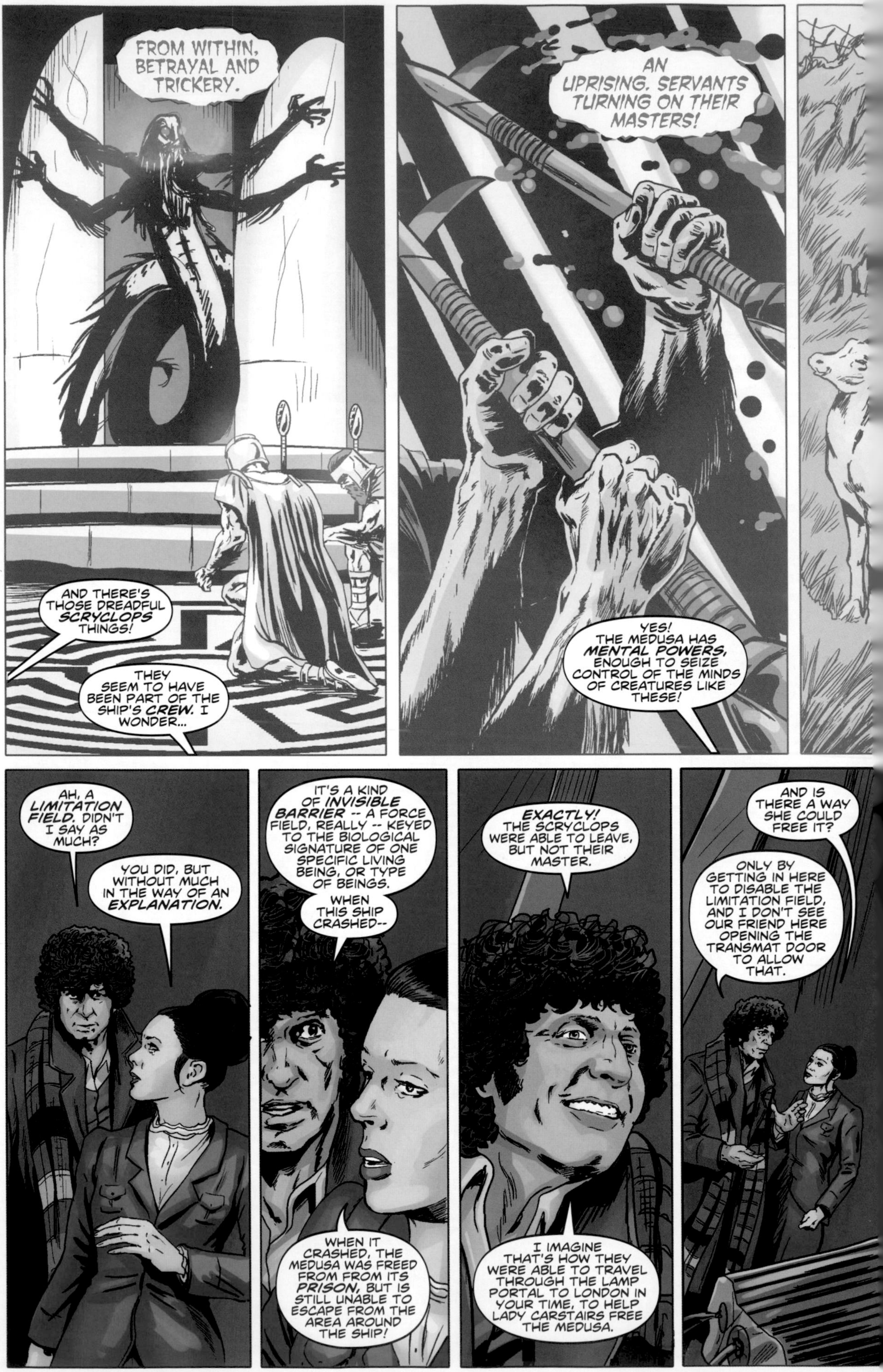
FROM WITHIN, BETRAYAL AND TRICKERY.
AND THERE'S THOSE DREADFUL SCRYCLOPS THINGS!
THEY SEEM TO HAVE BEEN PART OF THE SHIP'S CREW. I WONDER...
AN UPRISING. SERVANTS TURNING ON THEIR MASTERS!
YES! THE MEDUSA HAS MENTAL POWERS, ENOUGH TO SEIZE CONTROL OF THE MINDS OF CREATURES LIKE THESE!
AH, A LIMITATION FIELD. DIDN'T I SAY AS MUCH?
YOU DID, BUT WITHOUT MUCH IN THE WAY OF AN EXPLANATION.
IT'S A KIND OF INVISIBLE BARRIER -- A FORCE FIELD, REALLY -- KEYED TO THE BIOLOGICAL SIGNATURE OF ONE SPECIFIC LIVING BEING, OR TYPE OF BEINGS.
WHEN THIS SHIP CRASHED--
WHEN IT CRASHED, THE MEDUSA WAS FREED FROM ITS PRISON, BUT IS STILL UNABLE TO ESCAPE FROM THE AREA AROUND THE SHIP!
EXACTLY! THE SCRYCLOPS WERE ABLE TO LEAVE, BUT NOT THEIR MASTER.
I IMAGINE THAT'S HOW THEY WERE ABLE TO TRAVEL THROUGH THE LAMP PORTAL TO LONDON IN YOUR TIME, TO HELP LADY CARSTAIRS FREE THE MEDUSA.
AND IS THERE A WAY SHE COULD FREE IT?
ONLY BY GETTING IN HERE TO DISABLE THE LIMITATION FIELD, AND I DON'T SEE OUR FRIEND HERE OPENING THE TRANSMAT DOOR TO ALLOW THAT.

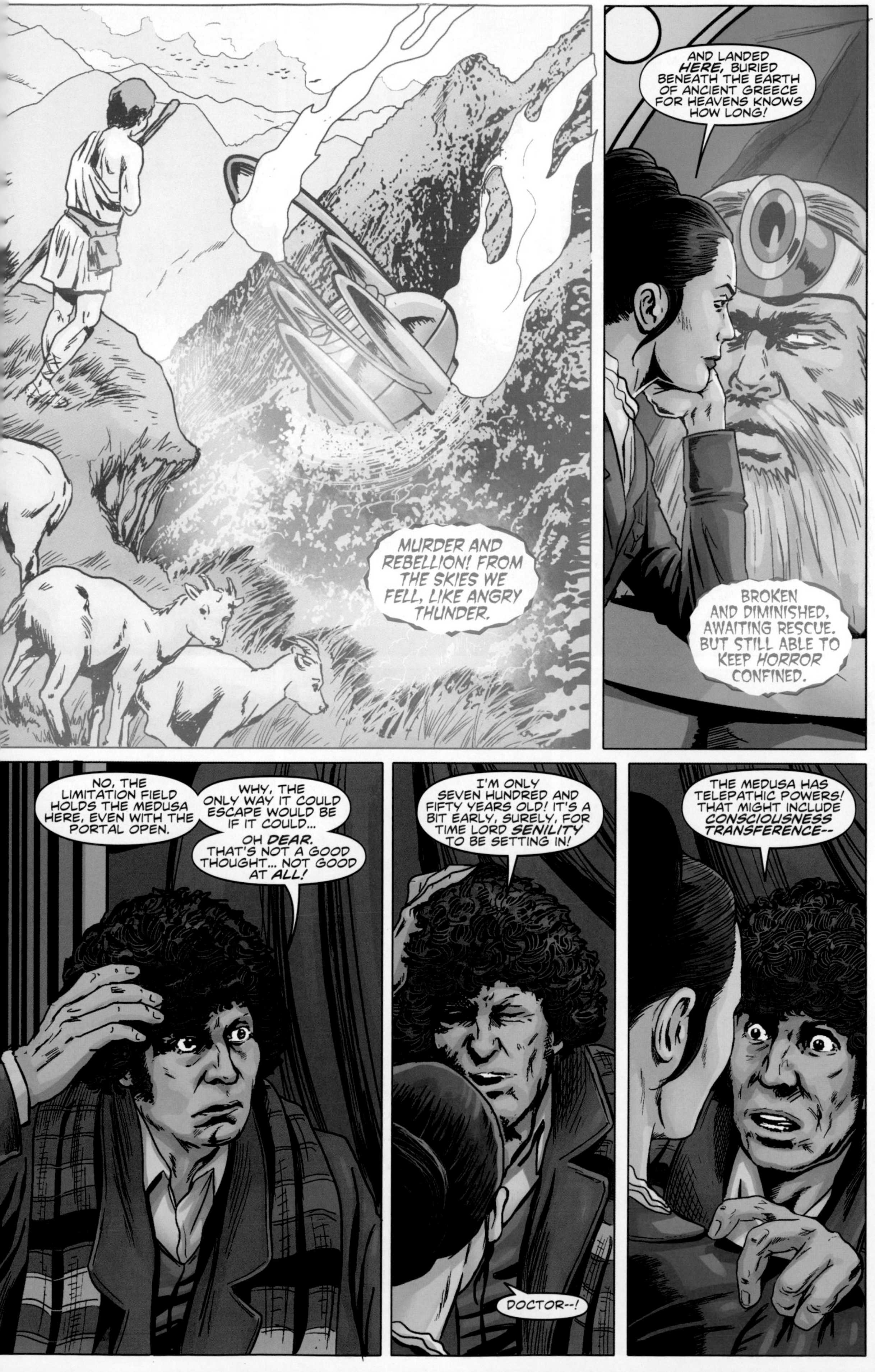
MURDER AND REBELLION! FROM THE SKIES WE FELL, LIKE ANGRY THUNDER.
AND LANDED HERE, BURIED BENEATH THE EARTH OF ANCIENT GREECE FOR HEAVENS KNOWS HOW LONG!
BROKEN AND DIMINISHED, AWAITING RESCUE. BUT STILL ABLE TO KEEP HORROR CONFINED.
NO, THE LIMITATION FIELD HOLDS THE MEDUSA HERE, EVEN WITH THE PORTAL OPEN.
WHY, THE ONLY WAY IT COULD ESCAPE WOULD BE IF IT COULD...
OH DEAR. THAT'S NOT A GOOD THOUGHT... NOT GOOD AT ALL!
I'M ONLY SEVEN HUNDRED AND FIFTY YEARS OLD! IT'S A BIT EARLY, SURELY, FOR TIME LORD SENILITY TO BE SETTING IN!
DOCTOR--!
THE MEDUSA HAS TELEPATHIC POWERS! THAT MIGHT INCLUDE CONSCIOUSNESS TRANSFERENCE--

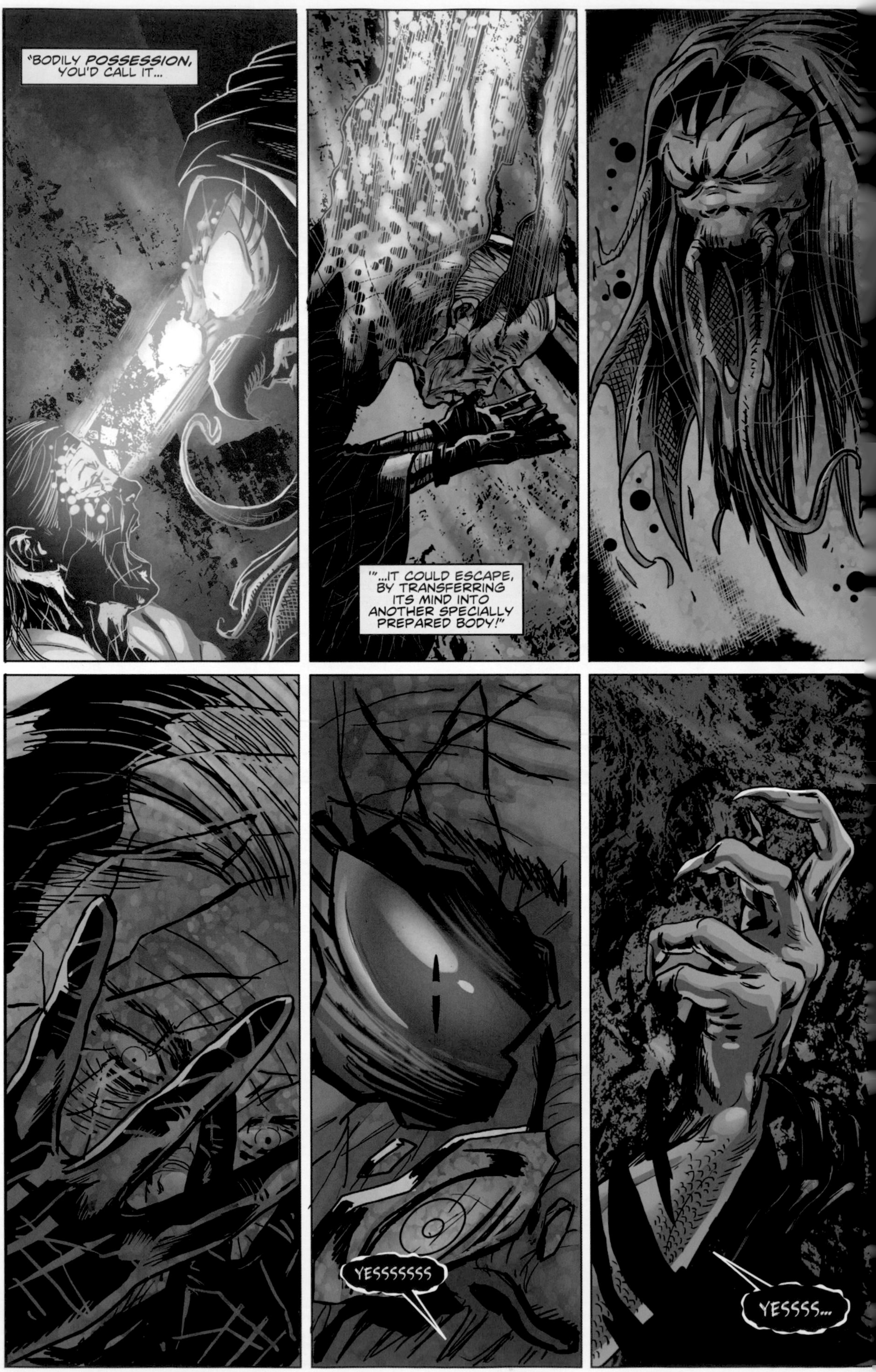
"BODILY POSSESSION, YOU'D CALL IT...
"...IT COULD ESCAPE, BY TRANSFERRING ITS MIND INTO ANOTHER SPECIALLY PREPARED BODY!"
YESSSSSSS
YESSSS...

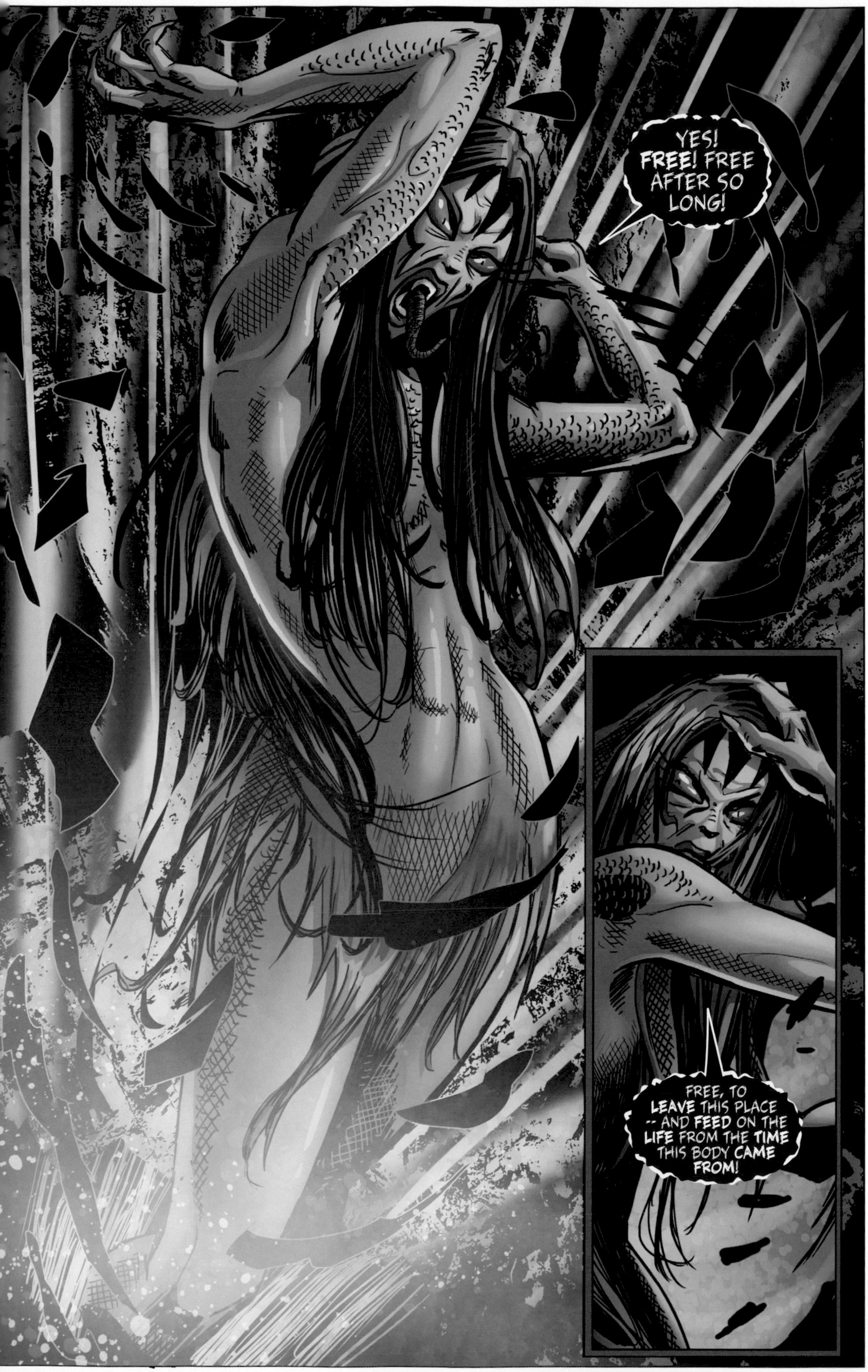
YES! FREE! FREE AFTER SO LONG!
FREE, TO LEAVE THIS PLACE -- AND FEED ON THE LIFE FROM THE TIME THIS BODY CAME FROM!

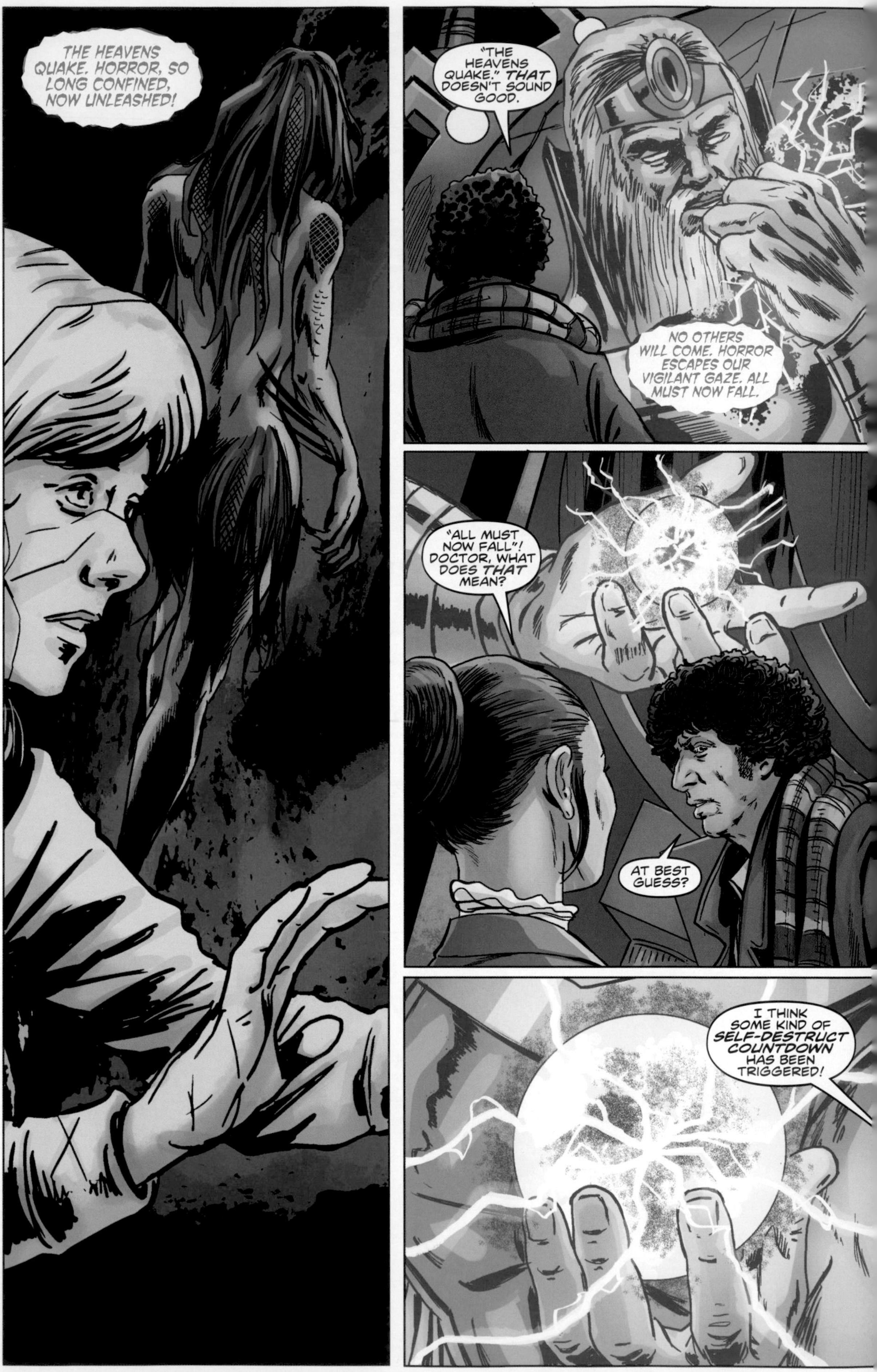
THE HEAVENS QUAKE. HORROR, SO LONG CONFINED, NOW UNLEASHED!
"THE HEAVENS QUAKE." THAT DOESN'T SOUND GOOD.
NO OTHERS WILL COME. HORROR ESCAPES OUR VIGILANT GAZE. ALL MUST NOW FALL.
"ALL MUST NOW FALL"! DOCTOR, WHAT DOES THAT MEAN?
AT BEST GUESS?
I THINK SOME KIND OF SELF-DESTRUCT COUNTDOWN HAS BEEN TRIGGERED!

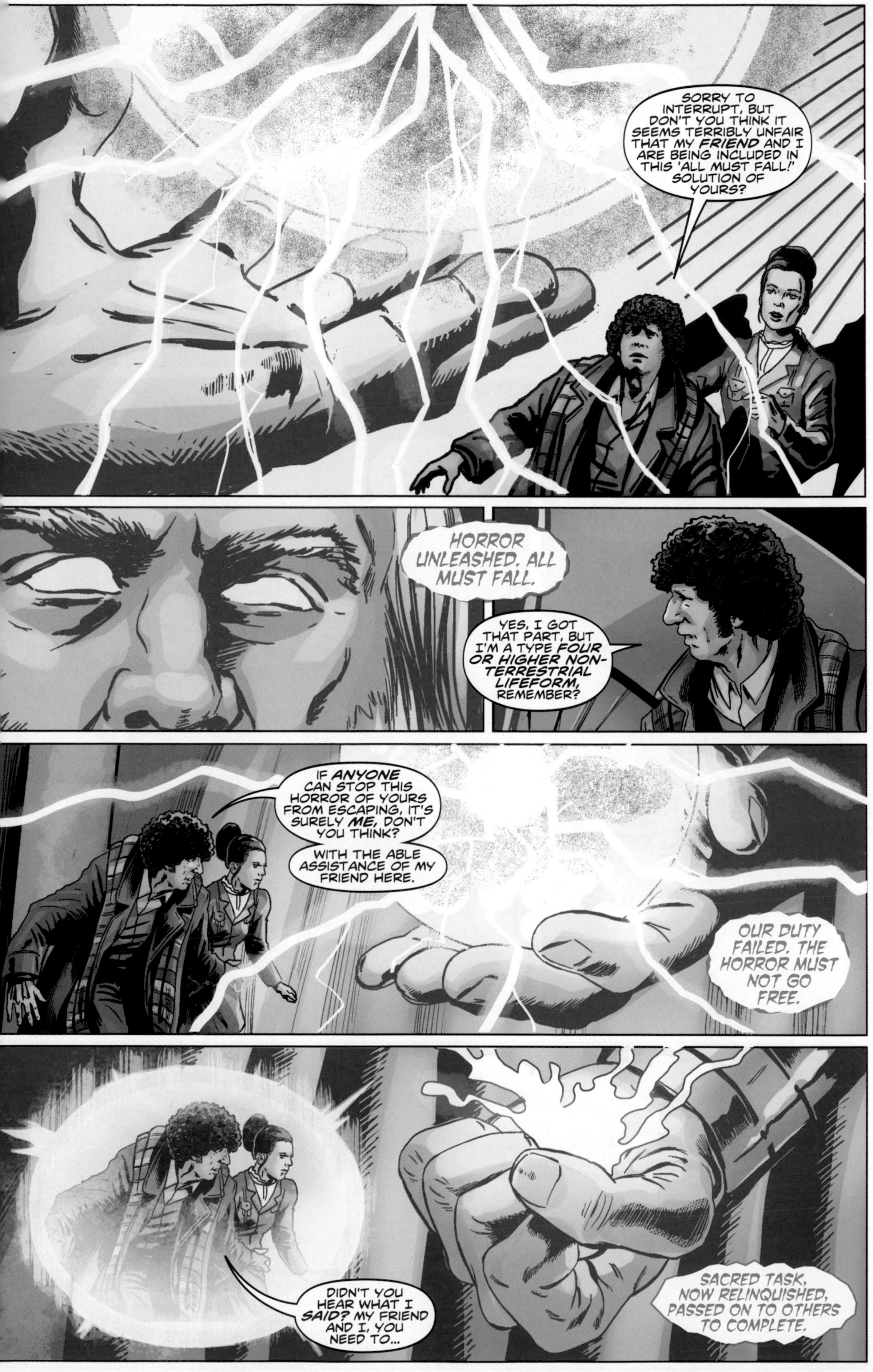
SORRY TO INTERRUPT, BUT DON'T YOU THINK IT SEEMS TERRIBLY UNFAIR THAT MY FRIEND AND I ARE BEING INCLUDED IN THIS 'ALL MUST FALL!' SOLUTION OF YOURS?
HORROR UNLEASHED. ALL MUST FALL.
YES, I GOT THAT PART, BUT I'M A TYPE FOUR OR HIGHER NON-TERRESTRIAL LIFEFORM, REMEMBER?
IF ANYONE CAN STOP THIS HORROR OF YOURS FROM ESCAPING, IT'S SURELY ME, DON'T YOU THINK?
WITH THE ABLE ASSISTANCE OF MY FRIEND HERE.
OUR DUTY FAILED. THE HORROR MUST NOT GO FREE.
DIDN'T YOU HEAR WHAT I SAID? MY FRIEND AND I, YOU NEED TO...
SACRED TASK, NOW RELINQUISHED, PASSED ON TO OTHERS TO COMPLETE.

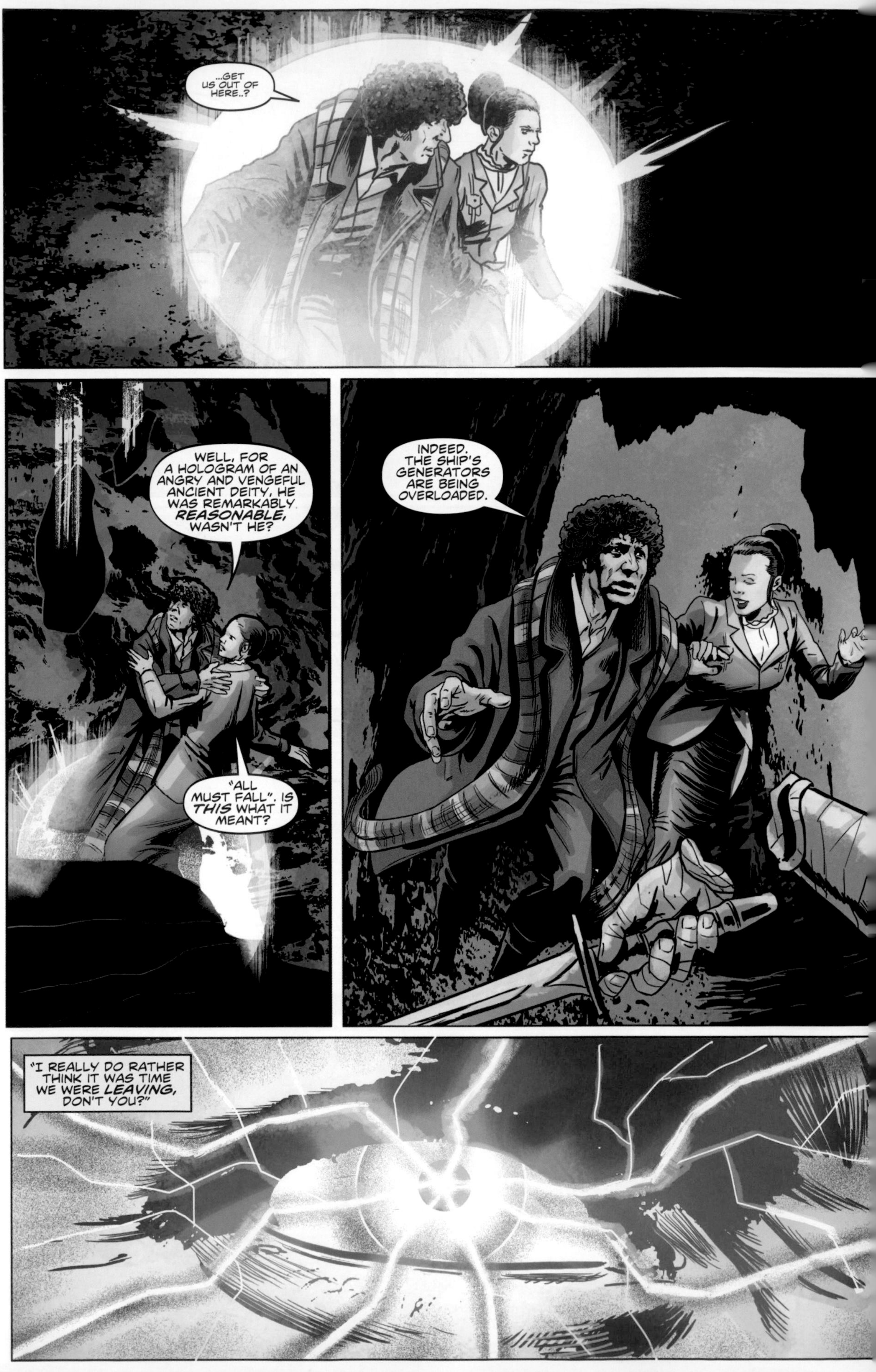
...GET US OUT OF HERE..?
WELL, FOR A HOLOGRAM OF AN ANGRY AND VENGEFUL ANCIENT DEITY, HE WAS REMARKABLY *REASONABLE,* WASN'T HE?
"ALL MUST FALL". IS *THIS* WHAT IT MEANT?
INDEED. THE SHIP'S GENERATORS ARE BEING OVERLOADED.
"I REALLY DO RATHER THINK IT WAS TIME WE WERE *LEAVING,* DON'T YOU?"

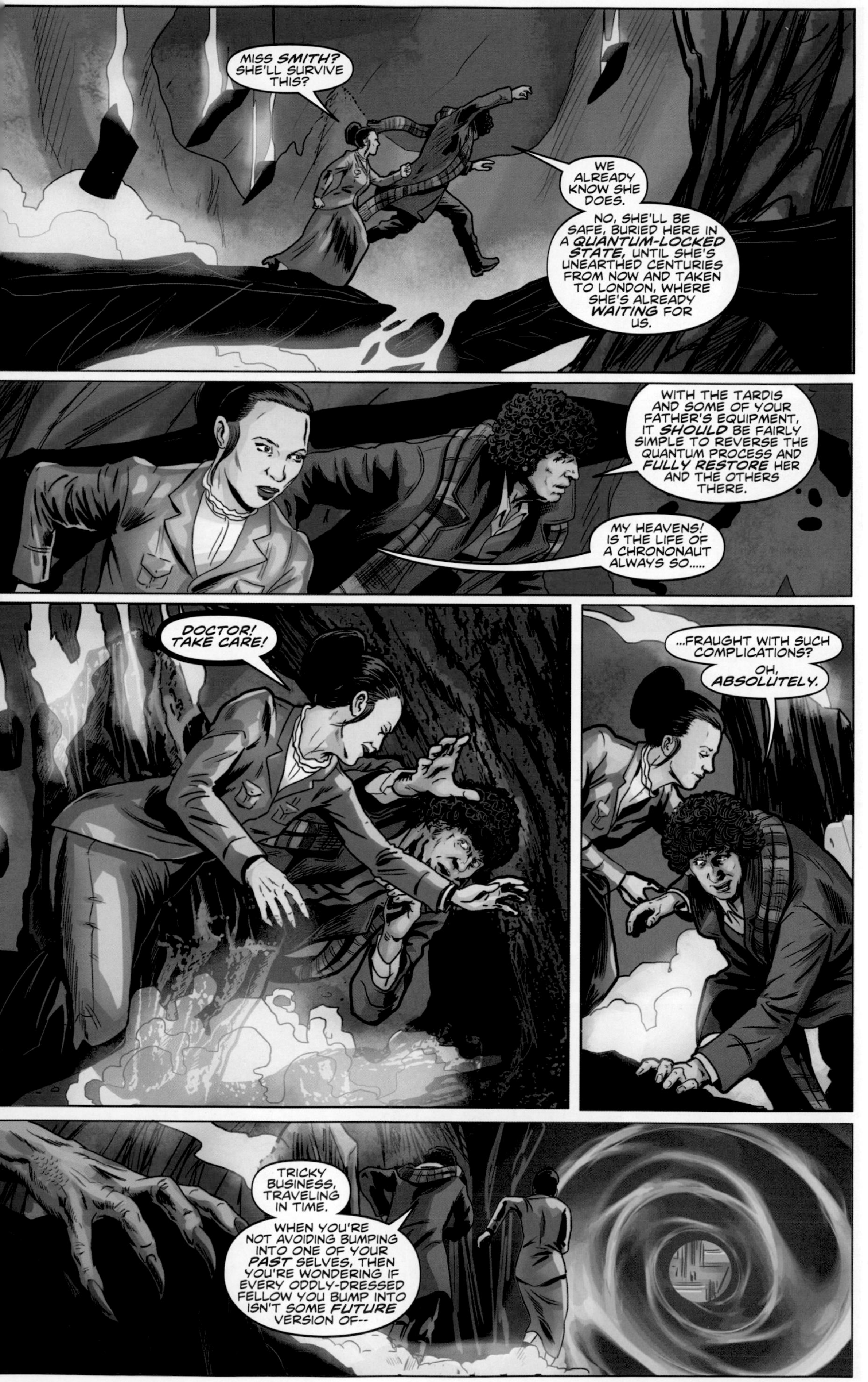

MISS SMITH? SHE'LL SURVIVE THIS?
WE ALREADY KNOW SHE DOES.
NO, SHE'LL BE SAFE, BURIED HERE IN A QUANTUM-LOCKED STATE, UNTIL SHE'S UNEARTHED CENTURIES FROM NOW AND TAKEN TO LONDON, WHERE SHE'S ALREADY WAITING FOR US.
WITH THE TARDIS AND SOME OF YOUR FATHER'S EQUIPMENT, IT SHOULD BE FAIRLY SIMPLE TO REVERSE THE QUANTUM PROCESS AND FULLY RESTORE HER AND THE OTHERS THERE.
MY HEAVENS! IS THE LIFE OF A CHRONONAUT ALWAYS SO.....
DOCTOR! TAKE CARE!
...FRAUGHT WITH SUCH COMPLICATIONS?
OH, ABSOLUTELY.
TRICKY BUSINESS, TRAVELING IN TIME.
WHEN YOU'RE NOT AVOIDING BUMPING INTO ONE OF YOUR PAST SELVES, THEN YOU'RE WONDERING IF EVERY ODDLY-DRESSED FELLOW YOU BUMP INTO ISN'T SOME FUTURE VERSION OF--

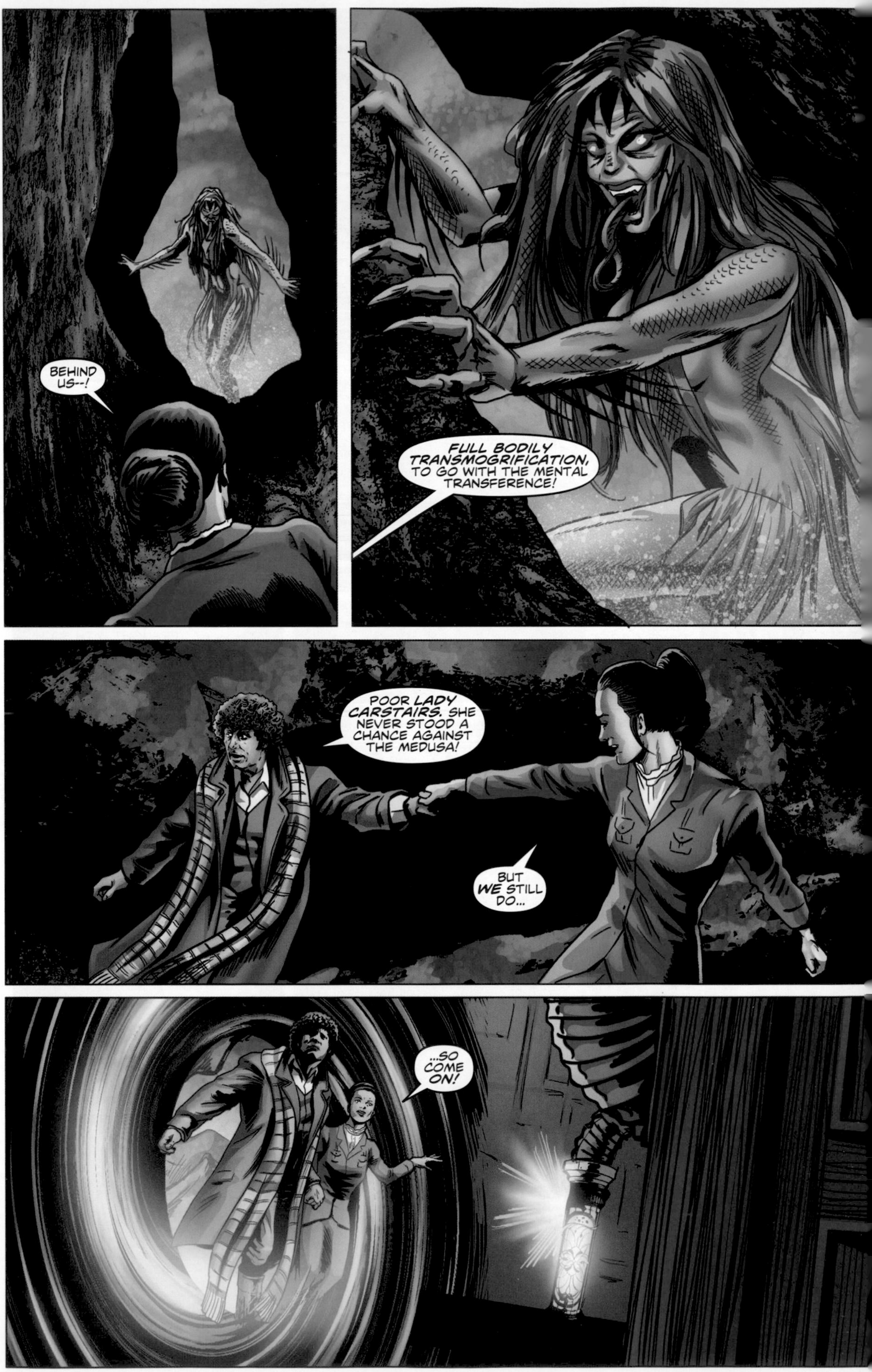
BEHIND US--!
FULL BODILY TRANSMOGRIFICATION, TO GO WITH THE MENTAL TRANSFERENCE!
POOR LADY CARSTAIRS. SHE NEVER STOOD A CHANCE AGAINST THE MEDUSA!
BUT WE STILL DO...
...SO COME ON!

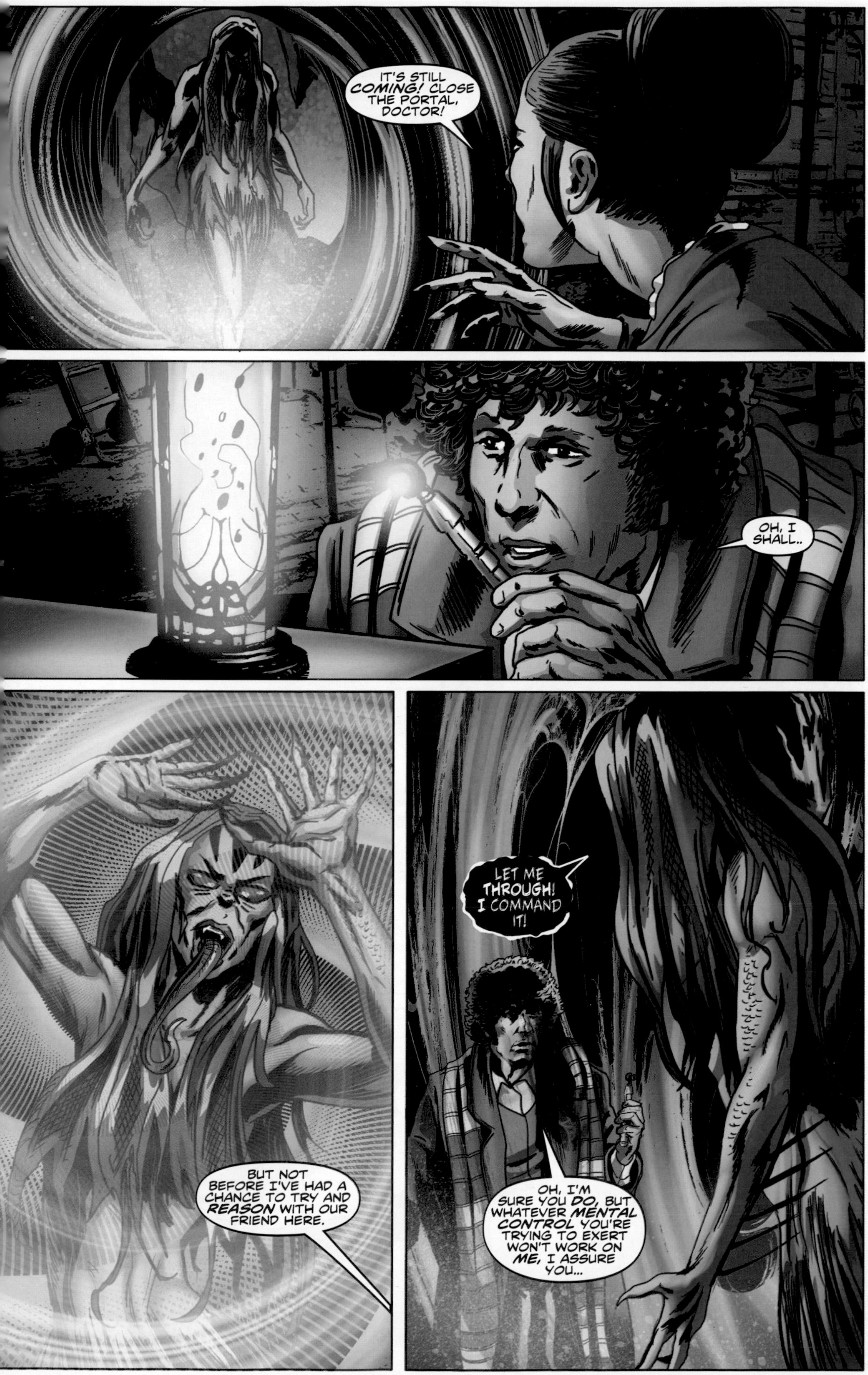
IT'S STILL COMING! CLOSE THE PORTAL, DOCTOR!
OH, I SHALL..
BUT NOT BEFORE I'VE HAD A CHANCE TO TRY AND REASON WITH OUR FRIEND HERE.
LET ME THROUGH! I COMMAND IT!
OH, I'M SURE YOU DO, BUT WHATEVER MENTAL CONTROL YOU'RE TRYING TO EXERT WON'T WORK ON ME, I ASSURE YOU...

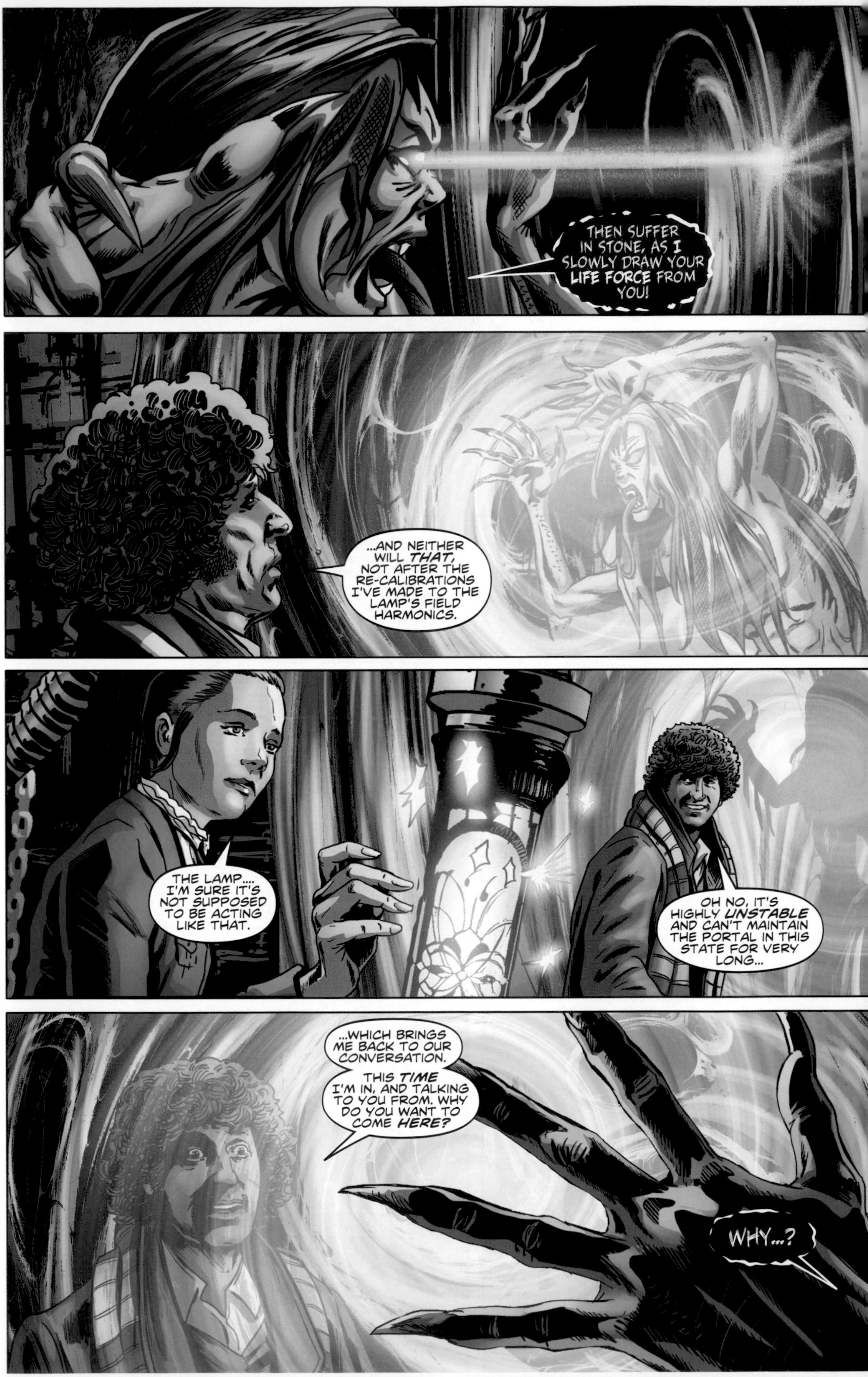
THEN SUFFER IN STONE, AS I SLOWLY DRAW YOUR LIFE FORCE FROM YOU!
...AND NEITHER WILL THAT, NOT AFTER THE RE-CALIBRATIONS I'VE MADE TO THE LAMP'S FIELD HARMONICS.
THE LAMP.... I'M SURE IT'S NOT SUPPOSED TO BE ACTING LIKE THAT.
OH NO, IT'S HIGHLY UNSTABLE AND CAN'T MAINTAIN THE PORTAL IN THIS STATE FOR VERY LONG...
...WHICH BRINGS ME BACK TO OUR CONVERSATION.
THIS TIME I'M IN, AND TALKING TO YOU FROM. WHY DO YOU WANT TO COME HERE?
WHY...?

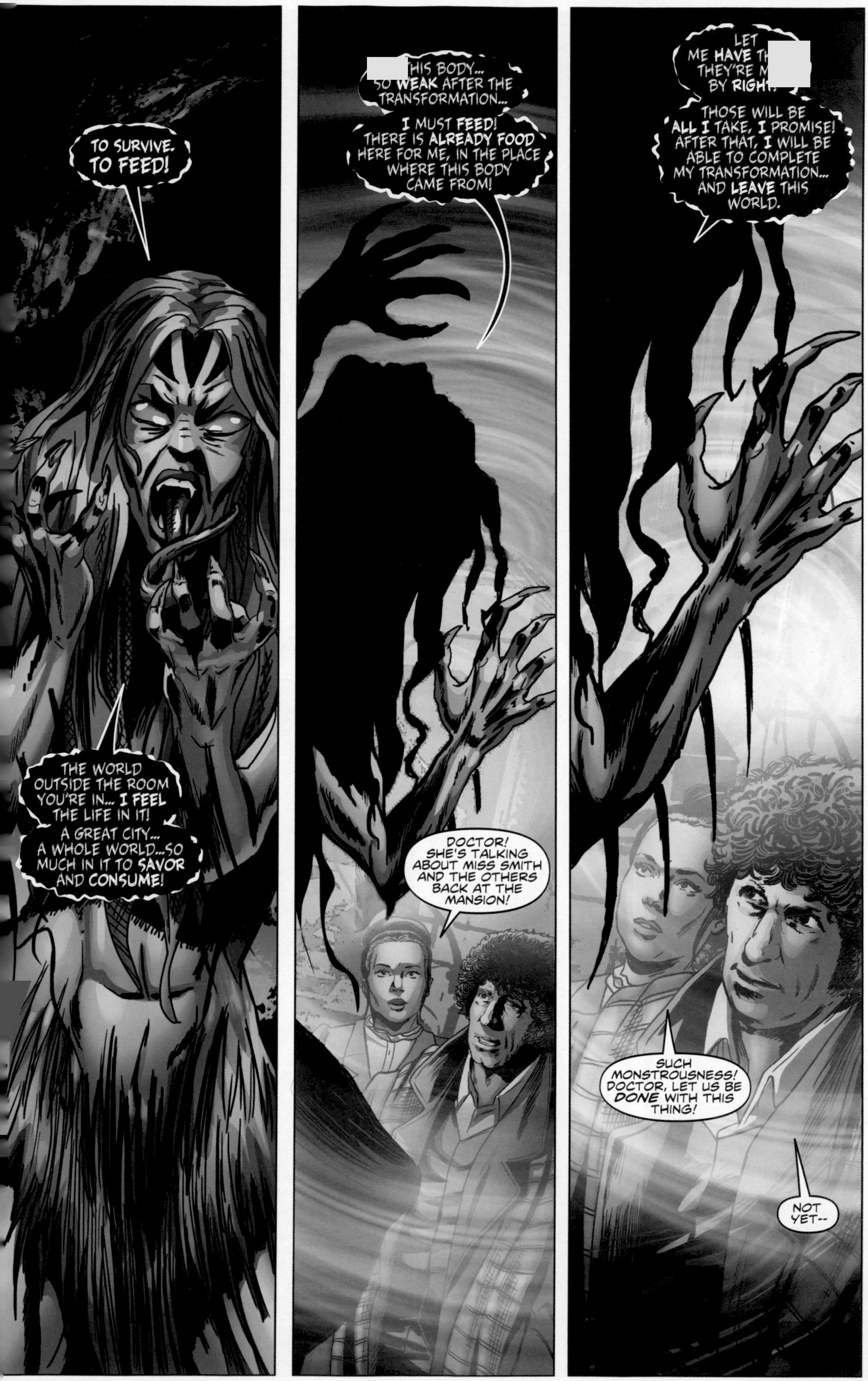
TO SURVIVE. TO FEED!
THE WORLD OUTSIDE THE ROOM YOU'RE IN... I FEEL THE LIFE IN IT!
A GREAT CITY... A WHOLE WORLD...SO MUCH IN IT TO SAVOR AND CONSUME!
HIS BODY... SO WEAK AFTER THE TRANSFORMATION...
I MUST FEED! THERE IS ALREADY FOOD HERE FOR ME, IN THE PLACE WHERE THIS BODY CAME FROM!
DOCTOR! SHE'S TALKING ABOUT MISS SMITH AND THE OTHERS BACK AT THE MANSION!
LET ME HAVE TH THEY'RE M BY RIGHT
THOSE WILL BE ALL I TAKE, I PROMISE! AFTER THAT, I WILL BE ABLE TO COMPLETE MY TRANSFORMATION... AND LEAVE THIS WORLD.
SUCH MONSTROUSNESS! DOCTOR, LET US BE DONE WITH THIS THING!
NOT YET--

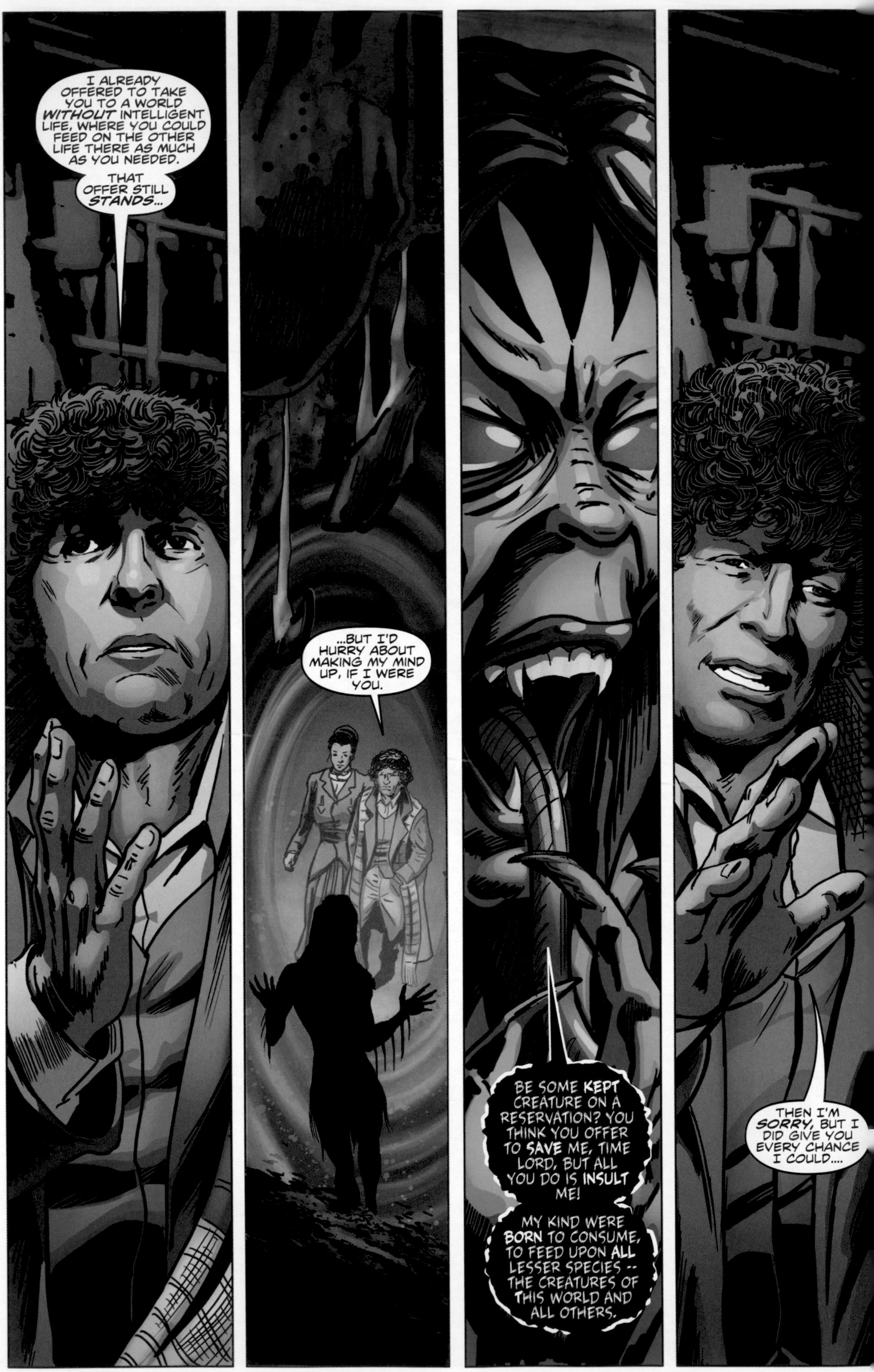
I ALREADY OFFERED TO TAKE YOU TO A WORLD WITHOUT INTELLIGENT LIFE, WHERE YOU COULD FEED ON THE OTHER LIFE THERE AS MUCH AS YOU NEEDED.
THAT OFFER STILL STANDS...
...BUT I'D HURRY ABOUT MAKING MY MIND UP, IF I WERE YOU.
BE SOME KEPT CREATURE ON A RESERVATION? YOU THINK YOU OFFER TO SAVE ME, TIME LORD, BUT ALL YOU DO IS INSULT ME!
MY KIND WERE BORN TO CONSUME, TO FEED UPON ALL LESSER SPECIES -- THE CREATURES OF THIS WORLD AND ALL OTHERS.
THEN I'M SORRY, BUT I DID GIVE YOU EVERY CHANCE I COULD....

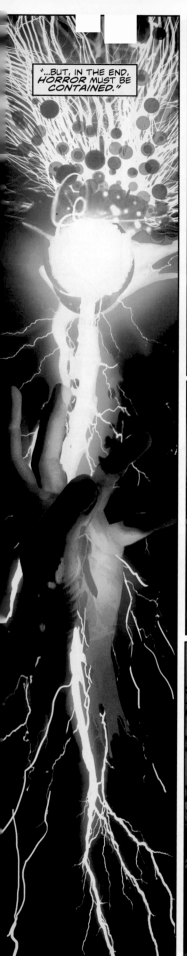

"...BUT, IN THE END, *HORROR* MUST BE *CONTAINED.*"

THE LAMP--!

OH YES, I'D ALMOST FORGOTTEN ABOUT THAT...

QUICK! INTO THE PORTAL WITH IT!

"IT'LL STAY THERE FOR TWENTY FIVE *CENTURIES* OR SO, UNTIL LADY EMILY'S HUSBAND DIGS IT UP AND STARTS THIS WHOLE PARADE ALL OVER AGAIN!"

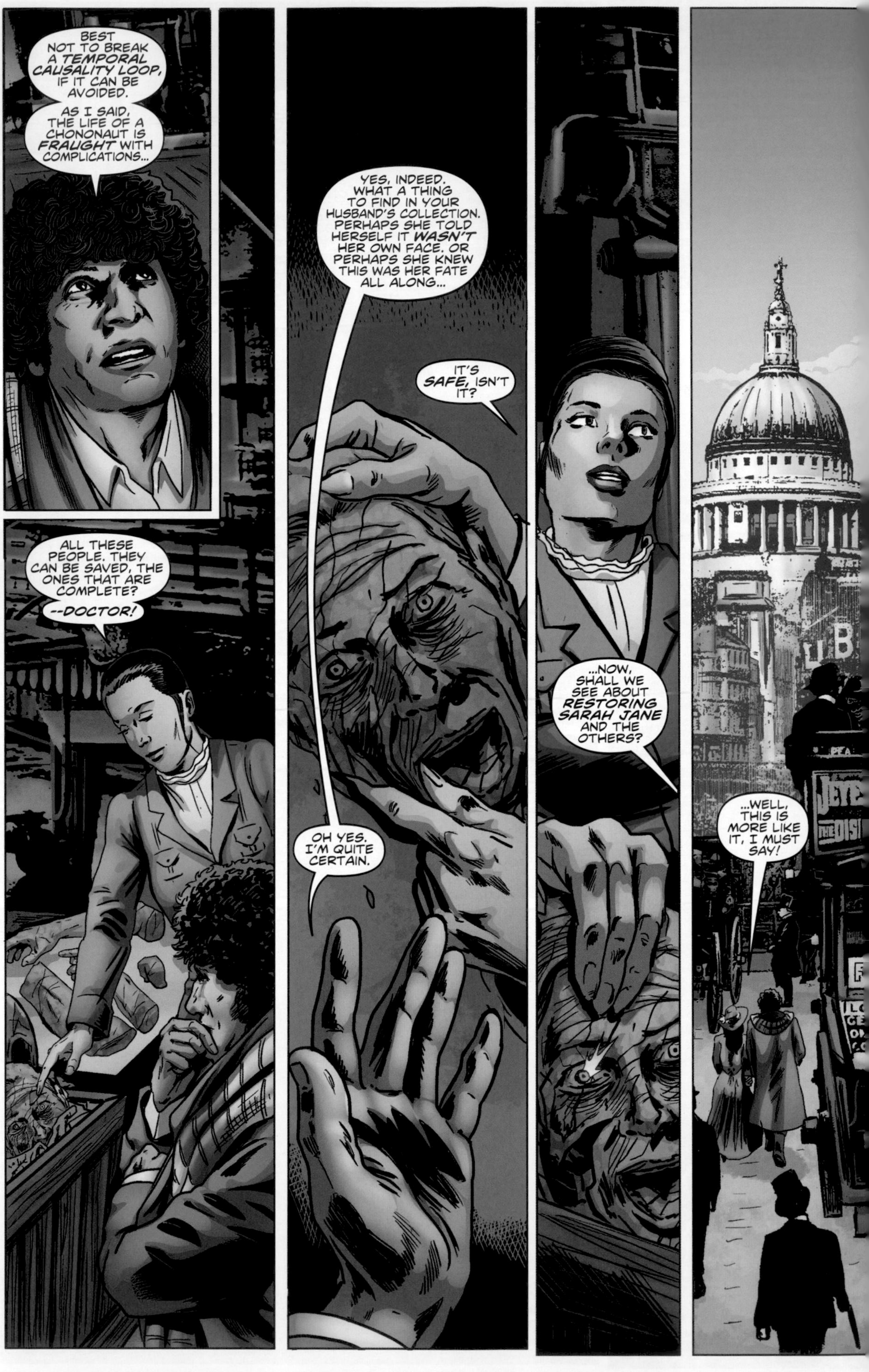
BEST NOT TO BREAK A *TEMPORAL CAUSALITY LOOP*, IF IT CAN BE AVOIDED.
AS I SAID, THE LIFE OF A CHONONAUT IS *FRAUGHT* WITH COMPLICATIONS...
ALL THESE PEOPLE. THEY CAN BE SAVED, THE ONES THAT ARE COMPLETE?
--DOCTOR!
YES, INDEED. WHAT A THING TO FIND IN YOUR HUSBAND'S COLLECTION. PERHAPS SHE TOLD HERSELF IT *WASN'T* HER OWN FACE. OR PERHAPS SHE KNEW THIS WAS HER FATE ALL ALONG...
IT'S *SAFE*, ISN'T IT?
OH YES. I'M QUITE CERTAIN.
...NOW, SHALL WE SEE ABOUT *RESTORING SARAH JANE* AND THE OTHERS?
...WELL, THIS IS MORE LIKE IT, I MUST SAY!

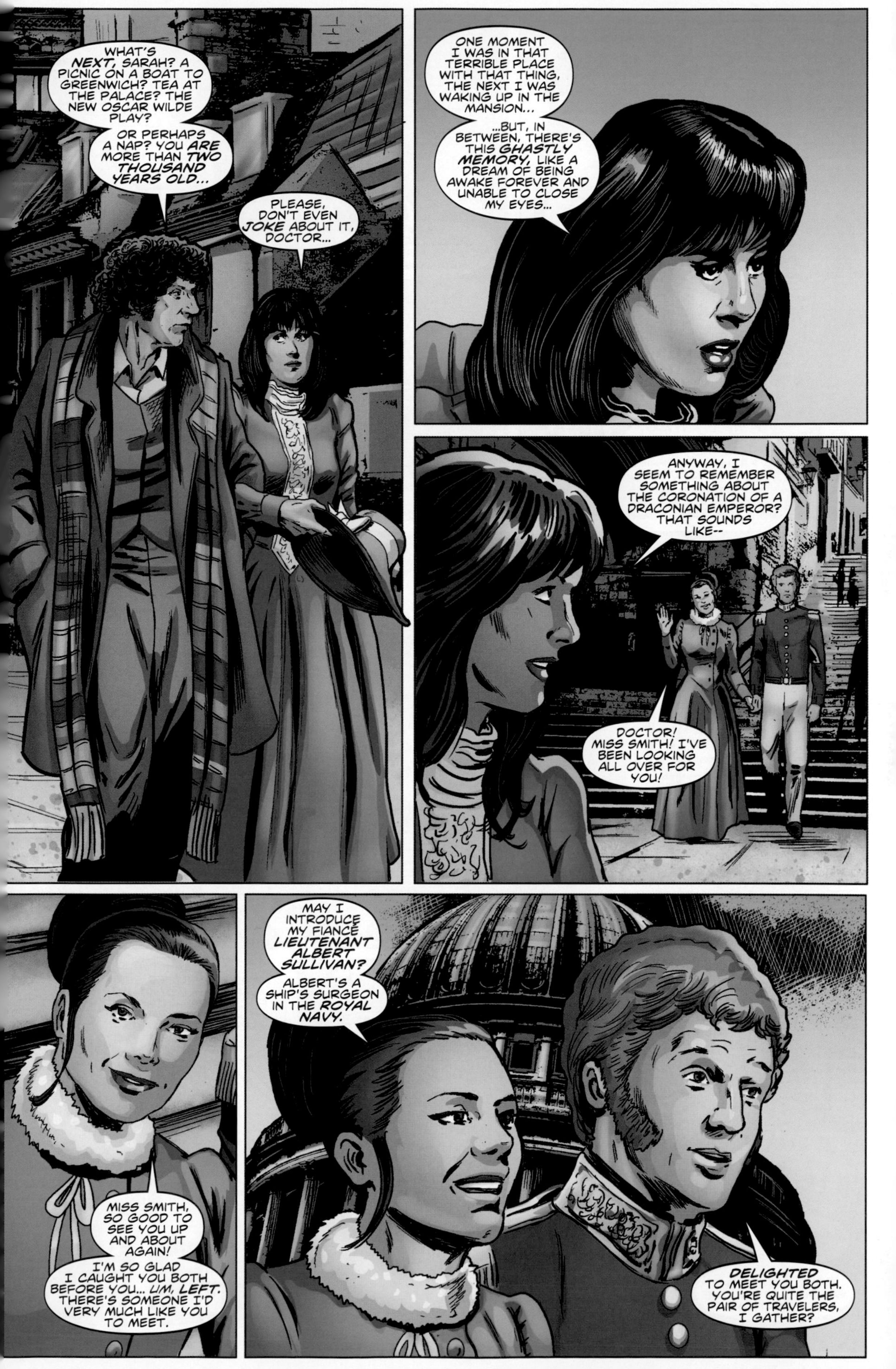
WHAT'S NEXT, SARAH? A PICNIC ON A BOAT TO GREENWICH? TEA AT THE PALACE? THE NEW OSCAR WILDE PLAY?
OR PERHAPS A NAP? YOU ARE MORE THAN TWO THOUSAND YEARS OLD...
PLEASE, DON'T EVEN JOKE ABOUT IT, DOCTOR...
ONE MOMENT I WAS IN THAT TERRIBLE PLACE WITH THAT THING, THE NEXT I WAS WAKING UP IN THE MANSION...
...BUT, IN BETWEEN, THERE'S THIS GHASTLY MEMORY, LIKE A DREAM OF BEING AWAKE FOREVER AND UNABLE TO CLOSE MY EYES...
ANYWAY, I SEEM TO REMEMBER SOMETHING ABOUT THE CORONATION OF A DRACONIAN EMPEROR? THAT SOUNDS LIKE--
DOCTOR! MISS SMITH! I'VE BEEN LOOKING ALL OVER FOR YOU!
MISS SMITH, SO GOOD TO SEE YOU UP AND ABOUT AGAIN!
I'M SO GLAD I CAUGHT YOU BOTH BEFORE YOU... UM, LEFT. THERE'S SOMEONE I'D VERY MUCH LIKE YOU TO MEET.
MAY I INTRODUCE MY FIANCE LIEUTENANT ALBERT SULLIVAN?
ALBERT'S A SHIP'S SURGEON IN THE ROYAL NAVY.
DELIGHTED TO MEET YOU BOTH. YOU'RE QUITE THE PAIR OF TRAVELERS, I GATHER?

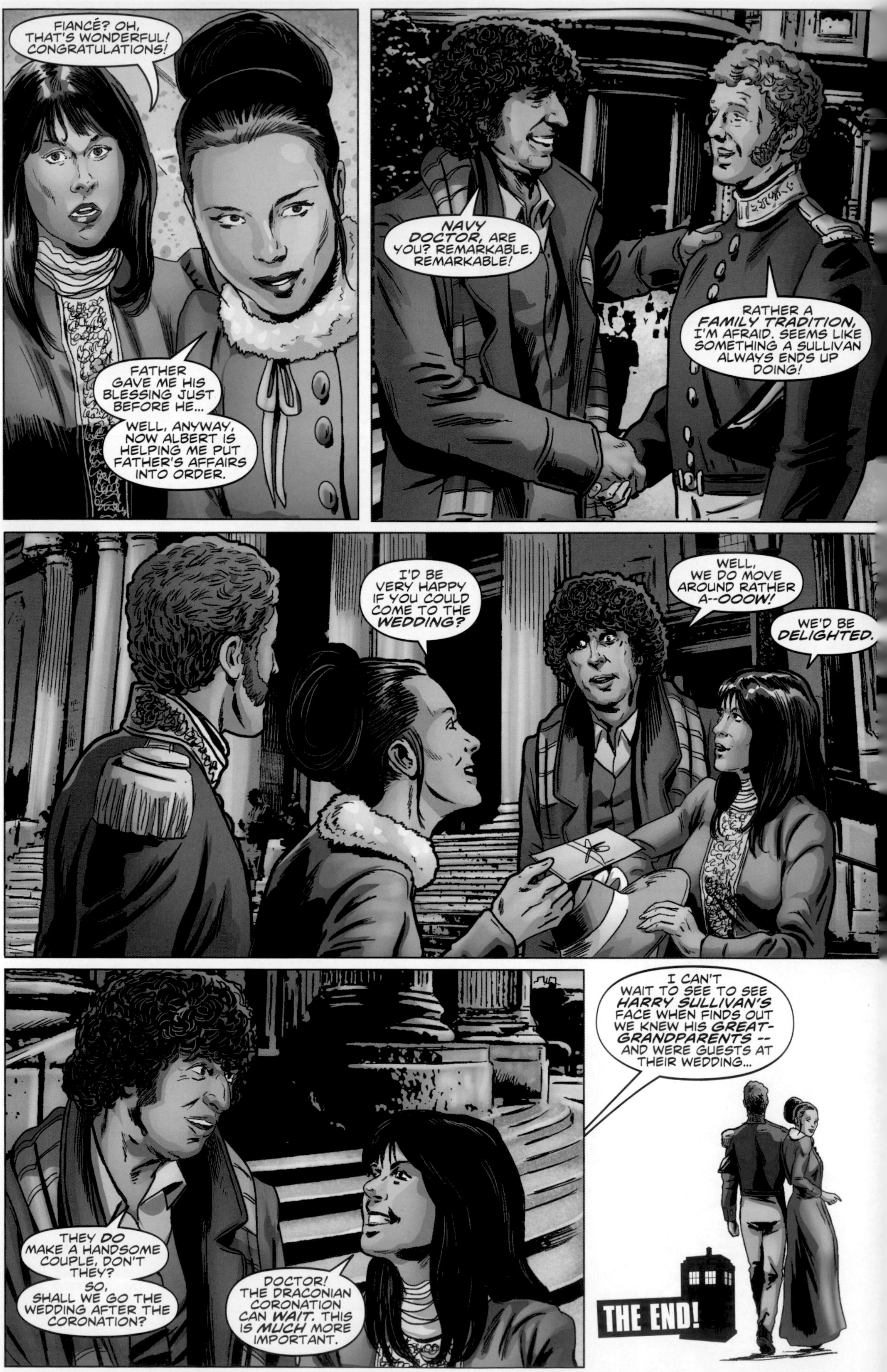
FIANCÉ? OH, THAT'S WONDERFUL! CONGRATULATIONS!
FATHER GAVE ME HIS BLESSING JUST BEFORE HE...
WELL, ANYWAY, NOW ALBERT IS HELPING ME PUT FATHER'S AFFAIRS INTO ORDER.
NAVY DOCTOR, ARE YOU? REMARKABLE. REMARKABLE!
RATHER A FAMILY TRADITION, I'M AFRAID. SEEMS LIKE SOMETHING A SULLIVAN ALWAYS ENDS UP DOING!
I'D BE VERY HAPPY IF YOU COULD COME TO THE WEDDING?
WELL, WE DO MOVE AROUND RATHER A--OOOW!
WE'D BE DELIGHTED.
THEY DO MAKE A HANDSOME COUPLE, DON'T THEY?
SO, SHALL WE GO THE WEDDING AFTER THE CORONATION?
DOCTOR! THE DRACONIAN CORONATION CAN WAIT. THIS IS MUCH MORE IMPORTANT.
I CAN'T WAIT TO SEE TO SEE HARRY SULLIVAN'S FACE WHEN FINDS OUT WE KNEW HIS GREAT-GRANDPARENTS -- AND WERE GUESTS AT THEIR WEDDING...
THE END!

COVER GALLERY

A

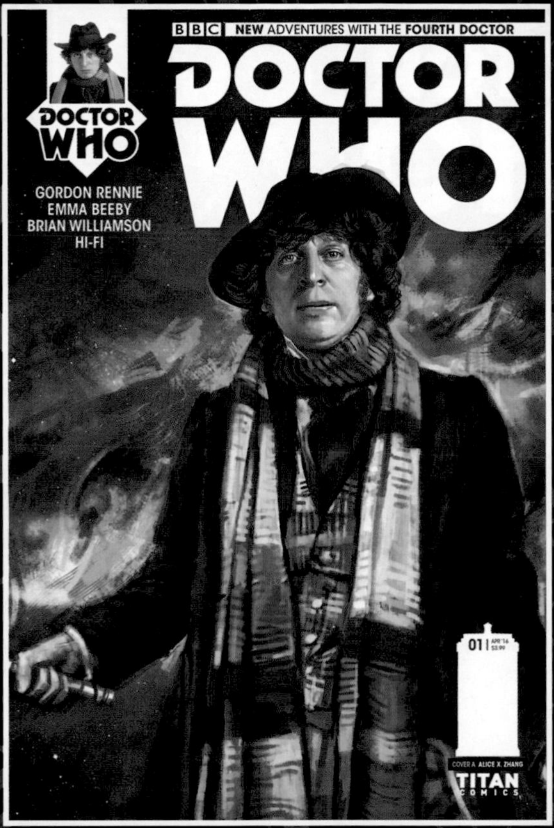
BBC NEW ADVENTURES WITH THE FOURTH DOCTOR
DOCTOR WHO
DOCTOR WHO
GORDON RENNIE
EMMA BEEBY
BRIAN WILLIAMSON
HI-FI
01 APR'16 $3.99
COVER A ALICE X. ZHANG
TITAN COMICS

B

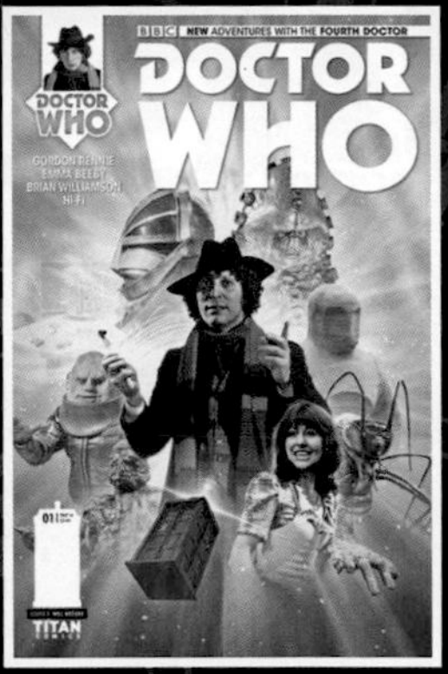
BBC NEW ADVENTURES WITH THE FOURTH DOCTOR
DOCTOR WHO
TITAN

C

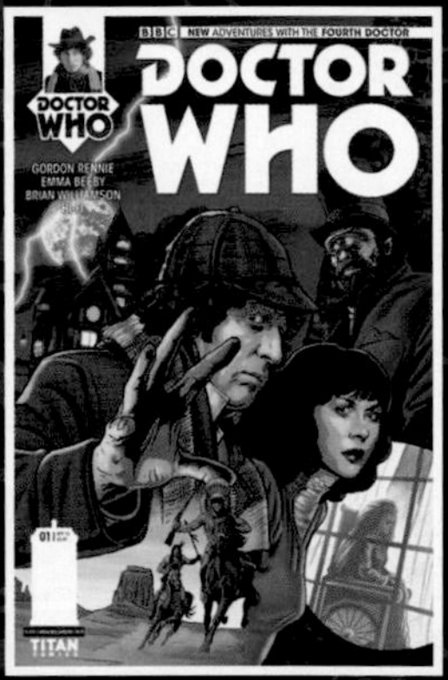
BBC NEW ADVENTURES WITH THE FOURTH DOCTOR
DOCTOR WHO
GORDON RENNIE
EMMA BEEBY
BRIAN WILLIAMSON
TITAN

D

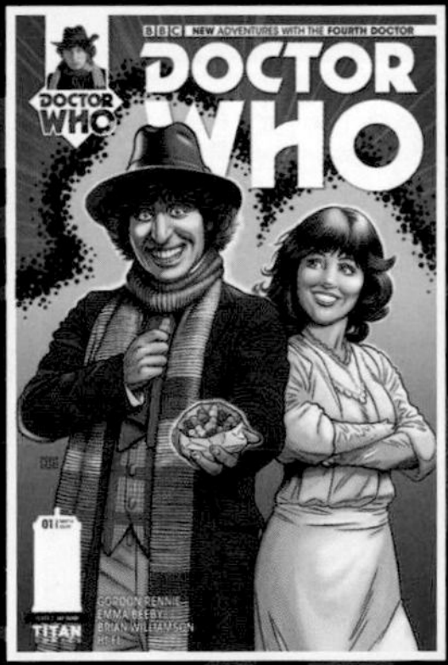
BBC NEW ADVENTURES WITH THE FOURTH DOCTOR
DOCTOR WHO
GORDON RENNIE
EMMA BEEBY
BRIAN WILLIAMSON
TITAN

E

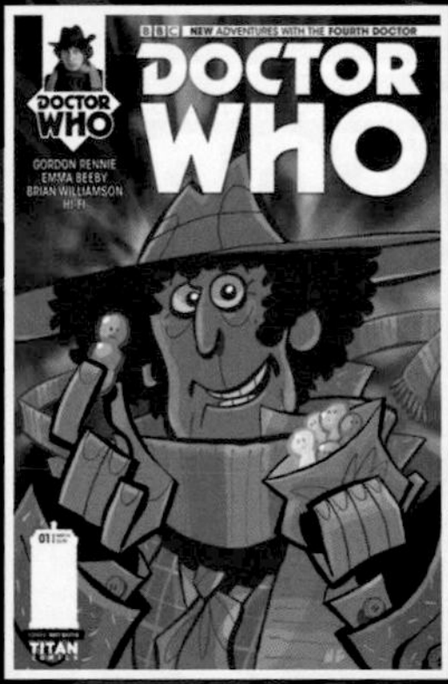
BBC NEW ADVENTURES WITH THE FOURTH DOCTOR
DOCTOR WHO
GORDON RENNIE
EMMA BEEBY
BRIAN WILLIAMSON
HI-FI
TITAN

F

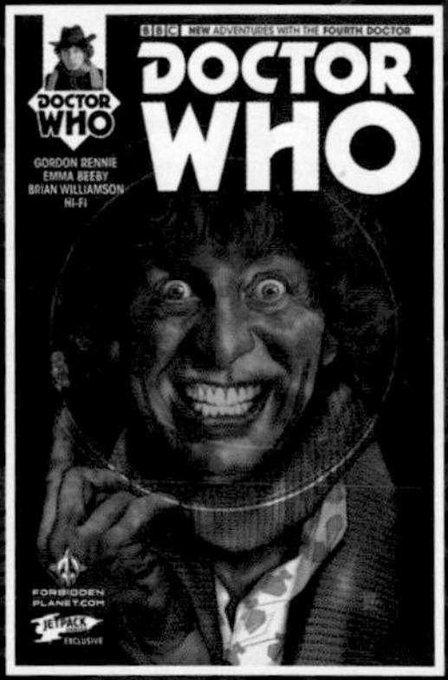
BBC NEW ADVENTURES WITH THE FOURTH DOCTOR
DOCTOR WHO
GORDON RENNIE
EMMA BEEBY
BRIAN WILLIAMSON
HI-FI
FORBIDDEN PLANET.COM
JETPACK EXCLUSIVE

G

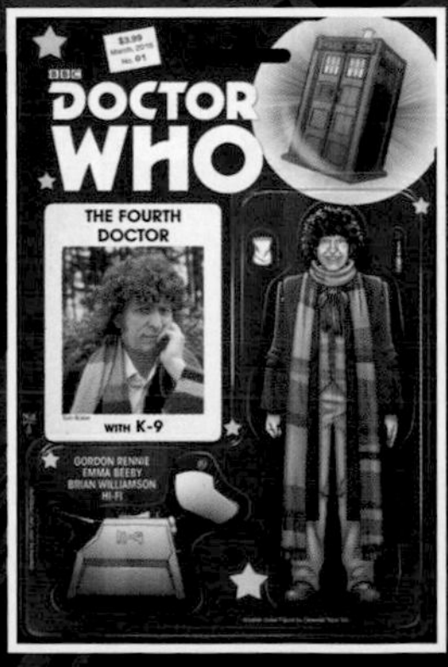
BBC
DOCTOR WHO
THE FOURTH DOCTOR
WITH K-9
GORDON RENNIE
EMMA BEEBY
BRIAN WILLIAMSON
HI-FI

H

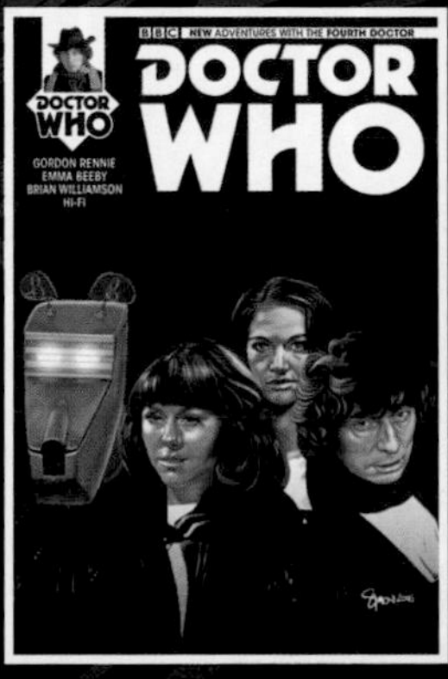
BBC NEW ADVENTURES WITH THE FOURTH DOCTOR
DOCTOR WHO
GORDON RENNIE
EMMA BEEBY
BRIAN WILLIAMSON
HI-FI

ISSUE #1

A. ALICE X. ZHANG
B. SUBSCRIPTION PHOTO – WILL BROOKS
C. BRIAN WILLIAMSON & HI-FI
D. JAY GUNN
E. MATT BAXTER
F. FORBIDDEN PLANET / JETPACK EXCLUSIVE BEN OLIVER
G. DIAMOND UK BLAIR SHEDD
H. AOD COLLECTIBLES SIMON MYERS

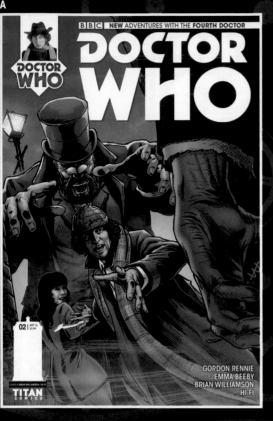

ISSUE #2

A BRIAN WILLIAMSON / HI-FI
B. SUBSCRIPTION PHOTO WILL BROOKS
C. MATT BAXTER

ISSUE #3

A BRIAN WILLIAMSON & HI-FI
B. SUBSCRIPTION PHOTO
WILL BROOKS
C. WARREN PLEECE
D. ROBERT HACK

A

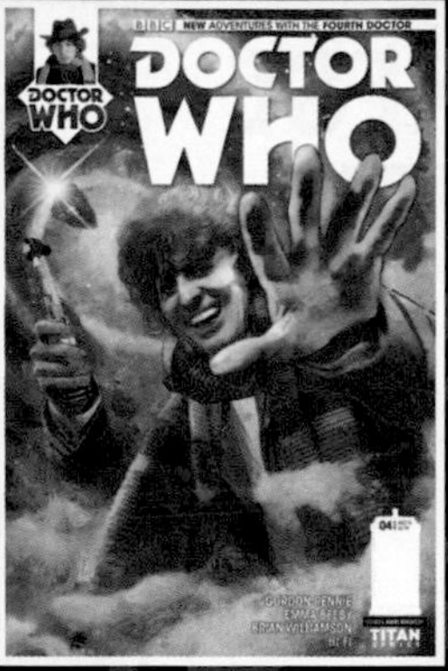
DOCTOR WHO
GORDON RENNIE
EMMA BEEBY
BRIAN WILLIAMSON
HI-FI
TITAN COMICS

B

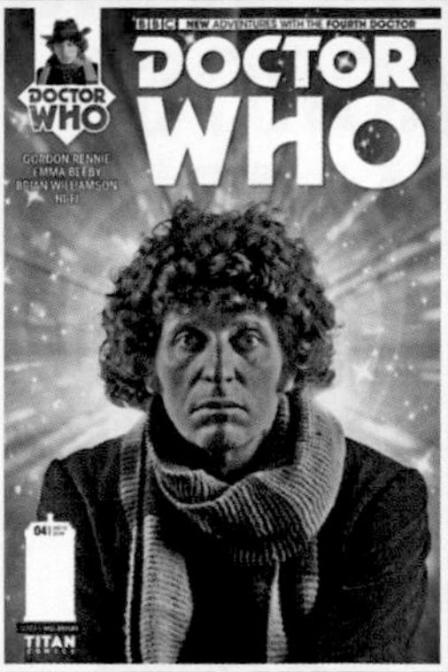
DOCTOR WHO
GORDON RENNIE
EMMA BEEBY
BRIAN WILLIAMSON
HI-FI
TITAN COMICS

C

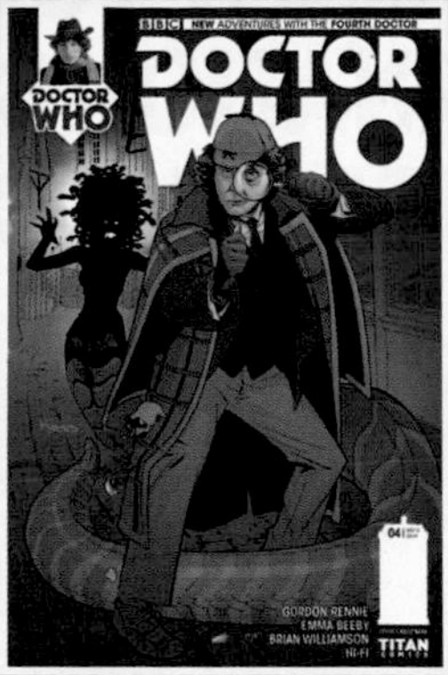
DOCTOR WHO
GORDON RENNIE
EMMA BEEBY
BRIAN WILLIAMSON
HI-FI
TITAN COMICS

D

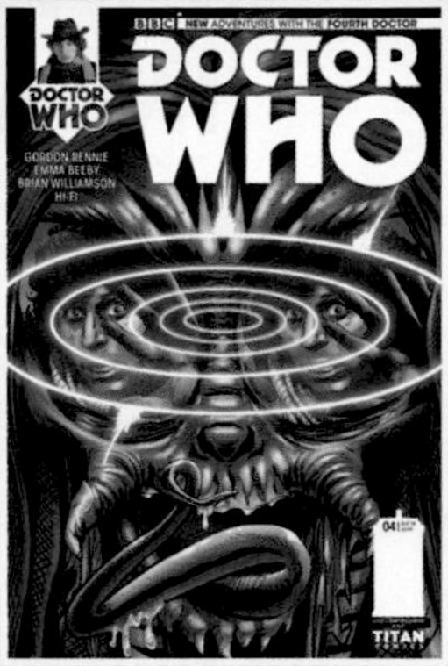
DOCTOR WHO
GORDON RENNIE
EMMA BEEBY
BRIAN WILLIAMSON
HI-FI
TITAN COMICS

E

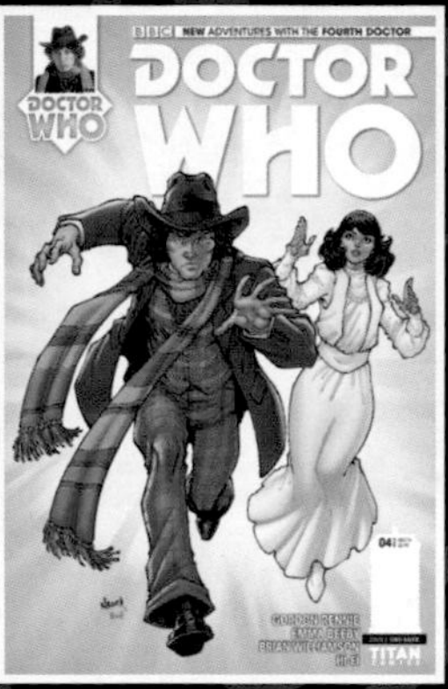
BBC NEW ADVENTURES WITH THE FOURTH DOCTOR
DOCTOR WHO
TITAN COMICS

F

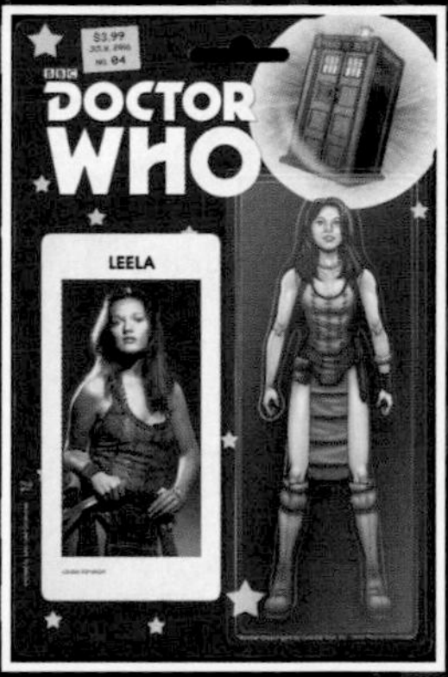
$3.99
NO. 04
DOCTOR WHO
LEELA

G

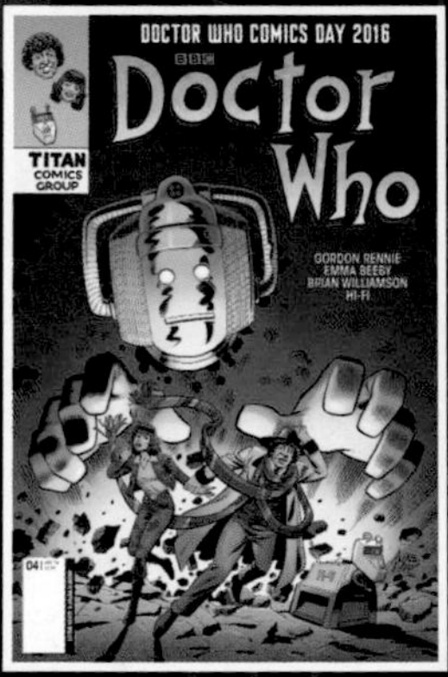
DOCTOR WHO COMICS DAY 2016
Doctor Who
TITAN COMICS GROUP
GORDON RENNIE
EMMA BEEBY
BRIAN WILLIAMSON
HI-FI

ISSUE #4

A. MARK WHEATLEY
B. SUBS PHOTO – WILL BROOKS
C. KELLY YATES
D. BRIAN WILLIAMSON & HI-FI
E. TODD NAUCK & HI-FI
F. DIAMOND UK ACTION FIGURE VARIANT BLAIR SHEDD
G. DOCTOR WHO COMICS DAY ANDREW PEPOY & JASON MILLETT

A

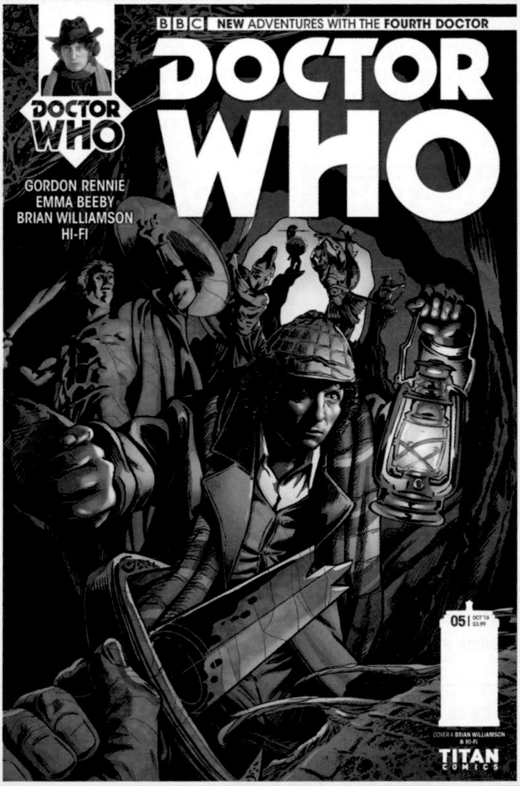
BBC NEW ADVENTURES WITH THE FOURTH DOCTOR
DOCTOR WHO
GORDON RENNIE
EMMA BEEBY
BRIAN WILLIAMSON
HI-FI
05 OCT '16 $3.99
COVER A BRIAN WILLIAMSON & HI-FI
TITAN COMICS

B

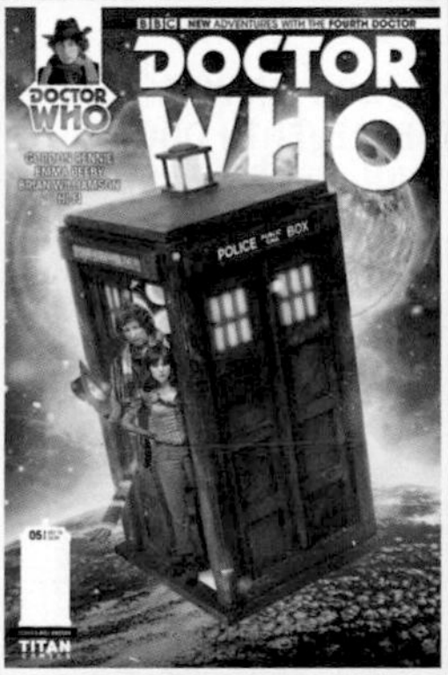
BBC NEW ADVENTURES WITH THE FOURTH DOCTOR
DOCTOR WHO
POLICE PUBLIC CALL BOX
TITAN COMICS

C

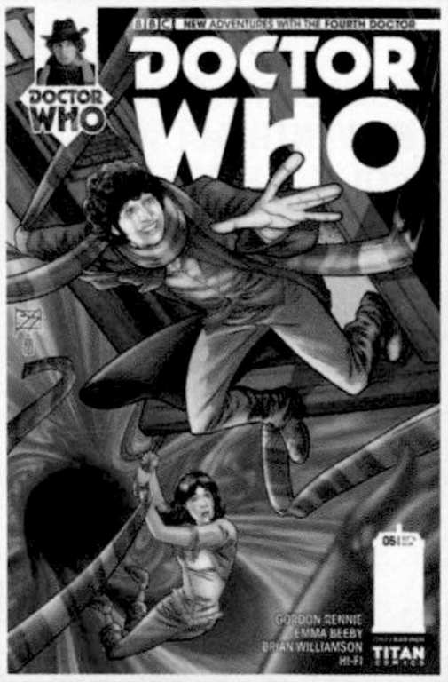
BBC NEW ADVENTURES WITH THE FOURTH DOCTOR
DOCTOR WHO
GORDON RENNIE
EMMA BEEBY
BRIAN WILLIAMSON
HI-FI
TITAN COMICS

D

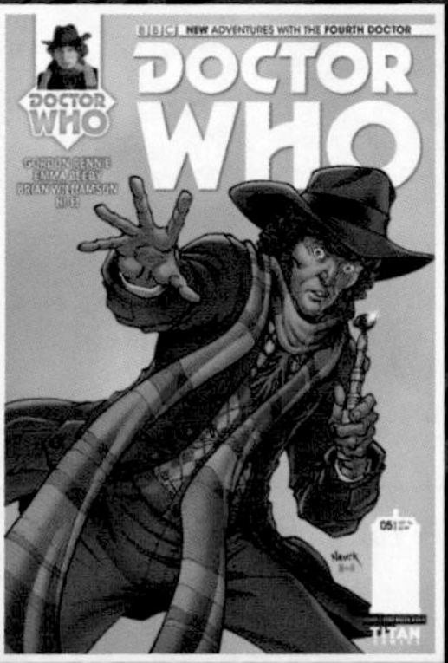
BBC NEW ADVENTURES WITH THE FOURTH DOCTOR
DOCTOR WHO
TITAN COMICS

ISSUE #5

A BRIAN WILLIAMSON & HI-FI
B. SUBSCRIPTION PHOTO WILL BROOKS
C. BLAIR SHEDD
D. TODD NAUCK & HI-FI

FOLLOW YOUR FAVORITE INCARNATIONS ACROSS THESE FANTASTIC COLLECTIONS!

DOCTOR WHO: THE TWELFTH DOCTOR VOL. 1:TERRORFORMER

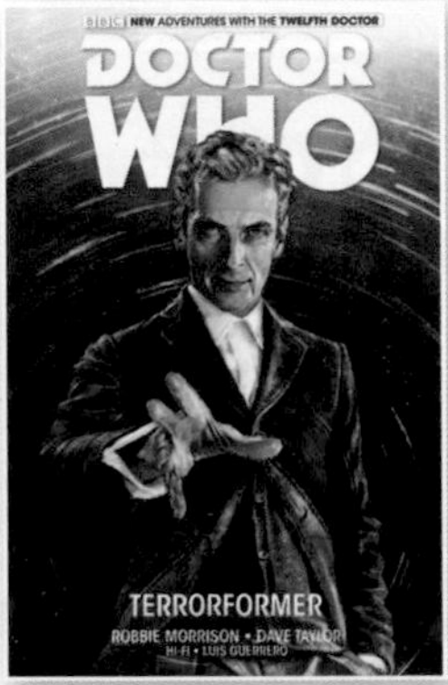
NEW ADVENTURES WITH THE TWELFTH DOCTOR
DOCTOR WHO
TERRORFORMER
ROBBIE MORRISON • DAVE TAYLOR

ISBN: 9781782761778
ON SALE NOW - $19.99 / $22.95 CAN / £10.99
(UK EDITION ISBN: 9781782763864)

DOCTOR WHO: THE TWELFTH DOCTOR VOL. 2: FRACTURES

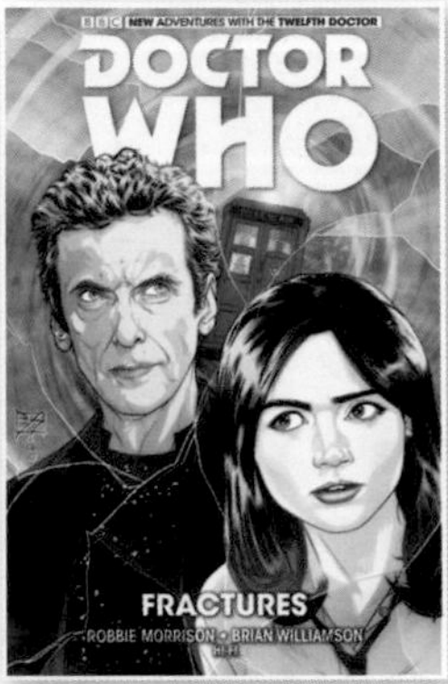
NEW ADVENTURES WITH THE TWELFTH DOCTOR
DOCTOR WHO
FRACTURES
ROBBIE MORRISON • BRIAN WILLIAMSON

ISBN: 9781782763017
ON SALE NOW - $19.99 / $25.99 CAN / £10.99
(UK EDITION ISBN: 9781782766599)

DOCTOR WHO: THE TWELFTH DOCTOR VOL. 3: HYPERION

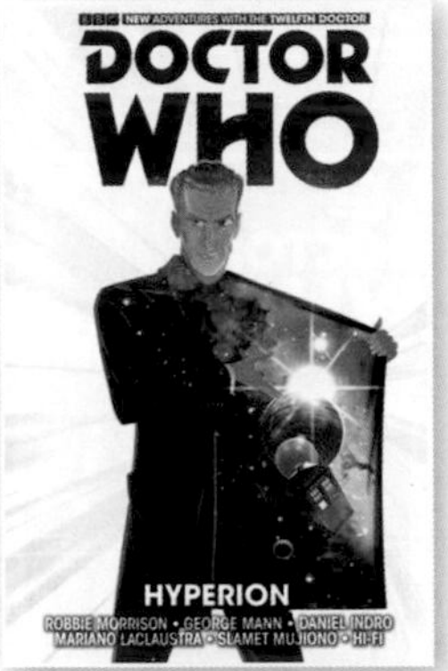
NEW ADVENTURES WITH THE TWELFTH DOCTOR
DOCTOR WHO
HYPERION
ROBBIE MORRISON • GEORGE MANN • DANIEL INDRO
MARIANO LACLAUSTRA • SLAMET MUJIONO • HI-FI

ISBN: 9781782767473
ON SALE NOW- $19.99 / $25.99 CAN / £10.99
(UK EDITION ISBN: 97817827674442)

DOCTOR WHO: THE TWELFTH DOCTOR VOL. 4: THE SCHOOL OF DEATH

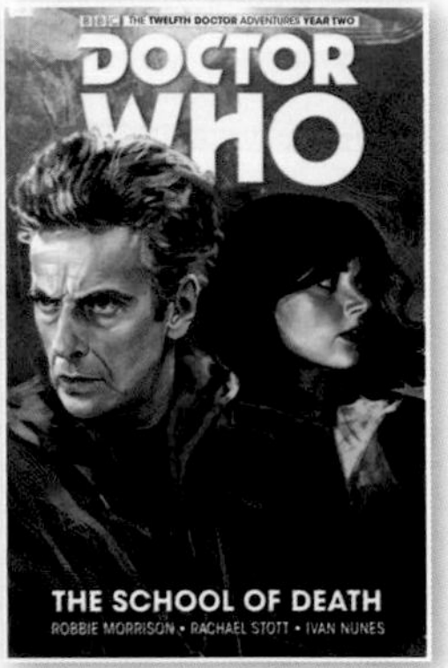
THE TWELFTH DOCTOR ADVENTURES YEAR TWO
DOCTOR WHO
THE SCHOOL OF DEATH
ROBBIE MORRISON • RACHAEL STOTT • IVAN NUNES

ISBN: 9781785851087
COMING SOON - $19.99 / $25.99 CAN / £10.99
(UK EDITION ISBN: 9781785851070)

DOCTOR WHO: THE ELEVENTH DOCTOR VOL. 1: AFTER LIFE

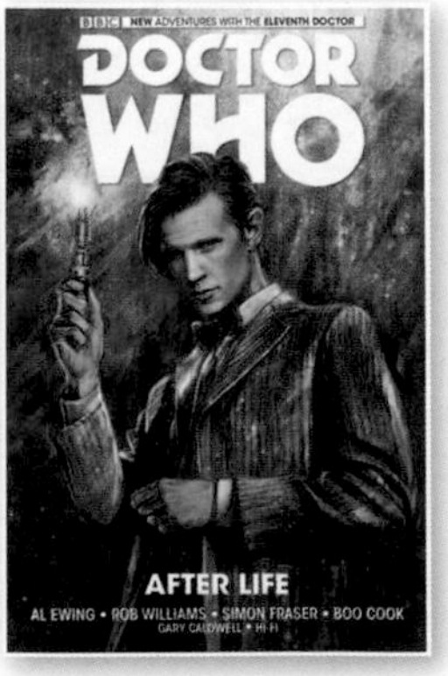
NEW ADVENTURES WITH THE ELEVENTH DOCTOR
DOCTOR WHO
AFTER LIFE
AL EWING • ROB WILLIAMS • SIMON FRASER • BOO COOK
GARY CALDWELL • HI-FI

ISBN: 9781782761747
ON SALE NOW - $19.99 / $22.95 CAN / £10.99
(UK EDITION ISBN: 9781782763857)

DOCTOR WHO: THE ELEVENTH DOCTOR VOL. 2: SERVE YOU

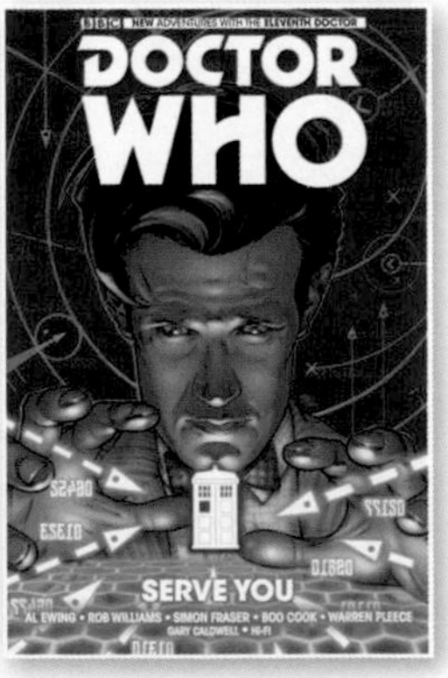
NEW ADVENTURES WITH THE ELEVENTH DOCTOR
DOCTOR WHO
SERVE YOU

ISBN: 9781782761754
ON SALE NOW - $19.99 / $25.99 CAN / £10.99
(UK EDITION ISBN: 9781782766582)

DOCTOR WHO: THE ELEVENTH DOCTOR VOL. 3: CONVERSION

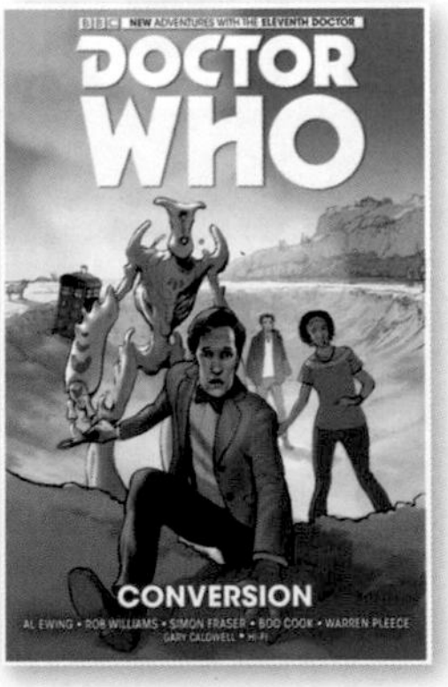
NEW ADVENTURES WITH THE ELEVENTH DOCTOR
DOCTOR WHO
CONVERSION
AL EWING • ROB WILLIAMS • SIMON FRASER • BOO COOK • WARREN PLEECE
GARY CALDWELL • HI-FI

ISBN: 9781782763024
ON SALE NOW - $19.99 / $25.99 CAN / £10.99
(UK EDITION ISBN: 9781782767435)

DOCTOR WHO: THE ELEVENTH DOCTOR VOL. 4:THE THEN AND THE NOW

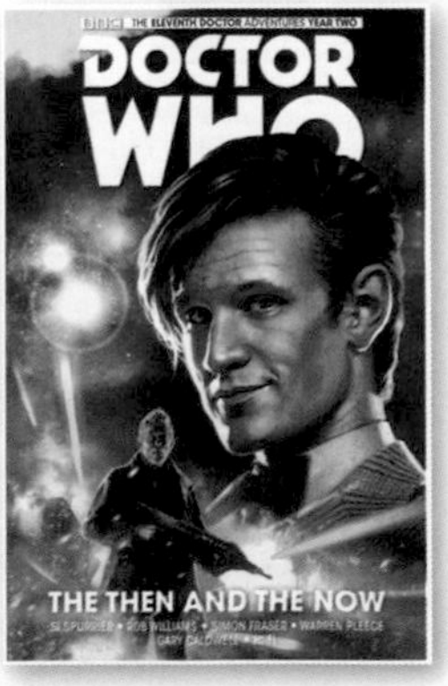
THE ELEVENTH DOCTOR ADVENTURES YEAR TWO
DOCTOR WHO
THE THEN AND THE NOW

ISBN: 9781782767466
ON SALE NOW - $19.99 / $25.99 CAN / £10.99
(UK EDITION ISBN: 9781722767428)

For information on how to subscribe to our great Doctor Who titles, or to purchase them digitally for your favorite device, visit:

WWW.TITAN-COMICS.COM

TITAN COMICS

COMPLETE YOUR COLLECTION!

DOCTOR WHO: THE TENTH DOCTOR VOL. 1: REVOLUTIONS OF TERROR

ISBN: 9781782761747
SALE NOW - $19.99 / $22.95 CAN / £10.99
(UK EDITION ISBN: 9781782763840)

DOCTOR WHO: THE TENTH DOCTOR VOL. 2: THE WEEPING ANGELS OF MONS

ISBN: 9781782761754
ON SALE NOW - $19.99 / $25.99 CAN / £10.99
(UK EDITION ISBN: 9781782766575)

DOCTOR WHO: THE TENTH DOCTOR VOL. 3: THE FOUNTAINS OF FOREVER

ISBN: 9781782763024
ON SALE NOW - $19.99 / $25.99 CAN / £10.99
(UK EDITION ISBN: 9781782767435)

DOCTOR WHO: THE TENTH DOCTOR VOL. 4: THE ENDLESS SONG

ISBN: 9781785854286
ON SALE NOW - $19.99 / $25.99 CAN / £10.99
(SC ISBN: 9781785853227)

DOCTOR WHO: THE NINTH DOCTOR VOL. 1: WEAPONS OF PAST DESTRUCTION

ISBN: 9781782763369
ON SALE NOW - $19.99 / $25.99 CAN / £10.99
(UK EDITION ISBN: 9781782761056)

DOCTOR WHO EVENT 2015 FOUR DOCTORS

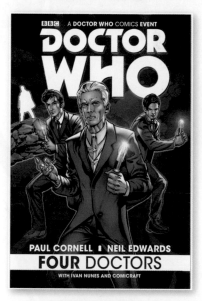

ISBN: 9781782765967
ON SALE NOW - $19.99 / $25.99 CAN / £10.99
(UK EDITION ISBN: 9781785851063)

AVAILABLE IN ALL GOOD COMIC STORES, BOOK STORES, AND DIGITAL PROVIDERS!

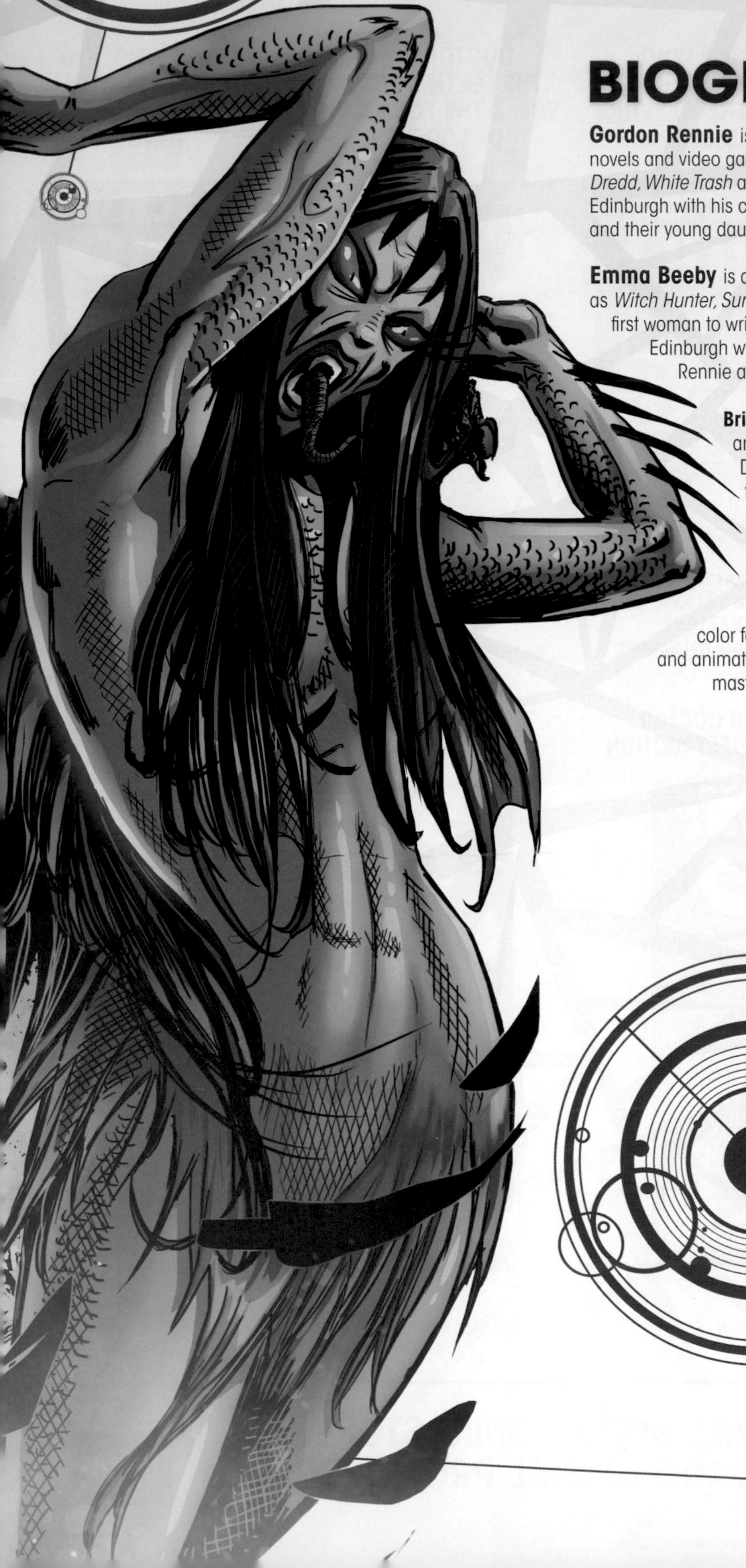

BIOGRAPHIES

Gordon Rennie is an acclaimed writer of comics, novels and video games, with titles including *Judge Dredd, White Trash* and *Dishonored.* He lives in Edinburgh with his co-writer and partner Emma Beeby and their young daughter.

Emma Beeby is a talented writer of titles such as *Witch Hunter, Survival Geeks* ,and was also the first woman to write for *Judge Dredd.* She lives in Edinburgh with partner and co-writer Gordon Rennie and their young daughter.

Brian Williamson is a British writer and artist, having worked for Marvel, DC and 2000AD and most recently for Titan Comics on the Twelfth and Fourth Doctors.

Hi-Fi Colour Design was founded in 1998 by Brian and Kristy Miller and provides digital color for comic books, toys, video games, and animation, and tutorials on color through masterdigitalcolor.com.